BETWEEN

EXPLORING BORDERLANDS, BOUNDARIES, AND EDGES

CollectiveInk

First published by Zer0 Books, 2026
Zer0 Books is an imprint of Collective Ink Ltd.,
Unit 11, Shepperton House, 89 Shepperton Road, London, N1 3DF
office@collectiveinkbooks.com
www.collectiveinkbooks.com
www.zero-books.net

For distributor details and how to order, please visit the 'Ordering' section on our website.

Paperback ISBN: 978 1 80341 862 9
eBook ISBN: 978 1 80341 863 6
PCN: 2025947192

A CIP catalogue record for this book is available from the British Library.

Design credit(s): Lapiz Digital

UK: Printed and bound by CPI Group (UK) Ltd, Croydon, CR0 4YY
Printed in the U.S. by S&S

The manufacturer's authorised representative in the EU for product safety is: *eucomply OÜ - Pärnu mnt 139b-14, 11317 Tallinn, Estonia,* hello@eucompliancepartner.com, www.eucompliancepartner.com

BETWEEN

EXPLORING BORDERLANDS, BOUNDARIES, AND EDGES

by

Martin Lee

zer0 books

London, UK
Washington, DC, USA

For the three without-whoms:
Ellie, James, and Tom

ON THE THRESHOLD

> In-between spaces are full of longing. Who knows what's waiting when we arrive? The space to process is a precious thing, anticipation, rest, the chance to change. We could all use some respite from the tidal shifts we're caught between right now. Uncertain times call for uncertain spaces.
>
> — Jan Carson, *Sea Border*[1]

There are two propositions that underpin everything you're about to read:

1. Borders are everywhere.
2. We are always between.

The argument of this book is that modern life is defined by a conundrum. On the one hand, we have a greater quantity of sharply drawn borders and boundaries than ever before in human history. At the moment of writing, there are 206 nation states that pass the test of statehood as defined by the United Nations. In 1900, the equivalent figure was 78. That also represents a huge increase in the number of borders worldwide. *Borders are everywhere*. In theory, you'd think that this would give all of us a secure sense of who we are, where we belong, and what our identity is. Because it's unarguable that when there are more countries, they are getting smaller on average, and received wisdom would tell us that it's generally easier to identify with small, tighter things than large, baggy things.

Yet at the same time, we exist in a transitional global culture, with more flux, more uncertainty, less clarity, fewer fixed truths. *We are always between.* For example, in principle, we now have unlimited access to information: it ought to be easier than ever to have certainty about facts and the truth. But we all know this isn't the case: in our era of deep fakes and viral stories of dubious origin, there is profound uncertainty about what is true, what is real. Maybe as a result, the number of people that now believe the Earth is flat has dramatically increased in recent years. Who saw that coming?

This book is devoted to exploring these types of puzzles. It's a fabulously rich landscape, and we will look at this picture from a variety of angles. It's in the nature of blurred spaces that they don't yield a precise diagnosis of our current condition. But the invitation is to step into borderlands of varied contexts, some of which are physical and geographic, some emotional and personal, some to do with the world of ideas, or time, or nature, and reflect on what it means for us to be living our lives in these transitional zones.

For my part, I have felt strongly drawn to borderland states for as long as I can recall, including all the things that go with them, such as edges, blurred boundaries, margins, grey areas, frontiers, thresholds, twilights, perimeters, liminal spaces, and so on. More recently, this attraction has accelerated, fuelled both by the conviction that borderlands are having a moment, and the realisation that I'm not alone. I have a tribe, however niche it is, and this brings me to the quote from *Sea Borders* at the top of the first page. Jan Carson is a writer from Northern Ireland. Much of her work is fiction, but in 2019, she created a half-hour meditation for the BBC. She has roots in both Scotland and Northern Ireland, even to the point of having an accent that defies being quite either, and she identifies with the idea of being caught between two worlds. Her piece centres around a ferry crossing between the two countries, evoking the thought of being in both locations at once, or maybe neither. An atmosphere of being in suspension hangs over the whole piece, and a particularly haunting quality can be felt in a couple of the phrases — 'In-between spaces are full of longing,' and especially the last — 'Uncertain times call for uncertain places.'

Both phrases resonate. The first captures an emotion that must surely be a common human experience. It's that feeling of not being settled because you are not at your destination, a bit like the impatient 5-year-old that calls out, 'Are we there yet?' while the plane is still heading toward the runway. You are on the way; you are journeying, but being right here, in transition, is not the point. I do think Jan Carson's use of the word 'longing' is perfect here. Longing has nuance to it — it could be something excitable, like anticipation, or indeed something heartfelt, like yearning. Either way, the longing is focused elsewhere. The significance is this: if we are indeed living in a time of continual transition — that we are always between — and if Jan Carson is right, as I believe she is, then we run the risk of spending a large part of our lived experience longing to be somewhere we are not. It's no wonder that life coaches these days encourage us to 'inhabit the moment'.

The second phrase is sister to the first. What Carson also identifies is that alongside experiencing our in-between time as a state of longing, we should relish it, learn to celebrate the opportunity it offers, dwell in it. If uncertainty is the default setting, then the way to deal with it is not to fight it, or yearn for an impossible stability, but to recognise the positives of uncertainty and embrace the environments that offer it. 'Uncertain times call for uncertain places' is like an emotional manifesto for this book, a north star.

Here is what lies ahead. Conventionally, in a work of non-fiction, you'd be reading something called 'Introduction' right now. Instead, it's called 'On the threshold', to start the process of immersion into all things liminal. Thresholds should feel exciting, and the ambition is that readers emerge at the other end of this book with a new-found pleasure at seeing the world through liminal lenses. I stress this because you could be forgiven for finding some of the opening mood anxiety creating. I've already used words or phrases like transitional, indeterminate, uncertainty, and blurred boundaries, and let's not hide from it. These words conjure up hesitancy, complexity, of not-knowing-where-we-stand. It's a human instinct to like conditions of certainty, but who of us looks around and sees any of that today? In case you are wistfully thinking back to some mythical golden age, listen to the opinion of French writer and thinker Voltaire, back in the eighteenth century. In a 1770 letter to Frederick the Great, he said: 'Doubt is an uncomfortable condition, but certainty is a ridiculous one.' Uncertainty is not going away anytime soon.

Within all that context, I propose that we label this period we are in as The Age of Between. I'll make the case that learning to thrive and prosper in borderlands is a modern life skill that we'd do well to acquire. But if that sounds arduous, I'll also argue that these spaces are constructive, stimulating, and enjoyable, rather than threatening. In-between spaces can be more creative, more entertaining, more insightful, more abundant, more filled with potential. It's in the borderlands that a lot of the fun stuff happens.

A WAY OF THINKING ABOUT BORDERLANDS

Almost by definition, the world of borderlands is a foggy topic. But there can be structure, and here is the organising model that I have settled on.

1. **Physical facts.** Those borders that exist independently of people perceiving them as borders — skin, cell walls, the seashore, the treeline, and arguably the precise moment of dying. I'd acknowledge that this is a borderline case, so to speak.
2. **Human inventions.** There are also those borders that are distinct from physical facts because they would have no independent existence if people hadn't created them — these are best demonstrated by geographical entities like national borders, counties, states, and parishes. But because humans have created these borders, they do exist and leave a visible mark, often on the landscape, and at the very least on maps.
3. **Mental ideas and concepts.** These are the most elusive of borders — they are abstract in that they exist more as ideas and because we *perceive* them as borders. They are a product of human behaviour, philosophy, and culture and are in continual flux. They are also everywhere in human experience — there are borders between truth and lies, between childhood and adulthood,

boundaries between people, even down to the very recent blurred boundary of hybrid working, and so on ad infinitum.

It is this third cluster that gives me the sensation that we are in a border-obsessed culture. If the quantity of international borders has grown over the last century, then this third group is in exponential growth. Our perception of transitional states is now more acknowledged, studied, and given language than ever before. Borders and borderlands multiply and are indivisible from each other. Each time that two borders or boundaries are defined, some new space opens between them. And even when only one border is identified, there is adjacent space on either side of it.

And because borderland thinking is part of the air that we breathe, it forces us to look back at the first cluster with fresh eyes. What if this notion of borders as physical facts is no different to the third cluster of abstract concepts? It's not to doubt the literal existence of skin, cell walls, etc. But the thought is whether other eras would have considered them borders at all. For instance, in the past, they probably wouldn't have looked at, say, ion channels in cell walls and then made a metaphorical leap to borders, but simply seen them as being ion channels in cell walls — er, that's it. Therefore, even attempting to make a case for 'physical facts' to exist as a distinct group of borders may be a sign of the time we are in — The Age of Between.

To examine all this, there will be nine broad themes, and sub-sections within them. The themes are distinct, but often interconnected, and so they'll often weave in and around each other, like dancers round a maypole, but to signpost them up front, here they are:

Section One — Words

Our relationship with borders and borderlands is experienced through words. Understanding the roots of the most important words we'll be spending time with helps to tell some of the historical story of how borderland thinking has evolved over time.

Section Two — Being Between — Liminality

The second and third sections both aim to explain why liminality is a hot cultural topic right now. This section addresses it head-on and gives a brief overview of how liminal thinking has taken root in Western thinking from its origins within anthropology and has now developed into a mainstream concept.

Section Three — Between Ideas

Other types of thinking have also got us to this point. This section will (very lightly) touch on other disciplines, principally physics and philosophy. The concepts we'll meet are not things that we're all immersed in all the time, but they are influential in the background and contribute to this Age of Between that we are in.

Section Four — the Betweens of You

Just as there are huge numbers of borders 'out there', there are borders inside you, inside each of us. In this section, we'll think about some of the internal borders that shape us. These include the relationship between the two hemispheres of our brains, and also consciousness, in the context of the border between you and non-you.

Section Five — Between Times

Closely related to the betweens of you is your own personal relationship to time. Time is an elusive commodity, and in the Age of Between, the thing we call the present is a curious entity that sits somewhere between the past and the future. But where exactly, and how do we make sense of it?

Section Six — Between People

The borders between people are far more talked about than used to be the case. Here, we'll start by talking about 'being boundaried', and this section dives into that territory. But it's not all about finding the point of separation between people; it's also about collaboration, and even shared memories. We'll also have a look at one of the defining borderlands between people — that of truth and lies. Finally, another important angle between people is the political realm, where borders that once were quite porous and overlapping are increasingly polarised.

Section Seven — Between Stories

One of the most enduring human activities since the start of civilisation has been storytelling — it's been a fundamental way in which we've learnt about our place in the world. And because stories either know no boundaries or know nothing but boundaries, storytellers have a lot to say on the spaces between.

Section Eight — Between Places

Geographic borders are the ones that are the most obvious — the ones we first become conscious about through education. Most physical borders tell a tale of conflict and therefore reveal a lot about our humanity. There are also a few borderland stories that are just too good to ignore, so let those tales get told.

Section Nine — the Betweens of Nature

Nature is full of liminal spaces: shorelines, the soil, woods, seas, and even times of day. Their appearance in this book is not to get into the science of them, but to see how people use them metaphorically. By coming to them last, they help to illuminate and distil the themes that we will have covered by then.

So that's the plan. A broad sweep, but no apology for that, because there's no realm of life, knowledge, or experience that doesn't have its borderlands.

Welcome to the spaces between.

SECTION ONE — WORDS

Most borders are not objective physical facts but human inventions. They are a product of our perception. Language is also a human invention, and it's through words that we have a tool for sharing and developing our thinking about ideas, including borders. It's one of two reasons that we're starting with words. To lay the ground for what lies ahead, it's good to look at the vocabulary of borders and all things between for the hidden clues that underpin our relationship to them. The way we describe them in language is part of the story. In my day job, we often talk about 'language leaks'; it's how hidden beliefs are inadvertently signalled by word choices and metaphors. When we get underneath the surface of words, there is often fresh insight, even when that hidden meaning is invisible to the person speaking the words.

The second reason is that there is no finer example of continual transition than language. It will be true of all languages, but to take English as an example, there is no single moment when Anglo-Saxon became Old English, and then when Old English became Middle English, and so on. A language never 'arrives'. Like us, it's only ever travelling from how it was to how it will be by way of how it is. The slippery impermanence of language is part of its joy and part of its strength. Just as culture evolves, so does the way we use words to describe it, and the words themselves. Our language today is like the time stamp of the era we inhabit.

This survey of words is organised in the approximate magnitude of their importance to the book, starting with the ones that will do the heaviest lifting, and coming to the supporting cast further on.

Between

What a great and underappreciated word this is. In fact, some of its wondrousness was hidden to me as well at the outset. However, once the thought of calling the book *Between* occurred, it was tempting to call this book 'Betwixt and between', and in fact both words are similar in meaning; it's only that betwixt is now archaic and barely exists in usage outside that phrase. Betwixt is just lovely, and I feel sad to be letting it go, but there are only so many battles you can fight.

But I will fight for between. To do the etymology bit, between comes from the Old English *betweonum*, and by the time of Middle English had evolved into *betwene*. It literally means 'by the two', or 'near both'. The tween part is related to twin. As the etymology implies, one great thing about between is that it can be fiercely spatial in the way that it is used. What this means in practice is that it's correctly used to specify the space that connects two (or potentially more) entities, such as in a sentence like 'She stood between her parents.' You get a sense of our unconscious rigour in using between correctly when you think about when it's *not* used. For instance, we wouldn't tend to say, 'I was caught between two minds,' because that's a metaphorical phrase, and between has more physicality than that, which at some level, native English speakers just happen to know without ever having it explained to them (I'd never given this a first thought, let alone a second one, before working this all through). Here's another example — we don't say 'You're between friends,' but 'You're amongst friends.' Again, it wouldn't *feel* right, and that's because we intuitively sense that the number of friends is not specified and so there is vagueness to the visualisation of this phrase. Contrast that with another case where we *would* use it, 'Between you, me, and the gatepost…' Here, the entities are specified, even though the gatepost doesn't exist.

Let's also not forget the lovely 'go-between', so much more resonant than the broadly synonymous 'negotiator' or 'intermediary'. For my taste, the extra dimension you get from go-between is the notion of physically transacting the space between two parties. Although it's a noun, it feels like a verb — the status of being a go-between can only be accomplished by doing some go-betweening (or should that be going-between?).

All of this adds up to *between* being a wonderful borderlands word — it's this evocation of actual spaces that connects people or things that is the source of its richness. Part of its attraction is also because it flies under the radar nearly all the time, having a kind of underdog status which appeals. It means that when it does get called out from time to time, it's surprisingly exciting, such as stumbling over this snippet on page one of Percival Everett's novel *The Trees*,[1] which was shortlisted for the Booker Prize in 2021. The narrator is introducing us to two characters, a married couple called Wheat and Charlene:

> Wheat was between jobs, was constantly, ever, always between jobs. Charlene was always quick to point out that the word *between* usually suggested something at either end, two somethings, or destinations, and that Wheat had held only one job in his whole life, so he wasn't between anything.

Exactly! Speaking personally, I find the spoken sound of the word quite beguiling, and even the look of it on the page. If it weren't so commonplace, there's a good chance that we'd venerate it more than we do. Someone who did venerate it was Horace Walpole, a dandyish, privileged individual of the eighteenth century who dabbled in travel, politics, architecture, and art history, and found the time to write the virtually unreadable Gothic novel *The Castle of Otranto*. I say he venerated between, but that is too generous — it may be more accurate to say that he couldn't leave it well alone. Not content with giving the English language the word 'serendipity' (which frequently ends up at the top of lists of people's favourite words), he also gave us 'gloomth' (a smooshing together of warmth and gloom), which defines a level of light so low as to induce physical and or psychological effects. To be fair to Horace, gloomth has a good liminal quality to it.

Anyway, not satisfied with these two coinages, Horace thought he could improve on between, and gave us 'betweenity', which he had down as meaning 'the state of being between, or of an indeterminate condition'. I'll confess that when I first ran across this, I wasn't convinced. My first thought was — isn't he just splitting semantic hairs here? The suspicion was that he was gilding the lily on an already entirely satisfactory word. But then followed the realisation that there was more going on here, because he was giving 'between' some status as a noun. I will certainly grant him that betweenity is a more elegant sounding word than betweenness, which is also a legitimate word, but not one that you will read again in this book. But it looks as if no one was ready for Horace's tweak, because there's barely been a flicker of usage of betweenity since 1850. I'd like to think that might change. And in fact, to give Horace some credit, there is a very strong case for needing a noun usage for this lovely word — so betweenity it is. In addition, let's also unleash onto an unsuspecting world the plural concept of 'the betweens' as the set of things that are between (although there is a risk that this makes them sound like a cosy set of villages in the Cotswolds, with Great Between, Little Between, and Much Between), and also 'betweenists', those people who are obsessed with all things between. Not satisfied with all this, it wouldn't be a surprise if I ended up deploying betweenish at some stage. Oh, I just have. You have been warned.

Liminality

For all that it has a Latin root, liminality is a recent word, dating only to the very end of the nineteenth century, turn of the twentieth, and making its first appearance then, at the point when anthropology became a recognised discipline. The Latin root word is *limen*, meaning threshold, in the literal sense of a doorway, but pretty much from the beginning, its usage was metaphorical, in that it was never used to describe a literal threshold. The anthropological sense is in describing rituals in which those who participate exist in a marginal state (liminality) from their pre-ritual state (whatever that was), but before they move on to their post-ritual state (whatever that will be). The most iconic of these rituals has historically been the one that celebrates the transition from puberty into adulthood.

It's a bit like a state of suspension, where the status of something is unknown or lacks clear definition. It has become such a prevalent cultural idea that many things that would never have previously been catalogued as liminal now are.

Linguistically, liminality has a cousin, in the Roman Catholic concept of limbo, another state of suspension — this time, the world that separates heaven and hell. We'll come back to limbo (how could we not? Borderlands hardly get more dramatic than that…), but for now, we're merely marking the fact of a related etymological root.

Liminality is so central to this book that it will have its own treatment soon, so there's no need to steal its thunder now, but it's worth making this observation. Recently, I stumbled across a German novel called *Liminal* by Roland Schimmelpfennig.[2] Sure enough, the book is full of liminal spaces — the murky zone of the Berlin underground scene, the central character's career hiatus as he's awaiting a possible criminal charge, the river as a symbol of impermanence, and so on. But here's the thing: you've read other books and stories before that have those kind of betweens, without having them pinned to an organising thought of liminality. Yet in this case, the title is a framing device, an organising idea that you can't escape from — you're more or less impelled to interpret events through that prism. It's further evidence of the contention that we are in a cultural moment where this kind of layered ambiguity is in the air we breathe.

Border

'Border' first crops up in the mid-fourteenth century as *bordure*, borrowed from Old French, and with a strictly heraldic use: to describe the coloured strip around the edge of a shield. Old English had a shorter word, *bord*, which meant 'side', demonstrating that there were a variety of European languages that had closely allied ideas and a similar root word. From that point, its meaning evolved from its heraldic use and was borrowed to describe other ornamental edges of things, such as crockery or even clothes. Now what's interesting about this usage is that it didn't imply a separation between two regions — it was simply decorating the edge of something. Of course, it's still possible to use the word in this way, but you wouldn't as a rule. You're more likely to say that a plate has a decorated rim or edge than a border.

The likely reason why we don't tend to use border that way is that by the beginning of the fifteenth century, the word was press-ganged into its modern geographical role of demarcating the partition between countries, and over time this has come to be the primary usage. To be explicit about it, we now have the idea of a border acting as a specific line between two states. Now, although I say 'line', it's not always quite so precise as that. Sometimes the border is more of a zone, or the immediate area leading up to the border. This is even more true in disputed and/or hostile borders, such as the demilitarised zone that separates North and South Korea. Semantically, I think we are obliged to say that a border is not as definitive as a boundary, and as evidence for this, we have the existence of the word borderland — the general area adjacent to the border itself. By contrast, we don't speak of the boundaryland. To cement this further, in the case of Britain, the area on either side of the England–Scotland border is often referred to as the Borders. It's not precisely defined but is generally taken to encompass the five counties on either side of the border itself, meaning Northumberland, Westmorland, and Cumberland on the English side, and Kirkcudbrightshire and Dumfriesshire on the Scottish side. Back in the sixteenth century, when the border itself hadn't been settled, this piece of territory was known as the Debatable Land, adding weight to the notion that borders are, and always have been, malleable and contingent, for all the apparent sharpness they like to convey on maps.

In summary, just as borders are in flux, across those centuries we see the word itself evolve from a visible ornamental shield edge to a conceptual mechanism for demarcating territory belonging to nation states. That's some linguistic transformation and reflects profound cultural and social change.

Boundary

A boundary describes the precise limit of a space: the line that marks the edge of a territory. In that very specific spatial and physical sense, a boundary is quite distinct from a border, which, as just described, is more indeterminate. Originally a bound (or *bunda* in medieval English) was a marker, a physical indicator of where the limit was. As a result, it carries a sense of constraint with it, which is detectable in phrases like fogbound, snowbound, etc. Nowadays, despite being far from an obsolete word, in everyday use we don't have that many uses for the physical use of boundary — outside of cricket, where it's alive and well. Some of its old usages, such as phrases like 'parish boundaries' are falling out of use. And way back in our history, and I'm talking of Anglo-Saxon times, there used to be an activity called boundary walking, or even more quaintly, 'beating the bounds', which was a custom of walking the village and parish boundaries as an act of remembering where the boundaries were. In the days before reliable cartography (the Ordnance Survey wasn't started until the nineteenth century), boundaries needed to be collectively remembered, to guard against encroachment or moving of the boundaries by people with colonising intentions. Traditionally, this activity was carried out at rogationtide, which is five weeks after Easter. The beating was carried out literally, with the bounds (the markers) beaten with branches of willow as a means of imprinting to memory the exact location of the boundary. In a practice that would be generally frowned upon today, children's heads would sometimes be knocked against the boundary stones, to make sure they didn't forget their position. (This was an era when 'beating some sense' into children was a physical process rather than a metaphorical concept.) Some groups, such as the Open Spaces Society in the UK,[3] keep this ancient tradition alive. Their contention is that although parish boundaries are still marked on modern maps, other boundaries, such as those that delimit common land and village greens, don't have that measure of protection, and in fact they are often unfenced. And because the Common Law operates on a kind of use-it-or-lose-it basis, unless villagers continue to beat the bounds, complacency can lead to the loss of publicly held space.

In our era, the word boundary has moved firmly into figurative usage, where the notion of our personal boundaries is beginning to dominate usage. It's not entirely clear why, but there's a clue in the phrase 'going beyond the bounds' (i.e., of acceptable behaviour). Because when someone does 'go beyond the bounds', they have an impact on others, and we talk about that as 'pushing the boundaries'. There's an interesting linguistic development of this in recent years, which is the rise of the word 'unboundaried'. If you check this out on Google Ngrams, which documents the ebb and flow of all words in the written record, the increase in usage of unboundaried is meteoric. The word has an emphatic pejorative flavour to it — you'd never hear it being used in an approving way. One way of looking at this rise of unboundaried is that perhaps as a population we've become surprisingly meek about public boundaries such as common land, but as a result become more militant about personal boundaries. That's where the greater battle around encroachment happens these days. Personal boundaries have an inbound (!) and an outbound dimension to them. As already implied, the inbound sense is when someone else invades your boundaries, perhaps through not being socially skilled, or just careless with etiquette. The outbound sense is when you are testing your own limits, which of course we all think is highly admirable, but perhaps comes with a lack of realisation that our testing of our outbound limits might well come at the expense of invading someone else's inbound limits. Maybe we need to rediscover the art of beating the bounds, but in terms of reminding ourselves of our own and other people's limits.

Frontier

Frontier has a fascinating etymology. It's hidden in plain sight, but frontier derives, of course, from front. As far as front is concerned, English annexed it from Old French, where it meant forehead or brow, and because a forehead faces forward, from about 1400 it started to be used metaphorically in both French and English to have a geographic sense of that piece of land that faces another territory.

And so things stood for a few centuries, but as the United States started its westward expansion in the nineteenth century, the word frontier started to take on almost mythic significance, indicating the separation between settled and wild land: the notion of the frontier comes into play as a potent cultural idea. Now a frontier necessarily lacks precision — we're not talking about a well-defined line that you could draw, so much as an area, the land that is just this side of a wilderness. Although this type of frontier border would exist in approximate territorial terms, it's as much a concept as a piece of geography. It was only later that there was an attempt to codify this, most specifically by Frederick Jackson Turner, an American historian from the late nineteenth and early twentieth century. His landmark 1893 essay was 'The Significance of the Frontier in American History',[4] later anthologised in one of his books. In the essay, one of his core definitions is given in terms of extremely low population density — 'What is the frontier? ... In the census reports it is treated as the margin of that settlement which has a density of two or more to the square mile.' Furthermore, it was American English that coined the idea of the frontiersman, to honour those individuals who lived their lives along that loose margin.

An interesting recent finesse on the subtle distinction between borders and frontiers has been suggested in a paper by the Czech geographers Dokoupil and Havlicek.[5] They make the point that, semantically at least, a border region implies a civil or political entity on both sides of a border line, whereas a frontier region suggests that on only one side. This tends to support the mythic idea of the American frontier mentioned above, which continued to creep ever westward until its ambitions were checked by the Pacific Ocean.

To bring this notion of how frontier is used right up to date, I've noted the recent use of the phrase 'jagged frontier' to refer to the development of AI towards the potential tipping point where humans lose control of technology and AGI takes over. It's a horrifying prospect in real life, but a thrilling use of language. Frontier is so much better deployed here than border would be — conjuring up a sense of an unmapped tech wilderness beyond what we currently know.

Middle

It's tempting to feel a bit sorry for the word middle. Instinctively, it seems to lack some of the linguistic glamour of between. You can sense that from some of the derivations that it's spawned over the centuries — middling, mediocre, middle of the road, middle class, middle ground, middle England, middlebrow. They don't stir the blood much, do they? It feels as if the very idea of 'middle' is going out of fashion. One of my colleagues, Sarah Jay, gave a prescient talk a few years ago called 'Death of the Middle Ground', anticipating the current culture of extreme opinion, at least some of which is attributable to the way in which social media algorithms promote more extreme content. And how remarkable that a venerable old county like Middlesex has been expunged from the map of England — even the racy suffix didn't save it. To add to the doldrums that middle finds itself in, there's very little drama to the story of the word. Our modern word comes from the Old English *middel*, which has a somewhat prosaic meaning, being just that spot that is equidistant from the extremes. And that's your lot. Two letters change position, and the meaning stays tenaciously the same, century after century.

In a way, it's quite a self-effacing word, and this could be the clue to both its durability and stubbornness to change in spelling or meaning. The point is, pretty much everything has a middle, but what that middle consists of (time, space, physical matter, a cultural concept) morphs in each case. The only connecting thread between radically different middles is their equidistance from whatever they are keeping apart. You could say (and so I will) that middle is the heavy-lifting shape-shifter of the borderland world. There's infinite flexibility here, and middle is perennially ready, on duty to provide whatever middle is required the instant that two ends of anything have literally come into being or simply been defined as an idea.

Twilight

Here's another beautiful borderland word. We'll revisit it much later, in the Betweens of Nature section, but here it's an example of the emotional impact of borders on our psyche. As we all experience every day, there is a real but hard-to-define bridge from day into night, light into dark. But in the natural world, that threshold into night has no intrinsic meaning beyond demonstrating the fact that the world spins on its axis during its journey round the sun. As far as we can tell, it's only we humans who have created metaphorical meaning there and imbued that time of day with a sense of unease, an indeterminate zone which is neither one thing nor the other.

The etymology of the 'twi' part is unclear (of course it is!) but appears to mean 'half', as if we have a time of day which is keeping its options open. It's perfect that the Sanskrit word for twilight is *samdhya*, which literally translates as 'a holding together, a junction'. It's a great mental idea, captured in a word; we have a time of day whose role is to bind together the day and night by acting as the buffer between them.

While on twilight, there is also the far less common word 'crepuscular', which also refers to twilight, but in the sense of being dim, indistinct, or obscure. It's a word that's been annexed by zoology to refer to those animals, like bats, that are especially active just before daylight or just as the sun goes down but lie low during full day and full night. Crepuscular deserves a wider audience, but then, that might destroy the point of it… Having said that, it's worth noting that the French word for dusk is *crepuscule*, and we shouldn't let mention of the French approach to twilight pass without commenting on their brilliant phrase for twilight, *entre chien et loup*, between the dog and the wolf. The point of the phrase is that there comes a point when the dog (symbolically standing for the day) and the wolf (the night) can't be distinguished from each other, but blend into one indistinct entity. Shivery in a good way.

Edge

Some of the words we're considering in this borderland lexicon have an implied breadth to them, including border itself, but also twilight, between, and middle. There's the sense of a lack of definition in space or time. Where is the border of a middle, or when is the exact moment when twilight is over? There's none of that with edge. The fact that even today we talk about a 'razor's edge' is a throwback to the Old English word *ecg* with its meaning of a sword's blade, and associated pin-sharp references such as point and corner. Even further back, the deeper-origin word suggests a sharpness so acute as to pierce. It's therefore unsurprising that edge still carries that sense of threat and uneasiness to this day. Something might be contemporary, but if it's also edgy, then that comes with a provocative, confrontational implication. In addition, something might set our teeth on edge, or it might tip us over the edge. It's all jeopardy and peril with edge — and of course, when you think of a sword blade, that must be right. There's lethal threat and a division between two sides that is so sharp that there is no resting place, barely even a visible juncture at all to the naked eye. It's no accident that in mountaineering, ridges are often called edges, which has the effect of increasing the sense of drama involved in the climb. Even a relatively modest mountain, like Helvellyn in the Lake District, has its Swirral and Striding Edges, and there's no doubt that the naming adds to the thrill of the climb for first-timers.

Margin

Margin came into English via Old French and originally from Latin (*marginem*). It started life in the mid-fourteenth century to specifically describe the edge of a sea or lake. But very quickly, with the rise of the printing presses from the fifteenth century, it was press-ganged into metaphorical usage, to describe the area after the end of a block of text up to the edge of a sheet of paper. There is a subtle shift that goes on there, from describing the edge of something, to the space between two things. What this allowed for was the notion that the paper margin allowed a little bit more space than you strictly need to fit all the writing on the page. And what that in turn did was to pave the way for the most contemporary evolution of the word into ideas like 'margin for error' and the financial sense of 'profit margin' — the gap between breaking even and making a profit.

And yet, even as this evolution was going on, 'margin' was also heading back a bit closer to its roots, with a phrase like 'becoming marginalised' describing the process of being pushed out to the edge. It's a fascinating case study of the way that words move about, always in flux, forever being redeployed to reflect cultural change.

Brim

Here's a lovely word, with rare, quite specific uses. But it has a story to it and helps to bring colour and shade to the language of borders. In daily use, it's most commonly used these days in a phrase like 'I'm full up to the brim', but what precisely is a brim — a word we use barely any other time? Taken back to its traceable roots, which may be Middle High German, brim means brink or edge, but with specific reference to the sea or sometimes a riverbank (although there is a possibility that it goes further back still to Norse, where *brrr* was interpreted as the sound of tides coming and going). What we've got, then, is this implication of being at the very point of overflow, where the water might be contained, just, or could spill. In his heartfelt book about shorelines, *Life Between the Tides,*[6] Adam Nicolson quotes a line from Seamus Heaney in which he talks about the shore being where 'things overflow the brim of the usual'. Arguably only a poet would know how to make good use of a word like brim these days, but we can all appreciate it. I can't think of the exquisitely delicate equilibrium that brim conjures up without also thinking of 'shifting sands', another metaphor for uneasiness taken directly from the volatility of shorelines.

Sayings, phrases, and proverbs

While still on language, there are further clues about our relationship with betweenity in some of the everyday phrases we use. Most of these are so familiar to our ears that if we use them, we do so unthinkingly, or if we hear them, we don't question them.

Phrases of certainty

It's a human instinct to like conditions of certainty. Granted, that is an assertion, but there is evidence embedded in language, and especially in some of our oldest proverbs and sayings. Reflect on these three seriously old examples:

'She lets me know where I stand.'
'A place for everything and everything in its place.'
'He calls a spade a spade.' (This one can be traced back 2000 years to Plutarch.)

There's an implied positive quality in all these phrases — there is not any hint of this certainty being, say, boring or bland. Knowing where you stand, you can get on with stuff. The sheer longevity of these phrases speaks to them coming down to us from an era of greater certainty and, as a thought experiment, it's hard to imagine a saying like any of these being minted in today's ambivalent mood. To give a further illustration of this, think of another ancient saying, still in regular use, 'being beyond the pale'. Pale, in this context, means a fencepost (or paling). Way back in British history, pales were used to demarcate the limit of a local jurisdiction, and so going beyond that pale was to step outside of your own space. As we all know, the phrase has an absolute sense of 'having gone too far', together with the implication that the person who has 'gone beyond the pale' should have stayed where they belonged. I'm even reminded of the original version of that cloying Victorian hymn, *All things bright and beautiful*, which includes the quite incredible verse (to modern ears):

The rich man in his castle,
The poor man at his gate,
God made them, high or lowly,
And ordered their estate.

I say original version, because you'll not find this verse in any recent lyric sheet (it was banned by the Inner London Education Authority in 1982). In all likelihood, you'd even struggle to find an opponent of political correctness who'd make a case for a verse like that today, so far has modern life moved on. I include it to illustrate the starkness of our cultural shift. Notice the physical separation here — the gate creates a barrier that is impassable, because in that era the class borders of rich are poor were seen as being ordained by God and therefore sacrosanct.

Phrases of uncertainty

By contrast, let's consider a handful of common phrases that describe someone who lacks decisiveness or clarity:

'They don't know whether they're coming or going.'
'I'm caught in two minds.'
'It feels like a grey area.'
'He's trapped between a rock and a hard place.'
'I'm in an agony of indecision.'

Whenever we hear any of these phrases, we know to interpret them as negative. The implication is one of mental turbulence, discomfort, tension. Whereas, as another thought experiment, imagine an alternative world where betweenism is celebrated and is the dominant mode of being. If you then heard someone describing a state of not having made up their mind, instead of saying 'I'm in an agony of indecision,' they might say 'I've got the luxury of choices ahead of me.' The tonal difference is absolute.

Phrases to do with boundaries

We also don't like it when there is no respect for boundaries in relationships, or when we are being asked to go past our own boundaries. We've already come across the notion of invading someone's personal space, and also being 'tipped over the edge', but consider some others:

'He's crossed the line.'
'She's overstepped the mark.'
'I'm outside my comfort zone.'

Notice a couple of things. Firstly, they tend to be more contemporary than phrases of certainty, speaking to the age we're in. Where the language of clarity belonged to our ancestors, we're creating a fresh supply of phrases for ambiguity to meet the increased demand. Secondly, all of them speak to the jeopardy of transgressed boundaries and the anxieties they induce. To state the obvious, in none of these examples is there an expression of pleasure in the crossed boundary. It's always negative.

Oxymorons

This is right up there amongst my favourite figures of speech. I said a few pages ago that I believe that it's in the borderlands that all the fun stuff happens, and oxymorons are great examples of wordy fun. For one thing, it's quaintly delicious that the word 'oxymoron' is an oxymoron itself. It comes from two Greek words: '*oxys*', meaning sharp, and '*moronos*', meaning dull.

Many oxymorons are now so embedded in language that the original oddness and oppositional nature from when they were first coined is lost on us — think of civil war, ill health, or lead balloon. It's the melting together of opposites that I love, the way that two ideas, coming from different positions, can joust and create something where the meaning is understood intuitively rather than rationally. The Greek philosopher Heraclitus (of whom more in due course) said, 'From the strain of binding opposites comes harmony.' It's unlikely he was referring to oxymorons when he said this, but it captures their magic perfectly. No one is or was better at it than Shakespeare (of course). Arguably, his defining oxymoronic moment is in *Romeo and Juliet*. He deploys them like confetti throughout, but it reaches its summit in this speech of Juliet's, after she discovers that Romeo has murdered Tybalt in a duel. The significance of this for Juliet is that Tybalt was her cousin, so the fact of her (now secretly married) husband having killed one of her relatives is a huge issue to confront:

Beautiful tyrant! Fiend angelical!
Dove-feathered raven, wolvish-ravening lamb!
Despisèd substance of divinest show,
Just opposite to what thou justly seem'st.
A damnèd saint, an honourable villain!

That's eight in five lines. We can legitimately conclude that her mind is in utter turmoil. These tumbling oxymorons are a demonstration of inner conflict. Mental states that would normally be separate have collapsed together into one roiling mass of irreconcilable opposites.

Or alternatively, maybe an oxymoron is more accurately thought of as a reconciliation of opposites. It's the new idea that is created when conflicting ideas collide. So in addition to being a window into confusion, their wonder is the way they open up creativity, creating a cerebral jolt, making the world feel new again. As mentioned above, the commonplace ones can lose their affect (think also of bittersweet for example, which is so steeped that it's a word in its own right that no longer even needs a hyphen). But when they hit you unprepared, they can still reframe the way you look at things. As a more contemporary example than Shakespeare, consider the oxymoronic phrase in Bob Dylan's 'Absolutely Sweet Marie', which goes, 'To live outside the law you must be honest.' Because it sits in a semantic borderland, it can create both a smile and a jolt each time you hear it, an elusive tang that the typical song lyric doesn't deliver.

As a final summary on all this, another language that needs a shout-out for oxymoronic joy is Euskara, which is the language of the Basque people, who straddle the France–Spain border. Euskara is famously hard to learn if you're not a native speaker. A good number of their words are oxymoronic, including '*harreman*', which means relationship (combining '*eman*', which means give, and '*hartu*', which means take); '*eztabaida*', which means discussion (and translates as 'yes it is no it isn't') and then rather poetically '*maiteminduta*', which means in love (combines '*maite*', which means love and '*min*', which means pain). Therefore, to fall in love in the Basque region is to be wounded by love. Even from this smattering of oxymorons, it seems to me that the Basques have a superb, intuitive grasp of the contingent nature of the ebb and flow of human interaction.

Hyphens

Finally, a note on a tiny punctuation mark — the hyphen. In the context of betweenity, there are two things to say. Firstly, at a literal level, hyphens sit between words. So that's one simple point to make. But there's more. During the research and reading for this book, it dawned on me that some of the authors who feel closest in spirit to betweenism use a similar construction to each other, using multiple hyphens to string words together into a single verbal phrase, like pearls on a rope. Examples include 'all these ways of being-a-self …' and '… revealing the experience of the *self-as-really-existing*' (both from Anil Seth's *Being You*), and also '… we need to redirect our attention to *what-out-there-is-not-us* in a way that rebalances …' (one example amongst many from Iain McGilchrist's *The Matter with Things*). It also made me think about the business I work for, where we frequently use the phrase 'the-me-that-I-am-when…' as a hyphenated phrase. There's something in common with these constructions, something about the flow of consciousness, when having separated, atomised words just won't do the job, and when the writing instinct is to snuggle the words all up together to express this sense of continuum.

SECTION TWO — BEING BETWEEN — LIMINALITY

Many popular concepts and ideas start their life in a very tight, specific fashion and loosen up over time as they enter the mainstream and develop a life of their own. This has happened to liminality. Let's start by giving it the historical precision it deserves and then follow its fantastic rise.

We have the early pioneering anthropologist Arnold Van Gennep to thank for indirectly introducing liminality into the English language. I say indirectly, because his ground-breaking book, *Rites of Passage*,[1] was only published in French, in 1909, and didn't get an English translation until the 1960s. The word *liminal* already existed in French, although not in great usage at the time, so it was relatively easy for Van Gennep to appropriate it into his book.

To reprise the introduction to liminality in the words section, in the strictly anthropological meaning, a liminal state is one where during a rite of passage ceremony, an individual is in a suspended state between two different phases of being. In Van Gennep's structure, there are three distinct phases — the separation phase; the ceremony itself, which is the liminal state (Van Gennep often calls these *rites liminaire* or *rites du marge*); and then the reincorporation phase, where the individual comes back into the group, but assuming their new identity.

Now this is where his original concept loosens up. He himself was clear that the liminal rite is not a 'transition'. The first and third steps were transitions, but the middle one wasn't. The loosening started with the first English translation (1960), which translated *rites du marge* as 'rites of transition' ('rites of margin' would have been a more strictly accurate translation). And as his ideas were increasingly popularised through the 1960s and beyond, most of the specificity of his critique rubbed away. We now have a more accessible, general sense of pre-, during, and post-, with the during being this liminal state. In fact, we can go further than this — it's very easy to come across someone using the phrase 'liminal space' without there being any implied pre- or post- to it. Rather, the concept of a liminal period happening *in a time sequence* can be replaced by it simply being a general, ill-defined state of suspension, or a synonym for a physical borderland like a shoreline, or even the type of physical space where you're just waiting for something else to happen, like at an airport. There is supporting evidence for its ubiquity as an idea. Using the handy Google Ngram viewer again, liminality is one of those concepts that rockets exponentially towards the end of the twentieth century, from barely having any existence at all prior to that. It starts to make a barely visible appearance in the 1890s, and makes small inroads for the next few decades, perhaps thanks to Van Gennep's work. But from the 1980s on (a while after the English translation of *Rites of Passage* and the popularisation of anthropology as an academic discipline), it starts to make a vertiginous climb in the quantity of its written appearances, a climb that shows no sign of levelling off.

And in this way, rather like a virus escaping from a laboratory, liminality has become epidemic in culture. Like most ideas that take flight, it's simple, malleable, and intuitive, and it is a fundamental concept that underpins The Age of Between.

In the rest of this section, we'll come at liminality from a few different directions. It's worth understanding more about rites of passage themselves because this is the proving ground for the current liminality obsession.

1. Rites of passage

In *Rites of Passage,* Van Gennep lists a few transitional states, including pregnancy, childbirth, marriage, and funerals. But it's fair to say that the one that has the most hold on our collective imagination is that which defines the transition from teenage to adulthood. It's worth pointing out that this wasn't only a discovery of field-based pioneering ethnographers in the early twentieth century. Similar traditions have been around for thousands of years and there are records of them in ancient texts. In *The Edge of the Plain,*[2] James Crawford gives an account of just such a process that existed in ancient Athens, 2500 years ago, using the present tense for dramatic effect.

> A group of young adolescent boys, known as *ephebes,* are about to begin a two-year stint of military training. At the end of this, they will become full *hoplites,* citizen soldiers, able to own land and property. But first they must leave the city, leave the countryside, and travel to the *eschatia.* That they will be known as *peripoloi,* those "who patrol around".

The eschatia was the uncharted land outside the city, and these boys became literal border guards, living outside the margins and becoming familiar with the wider territory within which Athens was situated. When that period finished, there was a rite of passage ceremony for them, in which they swore a highly resonant oath of allegiance to 'the boundary-stones of the fatherland, the wheat, the barley, the vines, the olive trees and the fig trees'. Take note of the prominence of the boundary stones in that oath — their literal and symbolic significance as demarcating all the cultivation that happened inside.

Now, ancient rites like those, and the more recent ones that Van Gennep and his colleagues were documenting over a century ago, are still with us. A lesser-known part of UNESCO's role (i.e., less well-known than their defence of world heritage sites) is supporting and safeguarding intangible cultural heritage. One such example is their listing of the initiation rites amongst the Maasai community in Kenya.[3] Three of these ceremonies are specifically called out by UNESCO, although the Maasai's own listing of ceremonies documents several others.[4] *Enkipaata* is chronologically the first of the ceremonies and is a rite of passage that boys undergo between the ages of 14 and 16. It has certain resonances to the process that Athenian boys underwent 25 centuries ago, including time spent away from their own homestead and sleeping in the forest — this is a quintessential pre-liminal aspect of such rites of passage, the separation rite. By spending time away from their home and family, it helps to formally mark the transition away from childhood. After the ceremony itself, which includes a day of non-stop dancing, the boys undergo a physical mark, such as circumcision, and have completed their transition into adulthood.

The point about the non-stop dancing shouldn't be glossed over. Part of Van Gennep's insight was realising how often, if not always, the literal threshold ceremony itself involves some physical activity on behalf of the initiand, in which they are mentally, emotionally, and/or spatially disoriented, symbolising the 'death' of their former self or status, before emerging on the other side of the ceremony with some new self or status. But there's also a physiology to this as well. Dimitris Xygalatas, in his 2022 book *Ritual: How Seemingly Senseless Acts Make Life Worth Living*,[5] talks about the way that in activities like synchronised dancing, endorphins are released that contribute powerfully to social bonding. And of course, in a rite of passage, members of a group are actively looking to cement the initiand into the group — the idea that the whole community cohere through shared physical exercise makes a lot of sense. Apparently, there are solid experimental findings to demonstrate that the more synchronised people are in their dancing, the higher the endorphin release, and the higher the trust between participants (as measured through trust games that are conducted after the experiments). He makes the point that you can also see echoes of this in activities like military drill. Even though no one marches into battle these days, and so there is no practical advantage to engaging in parade ground drill, these examples of synchronous movement encourage belonging. As he says, 'By acting like one, we come to feel like one.'

One point of fascination about these rites of passage is how structured they are. The traditions live on, and they are orchestrated by a senior elder within the community. As I've implied already, it's common for people to not enjoy borderland living, where the boundaries and rules are ill-defined. Their preference is for knowing where they stand and knowing their position. These rites of passage confer exactly that clarity, and part of *how* they do it is by demanding that the individual undergoing the transition must deal with the discomfort of having their certainties removed from them for a period of time.

2. **The West — young, free, and liminal**

In Western countries we no longer have these formal initiation rites. Teenagerhood is often talked about as a rite of passage, but it lacks true ceremony and precision. Perhaps there are some very faint traces of these ancient practices, such as in the mental dislocation experienced at raves, or in the recent gap year tradition, which at a stretch might connect to the notion of being separated from home to experience life outside. But none of this comes with any status being formally conferred in a public moment. There's no ritual, no boundary stone. The notion of coming of age as a celebrated event has weakened. Yes, there are graduation ceremonies, but in reality they are little more than a narrow recognition of educational attainment and lacking the life-changing significance of anything that people like the Maasai are marking in their ceremonies.

Instead of this, we have this enormous borderland, lasting for years. From puberty through to some vague moment in young adulthood (and increasingly not so young), people exist in a long liminal state. From a legal perspective, certain things happen in a very drawn-out fashion — in the UK, at each age between 12 and 19, and then finally again at 21 (the youngest age at which you can legally adopt someone), some new entitlement or permission comes into force. To spell it out, that's a 9-year gradual recognition from first acknowledgement of extra entitlement toward full adulthood. After 21, from an age perspective, any person is the same as any other as far as the law is concerned. But really, other than the occasion of someone's 18th birthday, and starting to appear on the electoral register, there's nothing to confirm to a person that they are a functioning adult and perceived as one by wider society.

I got an interesting perspective on the issues of young, Western liminality from an unexpected source. At one point in my research, I became aware of a literary journal, published in Dublin, called *The Liminal Review*. Out of pure intrigue and the hope of some fellow feeling around betweenism, I got in touch with one of the co-founders, Alix Berber, and was reassured to discover that she and her co-founder Shauna Smullen have similar sensibilities to the ones I've been chasing, but from a different generational perspective. They are both in their 20s and set up *The Liminal Review* because they sensed that the literary world was becoming ever more dominated by writing that explores transitional spaces of all types, and wanted to create a forum where that was an explicit part of the remit. In Alix's view, a tendency that was already strong has been accelerated by at least three factors:

a) the pandemic, which unmoored many people from their certainties.
b) the increasing dislocation of the digital world from the real world, with people having to exist and have personas in both.
c) the rise in the number of people that are living for far longer periods in rental property, which is a highly contemporary version of a liminal space. (We can add to this the huge increase over recent years of the number of young people who still live in their parental home, let alone in rented accommodation.)

In her view, all three of these factors have a disproportionate impact on young people, meaning that there is a generational overlay on notions of liminality. As much as many young people might yearn for concreteness, it's not on offer, so they learn to tack a course through these unstructured spaces. As Alix pointed out, many, maybe most, young people would be all too happy to have mortgages in their early to mid-20s and enjoy the relative securities that their parents enjoyed in the '80s and '90s, but in the absence of that, their choice is to either resent it or embrace the act of will to style it out and make it a decision. From their editorial perspective, judging by literary submissions, liminal themes appear to be a dominant concern amongst those younger writers who are mining their own lived experience for material.

3. The grey area

I was recently involved in a meeting that was going to have a professional impact on one of the people in the conversation. They had recently turned 50 and said, 'This feels like a moment of adulthood.' It was a joke of sorts, but it also registered with me as a sign of the immense age borderlands we have in our contemporary society. We have older people skewing younger (for many reasons, such as age denial, or having their own parents still alive well into their old age, or finding youth culture attractive), and younger people skewing older (because digital media makes the adult world available to them far earlier than in previous eras), all at the same time.

To underscore that, and moving on to consider the older end of the age scale, we also find it harder to know when we've finished. My grandfather, like everyone he knew, had a fixed retirement date, which coincided precisely with the arrival of his state pension. One day he was working in an iron foundry as a blacksmith, the next day he was retired. I was told later than on his last day there was a modestly early finish, a short speech of thanks from a manager, a presentation of a carriage clock (the great, ironic cliché of that era was that you'd be given a time piece to mark the decades of service that were now behind you), a slice of cake and cup of tea, and that was it. Fifty years in the same foundry summed up and underlined and dealt with. Just recounting it now feels almost brutal, compared to the long pre-retirement departure lounge that is increasingly common today. But in the way it was conveyed to me, there was no sense of it being savage at the time. Just a clean division between work and retirement. He knew where he stood (to use that phrase again), and so did everyone else. In that era (the 1970s), there was something implacable about the retirement age of 65 for men and 60 for women. Issues such as your own health, plans, finances, and so on didn't come into it.

But my father, by contrast, started planning for his retirement from about the age of 50, firstly by taking up golf, which he had marked out as his major time-filler and social life, and then from roughly the age of 55 by actively cutting down his hours year by year. Even after he finally left his teaching role at university, he continued doing summer school teaching for quite a few years into his retirement. A blurred work/retirement boundary of about 15 years.

I was reminded of my dad's approach during 2023, when I found myself, in the course of my own work, talking to groups of people in their 50s about their thoughts and plans around retirement. In nearly every case, their thinking about the date of retirement was entirely unfixed and bore very little, if any, relationship to the state retirement age. In as much as they had any guiding principle, it was financial — when could they afford to retire? And that is a fantastically hard question to answer. Several of them said a version of: 'The problem is, you don't know what you are planning for.' In other words, are you going to drop dead of a heart attack in your late 60s, or have a very long old age, with increasing need for support and care? Who knows? Therefore, in the absence of a social or regulatory mandate, it ends up being a very personal decision with no formal constraints, which can either end up being deferred, or alternatively brought dramatically forward.

In the latter case, it was widely documented that following the end of the pandemic, substantial numbers of people were permanently lost to the workforce, many in their 50s. A UK Government research briefing in August 2022 reported that post-pandemic there were just short of 400,000 more people of working age who were economically inactive than before the pandemic, despite there being record numbers of job vacancies waiting to be filled.

Anecdotally, a proportion of those people reported having had a taste of freedom during the furlough scheme and simply saw no compelling reason to go back to work. Of course, there's a lot more nuance than this — there were many reasons for the total figure, which the Office for National Statistics collected, but at least for some, the previously unchallenged expectation of being in the workforce as part of what it meant to be an adult was now up for review. From a liminal perspective, it's all evidence of phenomena that occur when previously unchallenged social behavioural boundaries get removed, and decision-making becomes a matter of personal circumstance and temperament. Of course, this is in no way a value judgement on anyone, but there's no doubt that there are implications at a social level. When these statistics emerged, there was a lot of subsequent debate about emergent skills shortages amongst the most experienced cohort of the workforce, and about how to attract them back. Decisions that feel very right for individuals generate complexity when multiplied up and demonstrate the intricate relationship between personal and social borderlands.

My instinct around all this is that there is a correlation between Western society becoming ever more individualistic and atomised, and having more feeble social ceremonies. Going back to formal rites of passage for a moment, one of the things that comes with initiation ceremonies is an ongoing obligation and clarity about how you fit into your group. Your identity as an adult has been publicly ratified and is not in doubt. The expectations that come with that are also clear. If that all feels like a sacrifice we're not prepared to make for the personal choice and freedoms that come with a Western lifestyle, it's worth hearing Dimitris Xygalatas out. He makes a powerful, evidenced case that people who experience strong social bonds and 'know their place' within their social group suffer less from conditions like high blood pressure or poor mental health. It's a trade-off — and much of it circles back to the contention that we're now living more of our life in borderlands of different sorts. Maybe something like imposter syndrome is partly due to the lack of formal initiation rites. At some level, we never quite know that we've arrived.

Usefully, Xygalatas creates a distinction between social rituals and personal ones, which he thinks of as routines. He explains that brains are essentially predictive devices but hampered by having no idea what's coming at them. Therefore, a personal routine, or call it a ritual if you prefer, offers the possibility of control over circumstance. Whereas uncertainty can breed anxiety, activities that are honed through repetition can calm the mind and persuade your brain that there is a measure of control and predictability that in turn leads to improved performance. Perhaps it's a bit like a see-saw — if we're not going to ever again have the certainty that things like fixed retirement gave us, then we need more personal routine as a psychological proxy.

4. **Flex is the new fixed**

We've considered the young and those approaching retirement, what about those who are solidly mid-career in the workface? What liminality do they encounter?

I want to go back in time to begin to illustrate this. When I was 16 and about to go into the sixth form, one of my schoolfriends, Nige, made a late decision not to study any more, but just take a desk job that was on offer in a local firm. He was very clear that he wanted money in his pocket straightaway. After his first week, I asked him how it was going. Apart from the money, the thing that most blew him away was flexitime. He went on and on about it. Of course, I can't remember it word for word, but the spirit of his amazement went a bit like this:

> "It's incredible. I have to be there before 9.30 and can't leave before 5.00, but apart from that, all I have to do is my hours each week, and I can figure it out for myself. And there's this clocking in and out system, where you put your own card in, and it reads your details. My dad reckons it's a skive, says he's never heard anything like it."

With the benefit of hindsight, flexitime didn't give employees a vast measure of control, but it felt like a breakthrough at the time, and certainly the older generation often couldn't get their heads round it. I knew Nige's dad. He was one of those affable men you see in every generation who are wry and likeable and do a good job of appearing to be entirely baffled by whichever iteration of the modern world they are encountering. I sometimes wonder what he would make of white-collar hybrid working. Even before the impact of the pandemic, there had been a gradual drift towards a more flexible, permissive attitude to a small amount of home-based working. So completely did the pandemic change working practices that I realised I had forgotten about 'dress-down Friday', which, while it was a thing, created an airlock between the working week and the weekend. I now see that quaint, short-lived tradition as a classic bit of liminality — turning Friday into a working day with a tacit degree of relaxation attached to it. It softened the edges of the weekend, and you'd hear people saying things like, 'Thursday is the new Friday.' In retrospect, it was a dainty step towards what we now have, but at the time, it had its own degree of controversy, at least from senior managers. In this current realm of hybrid working (2 or 3 days a week in the office, 2 or 3 at home), we're seeing something of a switch in the implicit or sometimes explicit contract between employers and employees in office-based workplaces. In our business, which is a classic small- or medium-sized enterprise

(SME) of 16 people, we have been feeling our way in this new landscape along with many others, but as part of our client work, we're also spending time listening to other employers talk about the challenges that running offices post-pandemic brings. Here's one of them:

> "Whereas we used to take it for granted that everyone would be in, with occasional exceptions made for a work from home day if someone needed solitude to work on something that needed concentration, now we have to coax them in. It feels like it's a question of we'll come in if we want to… And I don't want to be an enforcer, or take a register, but we do need people in, for all sorts of reasons."

The kinds of reasons she's talking about are things like team spirit, informal training for newer employees, creative thinking, pastoral support. Many of these rationales are intangible, but still feel real to employers. For employees, on the other hand, their rationales for working from home can feel entirely tangible, such as the cost of travel, work lunches, wear and tear from commuting. Now that the hybrid genie is out of the bottle, and everyone has found a way to make online video meetings work, it currently feels unlikely that this new-found flexibility will settle back to the previous rigid presenteeism, even though the pendulum has swung back somewhat. Like fluids, flexibility has a habit of moving in one direction. As anyone who works in a hybrid style now knows, there are common effects: a high level of variation with the quantity of people in on any given day; meetings where some people are physically present, and others are dialled in; having to formalise well in advance if everyone's physically needed; new etiquettes, systems, and processes to ensure decent coverage. Whereas office life had a predictably to it — it's where all or virtually all your work got done — now it's yet another liminal space.

Of itself, hybrid working could be shrugged off as a post-pandemic aberration, but when you add it to the other cases that we've looked at, it builds up into a bigger picture of people living without fixed points of certainty, or defined staging posts that represent a path through life itself, or even daily life.

Flexibility is not just about the days you work in the office, it's also about the work you do at all. One of the great markers of liminality in employment in our era is the rise of multiple employment. Figures vary, but research suggests that between 7% and 15% of the working population in the UK have more than one job. (The Office for National Statistics (ONS) are towards the low end, and a survey from Royal London Insurance in 2022 suggests the top end.) According to US Census figures, the figure in the States is over 15%. In the short term, these figures are rising due to the global cost of living crisis, as people take on extra work out of necessity, but there is also an underlying trend of multiple employment that was apparent well before the 2022/23 inflation spike. There are several names to describe this phenomenon. You can choose from slashie, diversified employment, or portfolio career. The grandest, with more than a touch of irony, must be the millennial multi-hyphenate. And we shouldn't forget the concept of the side hustle, which is adjacent to all this. If you take a positive view, then it's an empowered new way of working, where individuals get the chance to build skills and experience in parallel, rather than sequentially, as in the old model, and potentially having a passion project as one of the employments they are holding down. If you take a more jaundiced view, then you've got people being the servant of several masters at once, getting exhausted through shift juggling, and having no real security or long-term prospects available to them, or a solid-looking CV to show off.

Whichever way you look at it though, what multiple working does lead to is significantly more people having bespoke ways of describing what they do. That part of your identity that might have been quite clear cut — 'I'm a builder,' or 'I'm an accountant,' is more fluid and closer to being unique when it's 'I'm a D.J./copywriter/youth worker.'

5. **To have but not to hold**

My son Tom remarked to me a couple of years ago, 'In previous centuries, people used to be outlived by their possessions many times over, but now we easily outlive our possessions. The word "heirloom" will become obsolete in years to come — there won't be any.' His insight is undoubtedly correct, and his prediction could turn out to be correct too. A few years back (with the history of modern tech there's a need to be specific, so I'm talking of circa 2019), I had become attached to my increasingly venerable iPod, against all reason, other than a general resistance to overly convergent technology. This attachment had lasted for about 10 years, and the iPod was in danger of starting to look like the kind of nostalgic object you see in design museums, especially once the Bluetooth era properly kicked in: it had become almost wilful to still use it. There was then a moment in our office when younger colleagues gathered round and gawped at it with a sense of historical curiosity, as if it were, say, a slide rule, or one of those hand-operated meat mincers our grandmothers screwed onto the sides of their kitchen tops. I was bizarrely proud of the fact that I still had a bit of working electronic technology from before 2010. Well, I'm now here to tell you that it's broken, irreparably, and has demonstrated the accuracy of Tom's insight.

The current reality is that much of our consumer technology is intermediate, constantly being updated, or patched, a temporary staging post between one state and another. And because of that impermanence, consumer technology exists in its own liminal state, not expected to last longer than a decade, the maximum horizon of its likely utility. In a research project that we were running in our business on technology, one woman in her early 30s, quite a fan of tech, said something that many will identify with: 'Even though I've spent a lot of money on tech over the years, I still find that experience doesn't help me to know when is the right moment to buy that new thing. Is it going to be a good investment? Should I wait? It's really hard to know.' As a result, one of the great ironies of technology is that it promises to mitigate against human fallibility and make our lives less uncertain, and yet in practice its mayfly-like existence does the exact opposite.

If that is true of hardware, it's true of software too. Apps and software are continually updated; they're never finished. They are like the Forth Road Bridge of our era, being made new again continually. This state of perpetual liminality has an impact on notions of ownership too. Time was when you had to own music if you didn't want to be at the mercy of the radio to put on your favourite records. In the '80s, I had the experience of having my house broken into, and amongst other things, my entire music collection was stolen. I had to start over and rebuy the records and CDs I couldn't live without. By temperament, I'm still the type of person that would prefer to own all my music, but like most people, I don't. But for all that, it's still possible to have what you thought was yours taken away from you, such as the time quite recently when between 60 and 70 tracks that I'd 'purchased' from iTunes vanished overnight. Theoretically, I knew they were rented at the pleasure of Apple, but it didn't feel that way when they all tiptoed away while I wasn't looking. But such is the nebulous relationship that we have with products these days. Easy come, easy go.

6. **Caught in limbo**

So far, everything we've looked at in this section pushes in the direction of increased liminality in modern life. But ironically, for centuries, one of the main manifestations of liminality in the popular imagination was the Roman Catholic doctrine of limbo, and this has withered on the vine at precisely the cultural moment when liminality as a concept is going through an explosion. Is there some correlation going on here? It bears some examination. But before considering that, the tale of limbo is one that deserves telling for its own sake, and for what it tells us about human nature and notions of certainty and ambiguity.

If we broadly accept that, whilst alive, most people prefer clarity and certainty, where the end of life is concerned, the certain finality of death has not been a popular concept down the centuries. Instead, we have been happier to live with the ambiguity of the hope of the afterlife, in a physical or spiritual realm that is removed from our perception — meaning we must have faith in it. Our increasingly secular age is an anomaly in historical terms. It's been far more typical for cultures to soften the impact of death with the prospect of some version of an afterlife.

There is complexity here, though, and specifically because notions of heaven and hell, and their equivalents in non-Christian religions, create sharp binary boundaries that can be anything but emotionally comforting. Leaving faith to one side for a moment, and thinking about all this from a psychological perspective, it's not surprising that a middle ground sprang up, and in the case of Christianity, that middle ground was limbo. The name derives from the Latin *limbus*, meaning edge or boundary, and of course is closely related to *limen* or liminality. One of the interesting things about limbo is that there is no Biblical justification for it. It's an entirely man-made construct. I realise that many readers will believe and make the point that this is also true of the Bible itself and organised religion full stop. But for the purposes of this argument, I'm staying inside the precepts of religious doctrine and working on the premise that if grounds for doctrine and belief come from written authority, then in the case of limbo, a generous interpretation is that it's very thin. A less generous interpretation is that there isn't any. For instance, when Jesus is on the cross and still alive, and one of the thieves being crucified along with him repents, Jesus says to him, 'Truly I tell you, on this day you will be with me in paradise.' Not much room for limbo there. And presumably, if you believe in the divinity of Jesus, then you must allow that he's best placed to know.

In the interests of strict accuracy, there are some scholars who say that the meaning of Jesus's sentence hangs on the position of the comma, and they believe the comma is correctly placed *after* 'on this day', rather than before it, thereby leaving the door open for an interpretation as to the existence of limbo. I suppose as a lover of all things ambiguous, I should in theory take my hat off to those scholars, but if the existence of limbo hangs on punctuation, then even I am losing it at this point.

But standing back from the narrowness of that debate, the Roman Catholic limbo is part of a proud tradition of indeterminate afterlife states. Islam has *barzakh*, a word that tellingly is derived from the Persian word meaning barrier or partition, and is the place where souls go to after death, awaiting their ultimate fate on Judgement Day. Similar concepts to this can be traced all the way to Greek mythology. If you had been a hero in life, then your reward was the Elysian Fields, a place of celestial joy. And if you'd been evil, then you were bound for Tartarus, or hell. But for those who'd lived an average life, the destination was the Asphodel Meadows, the neutral space of no distinction between the two. (I have a mental picture of a well-educated town planner with an ironic twist of mind using it as a street name in one of those endless post-war suburban housing estates.) A very similar notion appears in Zoroastrianism, one of the world's most ancient religions, originating from Iran. *Hamistagan* is a neutral space for those who have lived a life that is neither good nor evil, and whose ultimate fate will also be decided on Judgement Day.

Returning to Catholicism, at least two specific limbos have been introduced over time, including the Limbo of the Fathers (designed as a kind of spiritual holding pen for Old Testament heroes like Moses and Abraham, whilst awaiting Jesus's reappearance on earth) and the Limbo of Infants (a space reserved for unbaptised infants, who hadn't had time to commit mortal sins that would send them to hell, but who hadn't received the baptismal sacrament that would give them automatic access to heaven). Again, you'll scour the Bible in vain to find hard or even soft evidence of these limbos.

To be abundantly clear, this is not a swipe at Catholicism, or organised religion in general. Rather, it feels to me that both concepts, along with the basic idea of limbo itself, in all its various forms across religions and epochs, conform to a psychological human need to allow for exceptional cases when, suddenly, the binary nature of life and death becomes too overwhelmingly hard to bear. They feel more like a response to an instinctive human sense of fairness, which should be celebrated. Banish Abraham to hell simply because of the accident of him being born before Christ? Outrageous! And babes in arms who have had no chance to commit a sin or make their own minds up about matters of faith? What we're seeing here are a set of exclusionary clauses, the creation of a supernatural borderland to allow for a merciful God, rather than a cut-and-dried set of extremes.

Whatever your own position on these theologically esoteric points of view about limbo, the Catholic church has often taken them to heart in implementing decisions out in the real world, and perhaps we need an example to see how it works out in practice. *In Stones of Aran: Pilgrimage*,[6] one of his two majestic books on the island of Aran off the coast of Galway, Tim Robinson tells a historical anecdote about certain burial traditions there:

> In the middle of this field of the fallen is a little hollow, between the road and the shore and about a hundred yards northwest of the consecrated graveyard, traditionally used as an infants' burial ground. Limbo, that neutral domain between the bliss of Heaven and the pains of Hell, invented by theologians to accommodate the afterlife of those who had not had life enough either to sin or to be saved, was until a couple of generations ago thought to be the portion of the stillborn or of babes who died unbaptized. Their bodies were discreetly buried in places that seem to answer to their spiritual abode: on *boundaries* between townlands, under *mearing* walls between holdings, on the *no-man's-land* of the seashore, in the ancient earthworks and *ring-walls* popularly associated with the non-Christian otherworld, or on the *margins* of consecrated ground. [My italics. By the way, a mearing wall is a boundary wall between properties.]

Now, before we leave this topic, there is an important bit of completeness to deal with. Previously, if I'd been forced to guess, I would have assumed that limbo and purgatory were essentially synonyms. But not a bit of it — they represent a kind of believe-one-get-one-free system. If you don't fit the criteria for the limbos mentioned so far, and let's call it out here, not one of you does, then there's the big catch-all of purgatory. If you haven't been following this closely, then purgatory can be thought of as a pre-heaven ante-chamber for all those who need an extra dose of purification before being allowed to enter in. As a mental exercise, imagine that it was your job to do the judging On That Day. You'd perhaps have little compunction in sending a few candidates to the fiery pit. You'd also acknowledge that some people display such saintliness that they were immediate candidates for heaven. Then you'd look at the rest of us, and you might conclude that there's plenty of modestly decent lives lived but falling some way short of having the adjective 'heavenly' attached to them. At that point, the notion of a celestial finishing school might come in handy, and towards the end of the twelfth century, that's pretty much what happened. Gradually, purgatory bubbled up as a cultural or theological idea, for obscure reasons, and over the course of a century of two, it developed a sufficient head of steam to turn into official Catholic doctrine.

There is a fascinating coda to all of this, because it is in the nature of borderland concepts to exist in a dynamic state of flux. And the Limbo of the Infants has fallen victim to these vicissitudes of theological fashion. What I haven't mentioned so far is that in 2007, Pope Benedict XVI, on the advice of the Vatican's Theological Commission, announced that the Limbo of the Infants would be abolished from Catholic teaching. It's an odd thought — for centuries after Christ there was no such idea, then it percolated into existence, was formally ratified, but suddenly it didn't exist again. Or maybe it never had. Who knows? Of course, it's a matter of belief. But of particular interest here is the wording of the Theological Commission:

> There is greater theological awareness today that God is merciful and wants all human beings to be saved. Grace has priority over sin, and the exclusion of innocent babies from heaven does not seem to reflect Christ's special love for the little ones. Our conclusion is that the many factors that we have considered … give serious theological and liturgical grounds for hope that unbaptised infants who die will be saved and enjoy the beatific vision. We emphasise that these are reasons for prayerful hope, rather than grounds for sure knowledge.

I'm especially drawn to the almost invisible use of the word 'today' in the first sentence of that judgement. In other words, by the turn of the twenty-first century, it no longer looks tenable in a contemporary cultural context to be hanging onto a notion that had reflected the cultural realities of the late medieval period.

Interestingly, purgatory is still very much alive and well in formal Catholic doctrine. Their teaching states that there are two types of judgement — the individual judgement of a person that dies, and then the general judgement at the end times. If you've been passed as fit for heaven, but still have a bit of purification to go through, you'll hang around in purgatory *between* the individual and general judgements, a bit like having to do a couple of important GCSE resits before being allowed in to do A Levels.

In summary, in the same way that limbo concepts came into being at a moment in time when religious culture had a doctrinal gap that needed filling, that need has ebbed away. The Church is also influenced by wider culture, and in an environment that is softer, less deterministic than it was, there is no need for a structural solution to deal with exceptional cases, like with unbaptised infants. We can allow the prevailing atmosphere of merciful ambiguity to do the job for us. Ironically, in liminal times, we don't need a formal limbo.

7. Section summary

Let's summarise what this survey of contemporary liminality has revealed.

a) We lack the clear markers that give sharp boundaries to various stages of life (leaving home, coming of age, unified age of retirement).
b) Hybrid working and multiple employments mean that, for millions of people, the workplace is a fluid concept.
c) Technology plays its part by creating a context where many of our most used possessions don't confer permanence or continuity in our lives.
d) Because liminality is the default setting, religious mechanisms like Limbo that were created in non-liminal times, have outlived their usefulness.

SECTION THREE — BETWEEN IDEAS

Liminal spaces, therefore, are everywhere we look. But in the world of ideas, they are not the only new kid on the block. There are other shaping forces too that contribute to the Age of Between. Yet to tell the story of those new factors, we need to start a long time ago, back in Ancient Greece, and then jump all the way forward again to a period much closer to our own times. In doing so, we're going to touch very lightly on topics that most people spend very little time worrying about in daily life, such as philosophy and physics, but not in a deep, immersive way. Our interest in dwelling on them briefly is for one purpose — to get insight into why liminal, betweenist thinking is suddenly a big part of the modern cultural soup, and why it's taken so long to take root.

The sequence of this section will run in this way:

1. **The dominant strain in Western thought** — a brief look at the main thrust of Western thinking in philosophy (and a bit on science), starting with the ancient Greeks in the fourth and third centuries BCE, and moving on to René Descartes (1596–1650) and the slightly later Sir Isaac Newton (1643–

1727), who are pivotal figures in ushering in Enlightenment thinking and the Scientific Revolution.

2. **Heraclitus — the lone Greek voice** — introducing the Greek philosopher from the fifth century BCE who preceded the main swathe of more famous philosophers and whose ideas stand in stark opposition to what was to follow.
3. **Process philosophy** — the body of new thinking that emerged at the very end of the nineteenth century and into the early part of the twentieth. These ideas can be traced directly back to Heraclitus but lay dormant for centuries while the dominant strand of Western thought held sway.
4. **The revolution in modern physics** — the dramatic breakthroughs in physics, popularised by Einstein and then a group of young physicists whose work has many parallels with the process philosophers, which were happening at the same time, in the early twentieth century.

We'll start to see how both strands of work, alongside the rise of liminality, started to challenge the orthodox views of Western thinking and laid the ground for the emergence of the Age of Between.

1. **The dominant strain in Western thought**

The Greek big hitters

The vast majority of us that live in the West have been profoundly influenced in our world view by a group of male thinkers that lived and worked in Greece nearly 2500 years ago. In addition to gender and an inclination to deep thinking, they were unified by having grand-sounding names like Socrates, Plato, Aristotle, Democritus, Parmenides, and Zeno, but there were a good number of others.

They didn't all agree with each other — far from it. But for our purposes, there's one key point to land about their legacy. There was a common obsession with trying to get to the essence of *what is*. What is the essential substance of which life consists? For example, Leucippus is credited with being the first person to invent the notion of atoms — separate elements of matter that can't be divided down any further and are too small for the human eye to see, meaning both invisible and indivisible. That's quite a leap to make before the invention of microscopes.

Some of their beliefs are in contradiction with ordinary daily experience, and yet they've still gone on to be foundational. As an example of that, Parmenides believed that all reality is timeless and uniform. One of his students, Zeno, took this one stage further and created a set of paradoxes to demonstrate that motion is essentially impossible. Perhaps the most famous of these is the one about the race between Achilles and the tortoise, in which Achilles gives the tortoise a head start. Despite being a far faster runner, Achilles never manages to catch the tortoise up, because in the time it takes him to reach the tortoise's starting point, the tortoise has moved on a small distance, and this continues to infinity, with ever-smaller distances. When you're thinking inside the world of this scenario, it's surprisingly hard to overturn the paradox, even though it's clearly nonsense as far as common sense is concerned.

To give another example of their output, one of Aristotle's foundational contributions was his *Categories*, in which he created a way of classifying objects and experiences of everyday life that we see around us. If this object is a table, and it has these attributes, can we predict that a similar object with the same attributes is also a table?

In very broad, overall terms, despite their differences, the Greeks were obsessed with notions of the material, the building blocks of life. It's all about things, stuff, substance. Even Plato, who is more concerned with the life of the mind, was committed to his notion of 'forms' as being identifiable, discrete mental states. They would accept that things move and change, yet were mistrustful of those phenomena as being superficial or even illusory, and instead put more emphasis on the eternal, unchanging essence of things as being a truer, deeper reality. In very broad terms, they are responsible for a whole branch of philosophy, called materialist philosophy, which has been the dominant strand of thinking that is embedded in Western minds.

The seeds of the Enlightenment and the Scientific Revolution

As evidence of this, we can come much further forward in time to René Descartes (1596–1650), often described as the founder of modern philosophy (at least in the West). For him it was straightforward to conceive of an entity like a mind as being able to exist by itself as an independent entity. His most famous phrase, 'Cogito, ergo sum' ('I think, therefore I am'), is possible because the mind doesn't have to be associated with its body for the act of thinking to validate the thinker's existence. Although Descartes liked to think he was making a sharp break with previous schools of thought, in reality his mind and body dualism was straight out of the materialist playbook. His thinking went on to become incredibly influential in creating the Age of Reason and Enlightenment thinking throughout Europe.

It wasn't just in philosophy that this type of confidence and structured thinking was in the ascendancy. It was true in science. A century after Descartes, Sir Isaac Newton in England was a mathematical and scientific colossus whose principles laid the foundation for centuries of classical physics that were to follow.

We're not focused on his science here. What we need to take note of is the *tone of certainty* that his science was grounded in. Take his first law of motion as a for instance: 'Every object will remain at rest or in uniform motion in a straight line unless compelled to change its state by the action of an external force.' Let's look closely at the language of this law, how it's expressed, by taking it in bite sizes. We have '**Every** object **will remain** at rest', and then 'or in **uniform motion** in a **straight line**', followed by '**unless compelled** to change its state', and concluded by 'the **action of an external force**'. It's gloriously certain. In a Newtonian universe, any object, be it a cannonball or anything else, would sit there politely minding its own business unless something came along and gave it a wee nudge, in which case it would veer off in a predictable fashion, like a snooker ball, based on the nature of those forces.

Just think of the impact of Newton's scientific revolution with these new certainties. Imagine yourself as a well-educated individual in the Enlightenment in Europe during the eighteenth century. It would feel like the march of science was unstoppable. Whole vistas of knowledge were being brought under the dominion of reason. Science and technology were even bringing themselves into the realm of trade and commerce, such as the way that John Harrison's ocean-going clocks finally solved the problem of finding longitude at sea in the 1730s. In overall terms, due to the dominance of science and rationalist thought, the prevailing intellectual mood was dominated by confidence in the ability to define reality; the organised classification of things; things being certain, knowable, and predictable; things being distinct from each other and having a clear independent existence; and things being stable, static, and inert as a default setting.

2. Heraclitus — the lone Greek voice

But Western thinking did not have to turn out the way it did: it wasn't prescribed or pre-ordained. It's not that way in the Eastern tradition, for example. Much of Indian and Buddhist thinking is taken up with notions of reality consisting of the interconnectedness of all things, rather than the independent existence of all things.

And curiously, it might not have been that way in Greece, either. Things could have worked out differently. For one thing, there was one lone voice, Heraclitus, who stood apart from the crowd of materialists, and had he had a much louder voice or his ideas taken root as orthodoxy, the history of Western thinking could have been very different.

The details of Heraclitus's life are elusive. We know that he lived in Ephesus, was active round about 500 BCE, and that he was by temperament somewhat misanthropic — or a bit mardy, as we call it where I come from. It's also a safe bet that he was a person of major standing within his city. But that's about it. We don't even have a complete book from him. It's believed by some scholars that during his lifetime he produced a book called *On Nature*, but if he did, it's been lost to history. What we have are a set of between 124 and 130 teasing fragments bestowed to us by other writers and thinkers of the time and attributed to him. Collectively, these are known as the *Fragments*, an entirely satisfying title in the context of this book. As unpromising as this sounds, these shards, which you could easily read in an hour or two, are closer to the zeitgeist now than they have been at any point over the last 2500 years. That's quite a slow burn by any reckoning.

As a thinker, Heraclitus stands in sharp contrast to the dominant strands of Western thinking laid down by the later Greek giants. If they have given us the basis of reason, logic, and a worldview based on stability and enduring substance, Heraclitus has done the opposite. His ideas centre around the concept of flux, emphasising that everything in the world is in a constant state of transformation. One of the fragments that is quoted by Plato sums this up as 'Everything flows, and nothing remains still.' He saw change and flow as *the* fundamental aspect of reality, asserting that all things are in a perpetual process of becoming something else. It's more radical than just acknowledging that all things are subject to change and flux. It's the change that is the point. Nothing is settled; it's all transitional. According to him, the universe is in this state of eternal churn, with opposing forces constantly interacting and balancing each other. And indeed, it's this fundamental idea of the unity of opposites which means that if there is ever a Hall of Fame for Betweenists, he's going to be in a position of ascendancy.

This notion of flow is seen through his imagery of choice — rivers and fire loom large in the fragments. Plato's mistranslation of Heraclitus gives us our most famous 'quote' of his: 'A man cannot step twice into the same river.' The implication of Plato's translation is that you're not the same man, and the river is not the same river, due to the processes of flow. In the context of this book, it seems pleasingly ironic that this most famous quote isn't even accurate, although in fairness it does seem to me to capture something Heraclitian for all that. A closer translation is: 'On those stepping into rivers staying the same other and other waters flow.' Eh? When you start to grapple with Heraclitus, you're often confronted with this sort of befuddlement — elusive meaning, verbal density, and ambiguity comes with the territory. I guess I ought to be delighted, but somehow, going with the flow feels like it should be a bit easier than this. Anyhow, after staring at it for ages, what I think this translation is driving at is that it's only possible to stay the same through experiencing continual change. A rather delicious paradox, but it feels right. It's when you discover that there is some core of you-ness that holds true, even when confronted by radically different contexts, that you feel some essential centre to what you're about as a person. Without that metabolic flux in your life, you wouldn't have this type of surround-sound insight into the you-that-you-are in any holistic kind of way.

At a grander level than the simple observation of people in rivers, his vision of flux is informed by a surprisingly modern grip on nature. He seems to have an intuition for the forces of change and inconstancy and finds expression for it. The Penguin Classics version of *Fragments* has been translated by a poet, Brooks Haxton,[1] and he has succeeded in retaining a sense of beauty in the language — and capturing the essence of the unity of opposites, which was central to Heraclitus's view — at the same time as expressing flow. (The numbers relate to the fragment number.)

23

The earth is melted
into the sea
by that same reckoning
whereby the sea
sinks into the earth.

25

Air dies giving birth
to fire. Fire dies
giving birth to air. Water,
thus, is born of dying
earth, and earth of water.

These fragments have some of the quality of extended Japanese haikus about them (a classic haiku is only three lines long, with a strict 17-syllable extent), and a similar sense of compression, together with that just-out-of-reach meaning that slips away the moment you think it's clarified. You are better off trying to feel them, rather than logically work them out. Even so, I don't think Heraclitus would have been troubled by the science if he'd been confronted by knowledge of plate tectonics, with our continents floating around on a sea of molten rock. It would have sat comfortably with his intuition and way of seeing the grand scheme of nature.

So what happened to Heraclitus's contribution? Put simply, his ideas didn't win out. Heraclitus's followers would literally have to wait millennia for his ideas to flourish, because the materialists were to hold sway for a long, long time. The world view of Aristotle and co., with its formal rigour and the comfort it provided about the unchanging nature of reality, carried the day, and continued to do so for centuries, as we've already seen.

However, to reuse his fragment: 'Everything flows, and nothing remains still,' it turns out that Heraclitus was to swing back into fashion, with his ideas eventually resurfacing after centuries of obscurity.

3. **Process philosophy**

By the very end of the nineteenth century, and certainly in the early years of the twentieth, a challenger to materialist philosophy finally appeared on the scene, and had he been around to witness it, there is no question that Heraclitus would have approved and been part of the gang. It's known as 'process philosophy', and their leading lights believe that qualities like interactions, the relations between things, interdependence, interconnectedness, inevitable change, and, of course, processes, are the very essence of reality, not just subordinate entities to objects, things, and substances. In this way of looking at the world, something like a tree does not have a meaningful independent existence — it only has any meaning within a context of its complete set of interactions: with the weather, or nutrients in the soil, or the fungal network that connects it to other trees in the same wood, or people taking shelter under it, and whatnot.

The metaphor of choice that process philosophers use to describe these interactions is 'web', and you can see the attraction. Think of spiders' webs, and the way that any contact or vibration at any point of the web is felt across its whole structure, and you have a good intuitive sense of how process philosophers feel about the intrinsic connectedness of all things. Of course, in our era, we have the ubiquitous World Wide Web, which cements the idea of connectedness and relational thinking. More recently, we've had the rather lovely coining of the wood wide web, which has come along to describe the underground connectedness between trees. In any case, it's worth taking note of how 'web' has come to be a dominant metaphor in daily life. These things are not accidents.

Why did process philosophy appear when it did? There's never one answer to a question like that, but we can use our handy new metaphor to say that a whole web of influences created the context in which Heraclitus's ancient idea about reality, lying dormant for centuries, along with co-existing Eastern ideas that are very similar, began to see the light of day again. I'd argue that some of these influences include the following:

a) The rise of democratic values, with a focus on the equal validity of each person's perception of the world, rather than some objective and static truth.
b) The influence of Charles Darwin. Once his theories about the influence of random mutations in shaping the course of evolution took hold, the world suddenly felt very different. The world was no longer ordained and prescribed by God, but subject to chance and the interactions of nature.
c) Let's also add in the increase in speed of the general rate of change. There was an exponential rush of change, in science, technology (the internal combustion engine, powered flight), and also the arts (think of the impact of cubism for example). Culture was on the move at a greater pace than ever before, with more momentum and more sense that change was a defining quality of modern life.

When you combine all of these, and probably other factors too, philosophy needed a new energy, a fresh discourse in its description of reality.

Early process philosophy pioneers

Several thinkers have been responsible for popularising process philosophy. In particular, towards the end of the nineteenth century and into the twentieth, there was the American William James (brother of novelist Henry James), and then the charismatic Henri Bergson from France, who managed the feat of achieving true A-list celebrity status as a philosopher — something we don't get to see a lot of in contemporary twenty-first-century culture, although one lives in hope.

James was by some years the elder of the two, but they still had time to meet each other and find real comradeship. James has a just claim to be the most influential of all American philosophers, having created pretty much single-handedly the doctrine of pragmatism. Pragmatism sits in a borderland, facilitated by the malleable intellectual and scientific atmosphere that presided at the time. Take his attitude to truth, which was sophisticated and nuanced. On the one hand, he didn't believe in one, eternal, fixed version of the truth. He believed that for each of us, truth is something we create as a product of our experience through life. But then on the other hand, he acknowledged that 'beliefs verified concretely by *somebody* are the posts of the whole superstructure'.[2] Because otherwise, there's chaos. I can't help but wonder what he'd make of the death of the middle ground we're experiencing now that I alluded to earlier, where at least some objective, verifiable truth that everyone agrees to respect feels like the rarest of commodities.

The pinnacle of James's output, published posthumously in 1912, was *Essays in Radical Empiricism*.[3] It's here that we see the seeds of process philosophy given full expression. For the longest time, philosophers had divided the world into the material and physical on one side, and the mental and cerebral on the other. With a single swat, James took issue with that, seeing both the material and the mental as subordinate to something he called pure experience, defined as 'the immediate flux of life which furnishes the material to our later reflection with its conceptual categories ... a *that* which is not yet any definite *what*, tho' ready to be all sorts of whats'. Notice the word 'flux', which takes us straight to Heraclitus, and look at the indeterminacy of what follows. He goes on to say that these 'whats' could be people, ideas, minds, objects. What is fundamental is not the independent existence of those entities, but the sequence in which they are experienced — or in other words, the *relationships between them*. The perceiver and the perceived are linked in pure experience.

Hot on the heels of William James came Henri Bergson. His prose style is more poetic than James's, and less academically rigorous, which perhaps accounts for his strong public persona, and maybe also for him being awarded the Nobel Prize for literature in 1928. Before the phrase of process philosophy was created, he was the great populariser of the central ideas, and in the sweep of his language, you can sense the urgency and force of his vision, even in translation. There's a great introduction to Bergson written by the Irish novelist and poet Michael Foley,[4] and he has captured some of Bergson's most vivid passages:

> Reality no longer appears essentially static, that affirms itself dynamically, as continuity and variation. What was immobile and frozen in our perception is warmed and set in motion. Everything comes to life around us, everything is revitalised within us. A great impulse sweeps forward beings and things.
>
> I believe that if one were convinced of the reality of change and made an effort to grasp it, everything would be simplified … the point is that usually we look at change but do not see it. We speak of change, but do not think about it. We say that everything changes, that change is the very law of things: yes, we say it and repeat it; but these are only words, and we reason and philosophise as though change did not exist.

It's impossible not to feel his passion for motion. Of all philosophers, he may have been the most influenced by dance and song, believing that it's a nonsense to think of a melody, for example, as a set of independently existing notes, when it only makes any sense to experience the unity of a whole melody.

A.N. Whitehead

Coming into prominence after Bergson was the English mathematician and philosopher Alfred North Whitehead. He gave the most rigorous intellectual gloss to the emergent movement with his book *Process and Reality*,[5] published in 1929. He argued for a reappraisal of the nature of reality, one where we 'see the world as a web [that metaphor again] of interrelated processes of which we are integral parts, so that all of our choices and actions have consequences for the world around us'. The best part of 100 years on, where liminal living is more mainstream, this reads as relatively uncontroversial, but back then, it was a breakthrough.

A brief mention of linguistics

As further evidence of the intellectual climate that was allowing these types of ideas to emerge, it's worth noting that in 1916, the Swiss linguist and philosopher Ferdinand de Saussure published his *Course in General Linguistics*.[6] Saussure is now thought of as one of the founding fathers of semiotics — the study of signs — and it was he who gave us the terminology of 'signifier' (e.g., the word 'chair') and 'signified' (the physical object, normally with four legs, that we sit on). Yet again, in a separate discipline, we're getting this backwards and forwards, this distinctive *relationship and interaction* going on. What's interesting is not so much the object itself or the word to describe it, but *what is happening between them*. The object and its descriptor are bound together in relationship.

Twenty-first century

To bring all this fully up to date, there are a group of thinkers now operating who are inheritors of process philosophy thinking. Perhaps one of the most powerful contributions to this interconnected way of seeing the world has been made by Iain McGilchrist. In the introduction to *The Matter with Things*,[7] he sets out the basis of his beliefs about reality, all of which are rooted in neuroscientific research, rather than just pure philosophical thought.

> I take it that there is something that is not just the contents of my mind — that, for example, you, my reader, exist. There is an infinitely vast, complex, multifaceted, whatever-it-is-that-

> exists-apart-from-ourselves. The only world that any of us can know, then, is what comes into being in the never-ending encounter *between* us and this whatever-it-is. What is more, I will claim that both parties evolve and are changed through the encounter: it is how we and it become more fully what we are. The process is both reciprocal and creative. Think of it as like a true and close relationship *between* two conscious beings: neither is of course "made up" by the other, but both are to some extent, perhaps to a great extent, "made" what they are through their relationship. If this seems at this point a step too far, the reader can, I hope, embrace a weaker position, that at least, as I say, our world is what comes into being in the encounter between us and this whatever-it-is.

For all the liminality that is expressed here — the thresholds that sit between the you and the non-you (and by the way, for the record, I'm loving his repeated italicisation of the word between), I find something pragmatic about his outlook here that I believe William James would have endorsed. He's not denying the essential reality of the world out there; we're not all caught up in some post-modern joke or mind-bending science fiction box set which makes us doubt our existence. In fact, it's more interesting and exciting than that. There is an exchange. That exchange is creative and transformative, and it's within that exchange, in the betweenity, that reality and true value reside.

4. **The revolution in modern physics**

> The atoms or elementary particles themselves are not real; they form a world of potentialities or possibilities rather than one of things or facts.
> — Werner Heisenberg

It wasn't just in the world of philosophy that ideas were becoming less deterministic. At the same time as process philosophy was finding its voice, there was a seismic shift in the world of physics.

We were last with physics a few pages ago, analysing the majestic confidence expressed in the writing of Isaac Newton. All of that was about to change in the early twentieth century. For centuries, the promise of science had been that it would replace ignorance and doubt with knowledge and certainty, chipping away at the unknown to give us the known.

It's instructive to glance again at the quote from Heisenberg at the top of this section and then compare that to Newton's description of the first law of motion, which for convenience is repeated here: 'Every object will remain at rest or in uniform motion in a straight line unless compelled to change its state by the action of an external force.'

For our purposes, the interesting comparison is not in the content, but in the difference in tone. What has happened? It's almost as if scientists have gone backward in terms of their confidence in what they can say about the nature of the world we live in.

To do some necessary storytelling, Werner Heisenberg was one of a group of physicists in the 1920s, alongside others such as Niels Bohr, Erwin Schrödinger, Max Born, and Paul Dirac. They were at the forefront of leading nothing short of a revolution in the practice of physics. A lot of their work came to be conducted in Copenhagen, where Bohr created the Institute for Theoretical Physics of the University of Copenhagen in 1921, which became a magnet for physicists and a place where these scientists could wrestle with complex problems that were often phenomenally abstract and conceptually hard to turn into mental pictures of reality. The label that has attached to this physics is quantum mechanics (we won't get caught up in the ins and outs of this). To give an inkling of the complexity they faced, one of the next generation of quantum physicists, an American called Richard Feynman, who won a Nobel prize for his contribution, famously said, 'I think I can safely say that no one understands quantum mechanics.' Whatever else one might think of quantum physicists, they must be given credit for being very comfortable with paradox. Here's Niels Bohr: 'It's the hallmark of any deep truth that its negation is also a deep truth.'

The new century trailblazer — Albert Einstein

We'll come back to the quantum guys soon, but a small bit of backstory is needed first. A couple of decades before them, Albert Einstein had been a pioneer, with his work on relativity. Because we don't want or need to get distracted by his science, the one thing of Einstein's to get our heads around is that he was the first person to realise that the speed of light must always appear constant to any observer, wherever they are, and whatever speed they happen to be travelling at. His other fantastic leap of imagination was to simultaneously realise that if light is always constant, then other things, such as time and space, must be *variable*. So compared to the rock-solid certainties of Newton, for the first time, Einstein gave the world glimmers of variability under certain conditions.

The theoretical implications of Einstein's work found their way into popular culture — they were too good to resist. The idea of twins, one stuck on Earth, and the other roaring around the galaxy at near-light speed and then returning to Earth to discover they were decades younger than their twin, became a staple of science fiction writers.

The quantum physics gang

Coming back to the quantum crowd, if Einstein had opened the door to some variability where none had existed, they were about to blow the whole house of certainty down. According to Heisenberg and his peers, certainty was no longer on offer; at the frontiers of science, the rules were different, and we had to be content with ambiguity and probabilities instead. The landscape they described was so confrontational, so destabilising, that even a scientific and intellectual giant like Albert Einstein couldn't accept it, coming out with his famous judgement on quantum mechanics, 'God does not play dice with the universe.'

And of course, when a discipline like physics — so traditionally associated with rigour, clarity of deterministic rules (if x then y), and laying out with precision information about how things work — starts to introduce ambiguity, doubt, and uncertainty, suddenly science feels provisional and maybe more fluid, just as philosophy was beginning to do.

To repeat, we're not here to get into the science of quantum physics; what we're interested in are those aspects that have found their way into culture and influenced our zeitgeist. For our purposes, let's dwell on just two aspects — Heisenberg's Uncertainty Principle, and the famous thought experiment known as Schrödinger's Cat, both of which have seeped into modern culture as part of the air that we breathe.

The Uncertainty Principle essentially says that it is not possible to precisely measure both the speed (momentum) and position of a quantum particle at the same time. The more you measure its position, the less you can know its speed and vice versa. What you can do is to measure first one and then the other, but, as Carlo Rovelli makes clear in his excellent primer on quantum physics, *Helgoland*,[8] the situation changes:

> But after the second measurement, the position will no longer be the same: measuring the speed loses information on the position, so that if we measure it again, we will find it changed.
>
> This follows from the second postulate, which says that even when we have gathered maximum information about an object it is still possible to learn something unexpected about it. The future is not determined by the past: the world is probabilistic.

Many physicists are exasperated by the way that the uncertainty principle has leached into popular culture. They think that the name of it is unfortunate, dumbs down the science, and is widely misinterpreted. It probably doesn't help that Heisenberg himself came out with the quote that we saw at the opening of the section. It's easy for non-scientists to run away with this ambiguous, hesitant picture of the state of physics, with further unsettling quotes like those of Einstein and Feynman adding further layers of mystery and bafflement.

If anything, the vivid, somewhat gruesome thought experiment of Schrödinger's Cat adds yet more exotic ambiguity to the popular perception of the quantum world. To reprise it briefly for readers who don't know it, we have a cat in an opaque sealed box, together with a device that has a 50% chance of being triggered by some quantum event. If it's triggered, poison gas is released and the cat dies, but if it's not, the cat continues to live. Because this event may or may not have happened, and we can't see the cat, in the normal world we all inhabit, you'd either say, 'I don't know,' or at most, 'It's either alive or dead.' More than that, you couldn't say. All very well, but Schrödinger conceived this thought experiment to illustrate the paradoxical notion of a concept known as the superposition of states — the idea that in the quantum world, unlike the normal human world, we have to assume that any condition *can and therefore does* exist, until we look at it, when the superposition collapses, giving us specific knowledge. Because of the bizarre way that quantum phenomena behave, the dominant interpretation at the time (1920s) had it that it was more accurate to say that the cat is simultaneously alive *and* dead, rather than it's alive *or* dead.

The impact has been to seed the notion of fundamental uncertainty into the fabric of modern life. Schrödinger's Cat has become a byword for indeterminacy and lack of certainty. You stumble across it all the time, again in science fiction, and in casual usage. References to it are rife on social media, where you can come across Schrödinger's Cat gifs, along with pleasingly erudite jokes, such as 'I asked the librarian for a book on Pavlov's dog and Schrödinger's cat. She said it rang a bell, but she wasn't sure if it was there or not.' One of my favourites was several years ago, just after the death of Alan Whicker had been announced, a celebrity TV travel presenter from the 1970s and '80s who had dropped out of public view for many years. I happened across a tweet (as it was called at the time) that said, 'It turns out that Alan Whicker has died. It turns out that he had still been alive. #Schrödinger's

Whicker.' Content like this demonstrates how embedded these scientific ideas have become, and shaped our worldview, dripping ambiguity and uncertainty into everyday experience.

We haven't quite finished with Schrödinger's Cat, because it does offer up one other intriguing insight. To reprise: for the observer outside the box, according to quantum theory, the cat is simultaneously alive *and* dead — it is in what quantum physicists call a superposition of states. So far, so good. But bear in mind that *inside* the box, albeit hidden from us, the cat is either alive *or* dead. Let's assume she is alive (cut me some slack here — the next few sentences become unnecessarily difficult if we assume she's dead). Therefore, the knowledge of her being either alive, or alive and dead, is relative to your position *vis a vis* the box. If you are inside the box, she's alive. That is a reality. If you are outside the box, she's alive and dead. That is also a reality. Paradoxically, both realities are true and allowed within quantum theory.

Can this paradox be reconciled? Perhaps. And since the 1990s, there has been an emergent interpretation of quantum theory gaining ground that might throw some light onto this and other odd quirks of quantum phenomena. It also chimes powerfully, even poetically, with the mood of the moment, by connecting to liminality and indeed to process philosophy. It's called the **relational interpretation of quantum physics**. Back in the early part of the twentieth century, the quantum pioneers were confounded by experimental findings that seemed to change, dependent solely on whether they were monitored. Put a sensor on a piece of equipment, and the particles behaved one way. Take the sensor away, and you'd get a different result. It was almost as if quantum particles seemed to know they were being watched and behaved differently as a result. This was, of course, a wild assault to common sense, but it felt like a reasonable conclusion when they watched it happen in front of their eyes, thousands of times. It was partly in response to this bizarre finding that Schrödinger came up with his famous thought experiment. Even in contemporary times, scientists who repeat the experiment, if only for their own satisfaction, and knowing full well what they are going to find, report being dumbfounded when seeing it for themselves for the first time.

The relational interpretation emphasises the significance of *relationships and interactions* in understanding quantum phenomena. Why 'relational'? Well, it challenges the notion of an objective, observer-independent reality and focuses on the relational nature of measurements and observations. It states that the properties of quantum objects only exist *in relation* to other objects or systems. In other words, the properties of a quantum system *are defined by its interactions with other systems.* These 'other systems' include the observer and the sensor. In other words, this interpretation isn't trying to claim that the particles know they are being measured and therefore behave differently. It's saying something both more mundane and more jaw-dropping — that all aspects of a system only exist in relation to each other. Reality is about processes and what is happening *between* entities. Heraclitus would be going 'Yep, I told you so. No one was paying attention.' And for a process philosopher like A.N. Whitehead, if he could have travelled forward 70 or so years to encounter this development, it would have felt entirely in line with his intuitions.

You could be forgiven for thinking that this is an isolated, esoteric physics debate, but in fact the mindset is everywhere. For example, in his 2024 book *The Art of Uncertainty*,[9] the eminent British statistician David Spiegelhalter, summarise his whole inspiration for the book as 'Uncertainty is a personal relationship with the world.' It's fascinating that a discipline like statistics, which, at least superficially to the layman, promises to give clarity and certainty about the nature of the world we live in from a statistical perspective, is now admitting to the fundamental lack of precision that data can offer. And why? Because the *sensation* of certainty or uncertainty is not objective, in his view, but contingent on your own relationship to the world.

In summary, let's look at the cultural legacy of quantum physics. We have radical uncertainty; a world where the solidity of physical matter is replaced by a set of probabilities; and now the absolute interdependence of all systems and objects, none of which have any meaningful independent existence. It is only in the properties of their interactions that they exist. If this isn't a liminal state, I don't know what is.

5. **Section summary**

Building on the language and liminality sections, what we now also have is this:

a) At the most profound level, the laws that underpin how the world works are governed by uncertainty and probabilities, rather than fixed principles.
b) The mind and body dualism that had dominated ideas about what it means to be a person in the world is now challenged. Ideas about the flow and interconnectedness of all things are increasingly in the ascendant.

SECTION FOUR — THE BETWEENS OF YOU

Maybe we all carry the lines with us. Maybe we are the lines.
— James Crawford, *The Edge of the Plain*

For all the insights we're getting from language, anthropology, physics, and philosophy, we shouldn't lose sight of the reality that betweenity starts at home. As individuals, we are chock full of borders and liminal spaces before we even step out into the world. Now is the time to think about some of them.

We came across James Crawford's book on borders in Section Two, in his account of initiation rites in ancient Greece. Beyond this historic story, *The Edge of the Plain* comprises some dozen or so visits to current border environments all over the world, including famously troubled ones such as those between Mexico and the United States, and Israel and Palestine. His journeys bring him face to face with many significant human truths that border thinking throws up — around conflict, inequality, scarce resources, growth, identity. It's a book rich in insight in every chapter, but for me, the most powerful thought of all is the one resting at the head of this chapter. What if it is the internal borders within each of us that somehow contribute to the external borders we see? Or beyond even that, what if we are made up of borders? In this section, we'll look at some of the key shaping borders that we toggle between as individuals. Some of these are physical facts, such as the ones inside our bodies, but others are the stacked identities that give us our sense of self, or indeed selves, and a few others are so inaccessible to us that we have no conscious feeling for them, but it's worth being aware of them, however briefly, in that they make life on Earth even possible in the first place.

1. The nested dolls

Like everyone, I am more than one person.
— Roberto Saviano, author and journalist

Each of us belongs as much to society as to himself.
— Henri Bergson, philosopher

Let's start this section on the betweens of you by embarking on a personal border journey, a guided tour of our own borders and liminal spaces. We'll take our cue from James Crawford's provocation because, even if only biologically, he's onto something. And these two quotes both make the case for nested identities — that we are never just one thing. You're never only, say, Scottish, or a surgeon, or a mother. You're always more. But how many levels of identity might you surf? Let's see.

Inside of you are approximately 50 trillion borders, give or take 10 trillion. Let's not fall out over the odd 10 trillion here or there. Nearly all of them are cell walls. And when things are running smoothly, there are no border disputes of any sort. Fifty trillion — it's a figure so large as to have nothing that we can realistically associate with it. It can only sit there as a statistic.

Up from those are thousands of other borders inside you: outer layers of tissue surrounding your vital organs, bones, muscles — essentially everything that is distinguishable inside you as a bodily entity that goes to make up you. A handful of times in your life, potentially, a surgeon may have to deal with those borders, but you'll know nothing about it.

So far, it's fair to say that you probably think about none of them on a daily basis, or possibly ever. Until we get to the next one out, which is a different matter altogether, because it's your skin. Which you care about because it's visible and you deal with it all the time, washing it, moisturising it, inspecting it, sometimes cutting or bruising it, tanning it, protecting it, complaining about it. Put this way, it feels disproportionate, doesn't it? 50,000,000,000,001 borders, and we only give a stuff about the last one, which is a layer of dead skin. I'm being unfair and provocative, because, of course, it's the only border that we feel says anything about us — the only one that feels like it's about our identity and the way we present to the world.

What's out from this? So far, we've had trillions that are physical but hidden and one that is physical and visible. Now let's consider one that is invisible and abstract, but you'll still have a strong feel for it, because it's your sense of personal boundary. This is a very malleable border. You'll let some people inside this boundary, based upon trust. More people you'll keep at a distance, based on either distrust, or just a sense of appropriate reserve. Notice that we're using metaphors of position here ('inside', 'at a distance') which we instinctively understand, but they're not literal boundaries. They represent a *feeling* of closeness or otherwise. With this boundary, you'll either 'let your guard down' or 'keep your guard up', not dissimilar to border guards. Friendly nations, such as those within the EU, keep their guard down to each other's citizens. Hostile ones have demilitarised zones, like between North and South Korea.

What comes next? Your family. This has its sense of identity, which often but by no means always involves a shared name and a shared home, but certainly has its membership, its stories, its traditions, its rituals, and so on. And although we have increasing numbers of blended families with blurring going on — with some family members belonging to more than one family at the same time — you'd still nearly always be able to say if someone is inside or outside your family, meaning that however fuzzy, there is still a boundary around its membership. And yet, those boundaries get reset, with events like divorce creating ambiguity and complexity around how someone who was inside your extended family border may now be outside it, even when they are still parents of children that are inside it. This is emotionally challenging for thousands of families. A large part of that is due to the lack of clarity around borders and how they get drawn and redrawn, especially because so much is implicit, and never dealt with directly in conversation.

Whilst still with your family, think about the place you live. Your home. If you own your home, you'll have title deeds that delimit the edges of your property. If you're lucky enough to have a garden, then those deeds will show who has responsibility for the upkeep of things like fences or walls. This is about the highly emotive topic of land. And even if you rent, there will be an agreement about the physical and contractual limits of your rental property, and where the edges of your responsibilities start and end in relation to your landlord.

As we move further out, there are more ambiguous or at least continually mutating human borders — the set of people who are your colleagues at work and, arguably even more so, your friendship group. These borders are full of leaky membranes. Neighbours come and go. Colleagues join and leave. In both cases, there is the somewhat queasy modern ceremonial of the leaver being cut loose (or not) from the relevant WhatsApp group. Friends? Some may well be lifelong, but others gently, almost imperceptibly wither on the vine, with no intention to fall out of touch, and yet it happens. As part of their ecosystem, Facebook were very happy to give you a precise quantity of 'friends', and for most members it was a flattering number, but everyone knows it's not like that in real life, and if you had to draw a border around the list of people you actually think of as friends, it would be a hard ring to define. Whilst still with human networks, you could belong to any number of them. They could involve political parties, religious groups, sports teams (either as a player or fan), hobby groups, activist associations, or neighbourhood groups. Many of these networks have a role in establishing aspects of your active identity — ways in which you describe yourself to others and to yourself. To take just one of these, there's something curious about football tribes that is useful to dig into, as an insight into the nested-doll theory of stacked identities. Once a fortnight, you stand or sit alongside people that you have just one meaningful thing in common with, and for that period of time, you're joined at the soul in craving just one outcome — victory. For most of the time, that allegiance is all about your own league team, and for as long as any player is 'wearing the shirt', you're on their side. And players of the opposing side are like enemy combatants. If those opponents happen to be top internationals, you'll cheer with great delight if they screw up. It's a visceral feeling of pure tribal identity. But the moment that the league focus switches to internationals, those opponents are suddenly your heroes, if they are playing for your country, with all your hope vested in them. Fans don't feel any contradiction here. Both identities co-exist, and it just depends on the context about which one dominates in the moment.

As we move further out, there is an entire web of physical borders, many of which interact with the ones we've already listed, and you will belong to all of them. They vary in their levels of definition. There is your neighbourhood. Rather like with your friends, you might know instinctively when a given street is outside your 'hood, but you'd be hard pressed to define it. It's nebulous. Even more nebulous for most of us is the idea of your community. That feels harder to pin down: it's a more emotionally loaded idea than neighbourhood, but with less definition.

Whilst staying in the immediate vicinity of your home, if you live in the UK, your home will be inside a parish with a defined boundary, but most people would have no idea where that boundary is, unless they consulted an Ordnance Survey map. Your home will also be in a village, town or borough, city, metropolitan district, unitary authority, and/or county. Some of these have clearly defined legal boundaries, others don't. But even when they don't, you have a feel for when you're inside versus outside.

A bit further out, and it could get very murky. What about your region? In the case of England, some counties confer a strong sense of identity onto their inhabitants, such as Cornwall and Yorkshire. But what about being a Northerner, or a Southerner? What attributes are you attaching to if you describe yourself as a Northerner? Hard to say precisely, but it is a descriptor that some people own for themselves. Less often do you hear anyone describe themselves as a Southerner. Why? And then again, what does it mean to be a Midlander, like me? A question I've been asking myself for decades. And how do you even define that in geographic terms?

Perhaps this all resolves itself if we zoom out further to nationhood? The question mark is because we all know it's not that straightforward, even if it used to be. You can have dual nationality or take out citizenship of a country that you end up living in which isn't the same one you were born in. One of my most emotional experiences at work was going to the citizenship ceremony of a couple that were originally from Kosovo but had to escape with their children with half an hour's notice to save their lives during the Balkan crisis in the 1990s. They found refuge in the UK and told me that they suspected that they felt more proudly British than the British-born people around them, putting that belief into action by attending every community meeting they could, picking up litter in the streets, and essentially doing everything they could to have a positive impact on their patch of the country. They were doing far more than I did (or do), in large part because they didn't take their nationhood for granted. They felt a degree of gratitude that you rarely feel when your nationality is a birthright.

Ploughing on, if you're a British citizen, you need to decide if you think of yourself as British, in addition to Scottish, Welsh, and so on. And even if you're say, Swedish, and don't have that type of historic layering to your nationality, you've still got the fact that you're a European. Is that continental border one that has any hold on you? Continental borders can also lack precision, such as that between Europe and Asia, where you have two continents but one land mass.

Assuming you get that nested doll sorted out, you might well think you can sit back and relax. But look up. What about the atmosphere? Where is the border to that? Well, it has a theoretical definition, for legal purposes. Known as the Kármán line, it is 100 km above sea level, beyond which space is technically free for all to explore. (Off you go.) But well before you got to the 100 km limit, the air would have been impossibly thin to breathe, or more to the point, fly a plane. For this reason, NASA has a different working definition, which is more like 80 km. The boundary between the Earth's atmosphere and the start of outer space must be the most blurred border we have on Earth. Having said that, it's not the most blurred boundary known to science. A stronger contender for that would be the heliosphere, which is a kind of solar bubble that surrounds the entire solar system and protects all the planets inside from extreme levels of cosmic radiation that would otherwise render all life on Earth impossible. One thing that the heliosphere shares with the collection of cell walls inside your body is that they are all borders that most people never think about from one year or decade to the next, despite us owing our existence to them. No doubt there are even more astonishing borders to grapple with further out in space, but we've got more than enough to deal with down here.

This personal identity flyby, with its dizzying set of borders to cross, is in stark contrast to how a similar hypothetical journey would have looked, say, three centuries ago. Let's imagine an agricultural worker living in an English village. At either end of the journey we've just been on, there would be nothing — no concept of internal borders within your body, and none to do with the outer atmosphere and space. The only ones that would be meaningful would be those that were close in, such as family, home, co-workers, parish, and village. Some identity borders that we experience as always being in perpetual flux wouldn't apply — no social media, dispersed friendship groups. Some of the more elective identity borders would also not apply — no sports tribes, political party affinity, and so on. Not only would the sheer quantity of items in your nested doll be far smaller, but those you had would be substantially more fixed, altered mostly only by birth and death. Crucially, the game-playing with identity and zooming in and out that is part of our learnt way of thinking of our identity wouldn't apply either.

In our business, we have a phrase to express the multiple, nested-doll identity syndrome, which I alluded to in the Words section. It's 'the-me-that-I-am-when…'. It's to capture that contemporary truth about how we learn to flex our sense of self as we shift from one context to another. I see that notion in the Roberto Saviano quote at the top of this section — 'Like everyone, I am more than one person.' He's a journalist, but of all professions, perhaps actors have the best grip on this identity slippage — it's literally part of their day job. There's a great knowing quote from Cary Grant that goes, 'Everyone wants to be Cary Grant. *I* want to be Cary Grant.' (This from a man whose name at birth was Archibald Leach, so there was a very knowing wink in this statement.) In a similar vein, the American actor Robert Duvall said this: 'I exist very nicely between the words "action" and "cut".' Finally, in the 2011 film *My Week with Marilyn*, Michelle Williams, who plays Marilyn, is at one stage just on the point of conducting a press conference, and before she does, quickly turns to one of the other characters and says, 'Shall I be her?' It's over in a moment but provides an insight into that gap between the you and the persona of you, which, even for all of us non-actors, is a symptom of multiple identities.

2. The ion gated community

The border journey that we've just been on started with internal borders that none of us have ever seen. They should have their moment, because we owe the ion channels in all those trillions of cell walls more than we could ever know. In biology, a living cell is an entirely bounded entity, a tiny bag of water and chemistry. But despite having their membranes, cells are anything but hermetically sealed. Some are charmingly named 'excitable cells' (which includes neurons and muscle cells), and they function by allowing a continual flow of electrically charged atoms and molecules (ions) in and out of the cell through portals in the membrane known as ion channels. These gates are often no more than an atom or so wide at their narrowest point, and when they open (in response to a chemical or electrical stimulus), a small electrical current is created by the ions that traverse the membrane. Sometimes, the stimulus for the opening of the ion channel is mechanical rather than electrical or chemical, such as touch receptor cells in human fingertips or, more gruesomely, in the case of the receptor cells in a Venus flytrap. Perhaps theirs should be renamed raptor cells.

The point of mentioning this at all is because our ability to perceive and move and think is entirely conditional on the performance of these ion channels — exquisitely tiny border crossings — and their ceaseless transmission of sodium and potassium ions from one cell to another, carrying electro-chemical messages. In some incredible way, we are able to decode them as 'You've scalded yourself on the oven door,' followed a little while later by a more metaphysical message such as 'When will you learn to use proper oven gloves?' which presumably still relies on the same type of cellular activity.

Beyond the astonishing biochemistry of all this, which is reason enough to engage with the life of the cell, the metaphorical power is something else. In effect, we have a situation with cells where the greater part of their effort is managing the internal drama within the cell wall — ensuring a continuous supply of carbon and energy, managing waste, and so on — and yet without the ability to transact with other cells through trading ions, the whole enterprise (i.e., keeping us going) would founder.

3. **In two minds**

Whilst still remaining inside the body, let's zoom out from cell walls, and think about the connective tissue between the left and right sides of the brain — the corpus callosum.

Like a lot of people, as a young adult I was somewhat influenced by a notion, very popular in the '80s and '90s, that most people were 'led' by one side of their brains. Early work in neurobiology, pioneered in the USA by Roger Sperry in the 1950s and '60s, had started to plot a path towards an understanding of the specific functions of the left and right hemispheres of the brain. But as often happens, the result of this work, at least as filtered down into popular culture, was a simplistic version of much more nuanced work. But precisely because it was presented in such a binary form, and was so easy to process, many of us wandered around with the notion that people that were dominated by their left brain strongly leaned towards being analytical, logical, and scientific, whereas right-brain people were imaginative, creative, and intuitive. I say, 'wandered around', but not if you were a left-brain person. You'd walk purposefully in a straight line.

Jump forward into the early 2000s, and a couple of things were coming together. Firstly, disparate work by psychologists in the realm of behavioural science was starting to coalesce under the umbrella term of behavioural economics and was gathering popular momentum. I was caught up with all this: behavioural principles proved to be a highly useful toolkit in the work undertaken by my colleagues and me, in understanding motivation and decision-making on behalf of commercial and public sector clients we were working with, and continue to do so. Secondly, at a deeper level, another half-century of work in hemisphere specialisation pioneered by Sperry and others, had continued, deepened, and reached a point of far greater precision and insight. Now, I've already briefly introduced Iain McGilchrist, but I want to turn in more detail to his thinking at this point. His *The Matter with Things* is a monumental 1400-page, two-volume book, published in 2021, that goes into rigorous detail about the current state of understanding of the role of both brain hemispheres. McGilchrist's own background straddles neuroscience, psychiatry, philosophy, and literature: it's the kind of boundary-crossing polymathy that used to be par for the course in Renaissance times and seems to be finally coming back into fashion (perhaps it's another welcome symptom of The Age of Between). This breadth matters in the reading experience because he synthesises across disciplines, making lateral connections much like the two sides of the brain do.

The absolute nub of his conclusions can be summarised succinctly. It turns out that the clichéd left-brain right-brain thing I grew up with has *some* basis in truth, despite being a truly woeful dumbing down. What it gets right is that there are significant differences in the type of attention that both sides give to the world. At the risk of duplicating the simplification of that previous era, the right hemisphere is more attentive to the big picture, or rather the whole picture, where the left hemisphere attends to the detail, the particular. Early in the book he produces a long, numbered list of instances of this distinction. I'm not going to reproduce all of it — a few edited highlights will give you a strong feel for them.

> 2. The LH [left hemisphere] deals preferentially with detail, the local, what is central and in the foreground, and easily grasped; the RH [right hemisphere] with the whole picture … including all that is not immediately graspable. The importance of the global (RH)/local (LH) distinction cannot be overstated.
>
> 4. The LH aims to narrow things down to a certainty, while the RH opens them up into possibility.
>
> 6. The LH tends to see things as isolated, discrete, fragmentary, where the RH tends to see the whole.
>
> 7. The LH's world tends towards fixity and stasis — that of the RH towards change and flow.
>
> 10. The RH understands narrative. The LH, if offered a story whose episodes are taken out of order, tends to regroup them so as to classify similar episodes together…

In summary, a healthy human brain has a forensic, episodic, literal, detailed left side, and a holistic, imaginative, sense making, empathetic right side, connected in the middle by the corpus callosum, which is like a long, thin junction box of 200 million nerve fibres that allows communication between the hemispheres.

But why? Firstly, it's worth pointing out that this division is also true of all vertebrate brains — it's an animal thing. And what do all animals have to do? Find food, while not succumbing to some other animal deciding that you are their food. That is the irreducible fact of life. This deep animal truth is lost to us now, because we can earn our next lunch by stacking shelves, or fixing damaged teeth, or flying planes. And no more than 0.1% of the human population is killed by animals each year, mostly by mosquitoes, so that relationship between killing and being killed has been severed, to all intents and purposes. But in evolutionary terms, this is a very recent development, and our brains are still coded according to deeper, prehistoric realities. In giving talks to clients on behavioural science, and specifically on phenomena like loss aversion, I several years ago settled on the soundbite of 'As an animal, you'd rather skip lunch than be lunch.'

I'm relieved to now discover that no less an authority than Iain McGilchrist confirms this. And the more precise neuroscientific exposition of that is around division of responsibilities in the context of survival. The left brain is primarily entrusted with the ruthless focus, the pure attention on capture to the exclusion of all else. Think of a cat stalking a bird in the garden. That's the left hemisphere in operation — it can't afford to be distracted by anything else. It's a specialist, and you need it to be relentless. It can't afford to be having idle thoughts about which cushion to sleep on later. And then the right hemisphere is taking care of not being eaten. It is aware of the entire picture; it is seeing everything. In the distant past, this was about being attentive to threat. The right hemisphere's role is to conduct a version of 'We're clear of danger, left hemisphere. Go to it! Bag us that rabbit, and I'll get the fire started.' Except of course, we don't experience it like that. To us, the whole enterprise of being conscious feels holistic; we have no sensation of a dialogue going on between two hemispheres. Inside ourselves, we have literally no intuition about our brains at all — under normal conditions, it gives us no signals about itself, unlike many other parts of our body, which are signalling away to the overworked brain the entire time, like the attention-seeking divas that they are.

The differences between the two hemispheres continue, the more you get into it. What my edited highlights of McGilchrist's list has left out so far is that the two sides of the brain also differ in terms of their levels of confidence, optimism, and self-esteem. Left to its own devices, the left side has a strong optimism bias — it overrates its own ability and likelihood of success in a task. The right side is the opposite of this — it is more prone to being pessimistic or at the very least realistic. Again, this makes perfect sense. For example, it's common knowledge that predators, like big cats, normally fail in an individual hunt. The statistics are not great. But if you're a lion, the last thing you want is your left hemisphere getting all gloomy over the odds based on prior experience. It needs to believe in itself *every time*. And yet there is a clear role for the right hemisphere: to weigh up the chances of an almost certainly fruitless chase across open savannah after a fully fit adult gazelle and rein in the left hemisphere to conserve energy.

The fantastic thing about all this is the notion of balance and co-operation between two sides of the brain that attend to the world in distinct ways. We need both perspectives, the zoom in and the zoom out, and we need them to be able to toggle backwards and forwards continually in the interests of good decision-making. And for all that, we've got no awareness of this going on. The reality is that the great internal hemisphere boundary, the corpus callosum, is working away inside you the entire time, organising communication between the hemispheres, in the interests of keeping you at the same time sufficiently focused and sufficiently broadly aware.

Incidentally, one of the reasons why so much is known about this is due to decades of painstaking work done by neuroscientists following brain injuries and strokes. Typically, lesions that happen to the right hemisphere are far more debilitating than those that happen to the left. The reason for this is that the right side, with its big picture perspective, can compensate for, or at least disguise, damage to the left side far more easily. But the left side can't make a similar compensation. Its fragmentary outlook means it can't stitch together successful whole-picture narratives, and therefore the real-world impact to those individuals is significantly more disabling. That's not to say it doesn't try to stitch a cohesive picture together: it has a go, because it doesn't like the uncertainty, but it gets it wrong, because that's not how it attends to the world, and this presents outwardly in the form of phenomena like delusions.

4. **Hemisphere collaboration in practice**

What this adds up to is that, in a healthy brain, there is a principle of co-working and balance between the hemispheres, and a vast amount of integration and processing of messaging across the corpus callosum the entire time, most of which is below any level of consciousness. We're slipping between intuition and judgement continually, and amidst all of that, decisions emerge. For most of us, those decisions are banal, but it's instructive at this point to introduce an insightful quote from David Bodanis's 2016 book *Einstein's Greatest Mistake*,[1] where the American science writer makes an empathetic observation about what it must be like to be operating beyond the realm of ordinary people.

> Geniuses have to push hard to come up with their first ideas. Almost always, they're going far past what everyone assumes to be true and have to be confident that they're right. That involves being stubborn. But they also need to be supple, making sure their breakthroughs incorporate all the relevant

> factual information, then keeping their later work responsive to what others are finding out, too. The trick is to surf this line between the supple and the stubborn without straying too far to either side.

That surfing trick is a key life skill for geniuses and ordinary mortals alike and takes on a whole new dimension when seen within the context of this interaction between the hemispheres.

You might be thinking, how might this look in reality? By way of an illustration, for a while I worked with Michael Wolff, co-founder of the brand strategy company Wolff Olins. Michael himself operated on the cusp between design and strategy and used a simple metaphor to describe the process of creativity. In the metaphor, there are four rooms in which you can attempt to be creative, all of which have some validity:

1. The first is the room of great work, where your starting point is to take inspiration from what has been done already by other people.
2. The second room is the room of reason, where you begin from a position of logic and analysis.
3. The third room is the room of precedent, which differs from the first room because it's the things you've done yourself in the past (that have worked).
4. The fourth room is the room of not knowing, where you trust your imagination and your creative instincts, whilst being informed by what you've learnt in the other three rooms.

The point of sharing this metaphor is to link back to the relationship between the hemispheres — the first and fourth rooms both have some right-side emphasis (the fourth in particular) and the second and third lean into the left side. Now, in daily consciousness, we've got no access to the way in which the two hemispheres are connecting and communicating with each other, but having a schematic like this metaphor equips us with the wherewithal to ensure that we're not being overly led by either rigid logic or aimless brainstorming but holding inputs in balance to achieve nuanced decisions in whatever we're trying to resolve. Incidentally, when I think of Michael's intriguing but somewhat unnerving room of not knowing, I sometimes get reminded of Einstein's reflection on why he, Einstein, was held in such esteem. He said, 'The magic of incomprehension attracts the reader.' There is something seductive in those things that are either at the edge or just beyond our ability to immediately grasp them.

5. You and non-you

> What it means for something to exist is that there must be a difference — a boundary — between that thing and everything else. If there were no boundaries there would be no things — there would be nothing.
>
> This boundary must also exist over time, because things that exist maintain their identity over time. If you add a drop of ink to a glass of water it will rapidly disperse, colouring the water and losing its identity.
>
> — Anil Seth, *Being You*[2]

Having paid our dues to the role of ion channels in keeping our bodies alive and looked at the interaction between brain hemispheres in keeping us balanced in our attention and productivity, we still have the question of our essential self, our consciousness.

Anil Seth is a leading neuroscientist, based at the University of Sussex. The quote above is very much his starting point. Without a boundary, like skin, there are no conditions for any notion of individual living existence. In addition, that separation must exist over time — the image of the water droplet is intuitive. He then goes on to point out that the difference between living systems and things that simply exist is that living systems actively work at preserving their boundaries. A rock will easily outlast a human, but it does literally nothing to stop its boundaries (i.e., surfaces) from being eroded by weathering. It has no agency to prevent it and no instinct to prevent itself being turned into millions of grains of sand. Whereas a body, human or otherwise, works tirelessly to sustain its status as a living entity — even though it's fighting a battle it's certain to lose. And that's the point of the distinction. On reflection, the word 'tirelessly' may be misleading here, because sustaining life is enormously costly in energy, and in the end every living system, even if not eaten or killed by another, will eventually die — partly through the sheer effort of self-defence. Could rocks last as long as they do if they had to put effort into preventing themselves from being eroded?

But is being a living system that defends its boundaries the same thing as being conscious? A tree will make efforts to repair its bark if it's invaded by burrowing insects, but is it conscious? These questions are partly metaphysical, but what is clear is the prevailing direction of travel. If we settle on consciousness as being 'aware of your own existence', scientists continue to expand the number of species that pass that definition. Because this book has boundaries (it may not have much else but boundaries), we'll leave other animals to one side and concentrate on human animals.

In thinking further about consciousness, Seth goes on to consider the impact of one very uncompromising boundary: the skull. He asks us to think of it from the brain's point of view. The poor brain itself has no direct experience of the world, ever. Inside its skull, it's got no independent sight, hearing, smell, touch, taste, or balance. None at all. In there, it's silent, utterly dark, and the brain has no connection of its own with the outside world. It gets everything second-hand, via messages from sense organs or the nervous system. It therefore must intuit what's going on in the outside world by piecing together evidence from all these inputs it gets and trying to create a coherent picture.

So far, we could have got that much on our own. But what comes next is the deeper revelation, which I've already alluded to, when quoting Dmitri Xygalatas as saying that brains are predictive devices. Seth agrees with this. He makes the point that the way the brain learns over time is not by just waiting passively for the information to come in, making sense of it, and then alerting you to, say, jump out of the way of a speeding car. That's all too slow for short- or long-term survival prospects. In layman's terms, it starts to send out a stream of pro-active guesses that meet the incoming signals halfway. In this way, you end up back on the pavement in the nick of time.

Consequently, instead of a linear 'inputs in, instructions out' approach, what you get is a more creative, sense-making interaction between your own unique prior set of experiences, memories, and associations that are stored in your brain, together with fresh sensory inputs streaming in. Seth has an intriguing phrase for this phenomenon, which has a betweenist sense to it. He calls it a 'controlled hallucination'. This is because part of the picture that's created in your mind is the result of your brain's best guesses, rather than from what is literally out there (whatever that is). Common-or-garden statements like 'Nobody sees things the way I do,' which you might otherwise dismiss as the solipsism of your inner teenager, may turn out to be neurologically correct.

6. **Merging with non-you**

Before moving on from Anil Seth's quote, let's look at it one more time, and with an even closer examination of the phrasing in that passage. I'd stake a modest bet that the premise in that quote felt entirely straightforward for the majority of people that read it. Think again at the emphatic language that he uses — 'there *must* be a difference — a boundary' (my italics) and 'if there were no boundaries there would be no things'. There's no ambiguity here; he's not entertaining any doubts. If my bet works out, and you didn't question that forceful clarity when you read it, it's likely because you've absorbed that system of thinking as being axiomatic, even if you've not had that precise insight before. In modern

Western culture, we accept and celebrate the distinctiveness of the individual — it's how we roll. Our perceived self-identity as individuals is in large part established in contrast to everything that isn't us. This goes right back to the system of Western thinking that was established by Aristotle and those other Greek philosophers we were thinking about in the last section. It's so deep in us that it's hard to stand outside of it.

But some worldviews would be more ambivalent than this. If we think about Buddhism, for instance, the highest attainment is to so minimise your personal sense of self as to set aside personal desire. The type of dualism represented by Seth's worldview is one that a Buddhist is trying to ease out of their way of being. The Zen Buddhist branch is a system of being that celebrates holism to such an extent that in a state of perfect enlightenment, identity borders don't even exist. In his 1970s classic *Gödel, Escher, Bach*,[3] the American mathematician and cognitive scientist Douglas Hofstadter considers this notion with reference to a particular koan — a paradoxical question, statement, or story designed to illustrate a Zen principle.

Zen is holism carried to its logical extreme. If holism claims that things can only be understood as wholes, not as sums of their parts, Zen goes one further, maintaining that the world cannot be broken into parts at all. To divide the world into parts is to be deluded, and to miss enlightenment.

> A master was asked the question, "What is the Way?" by a curious monk.
> "It is right before your eyes," said the master.
> "Why do I not see it for myself?"
> "Because you are thinking of yourself."
> "What about you: do you see it?"
> "So long as you see double, saying 'I don't', and 'you do' and so on, your eyes are clouded," said the master.
> "When there is neither 'I' nor 'You' can one see it?"
> "When there is neither 'I' nor 'You', who is the one that wants to see it?"

Apparently, the master wants to get across the idea that an enlightened state is one where the borderlines between the self and the rest of the universe are dissolved. This would truly be the end of dualism, for as he says, there is no system left which has any desire for perception. But what is that state, if not death? How can a live human being dissolve the borderlines between himself and the outside world?

To a modern Western mindset, this is an almost obvious question. How indeed? The worldview division that separates Zen from much of Western thinking and philosophy is a chasm.

7. And they say Romanticism is dead

I qualified my last sentence with the word 'much', the reason being that there is the notable exception of the Romantic movement, which is something of an island in Western thought. Romanticism came about partly in reaction to the dualist philosophy of the Enlightenment era that came before it, as well as responding to the social upheaval caused by the French Revolution of 1792, which overturned the established order and caused shock waves across Europe. British Romanticism was also in opposition to the Industrial Revolution, especially the rise of urban culture and grim cityscapes. Romanticism had some core beliefs: celebrating nature, the self, the imagination, and the central role of intense emotion in conveying this aesthetic sensibility. In historical terms, Romanticism didn't last that long (from roughly the end of the eighteenth century through to about 1850). But in terms of its underpinnings, it had more in common with Buddhism than any other major artistic or philosophical tradition originating in Europe. Any number of Romantic thinkers yearned for a dissolution of boundaries, and an elevation of nature and unbounded natural living versus the hemmed in, claustrophobic experience of city life that was burgeoning across the continent, led by Britain. The Frenchman Jean-Jacques Rousseau laid the groundwork for a lot of this thinking during the middle of the eighteenth century, expressing an aversion to the overly structured growth of European civilisation and its demarcated social structures, writing the following in 1754:

> The first man who, having fenced in a piece of land, said "This is mine", and found people naïve enough to believe him, that man was the true founder of civil society. From how many crimes, wars, and murders, from how many horrors and misfortunes might not anyone have saved mankind, by pulling up the stakes, or filling up the ditch…

It took some time for this type of thinking to find its way to America, but similar types of yearning were still being expressed by the unorthodox thinker and essayist, Ralph Waldo Emerson, nearly a century later, in his famous essay 'The Over-Soul', published in 1841. Emerson had been influenced by several oriental religious texts, and that influence is obvious in the collision between classic Western observation of how we live, and the role of the over-soul that he proclaimed:

> We live in succession, in division, in parts, in particles. Meantime within man is the soul of the whole; the wise silence; the universal beauty, to which every part and particle is equally related, the eternal ONE. And this deep power in which we exist and whose beatitude is all accessible to us, is not only self-sufficing and perfect in every hour, but the act of seeing and the thing seen, the seer and the spectacle, the subject and the object, are one. We see the world piece by piece, as the sun, the moon, the animal, the tree; but the whole, of which these are shining parts, is the soul.

The irony is that the last thing the Romantics wanted was to be so subsumed into nature as to lose consciousness of it — they wanted to exist, at least emotionally, on the exact cusp of sensing and being. That much is clear from Emerson, as he writes of 'the act of seeing and the things seen'. The Romantic sensibility is a massive tease and involves a significant navigation of a borderline state. Rousseau himself understood this, with his celebration of an idealised version of mankind as a '*sauvage*', halfway between a brute animal and an enlightened civilian.

Never was the Romantic desire to have your cake and eat it better exhibited (literally, as we're about to discover) than by another great American Romantic, Henry David Thoreau, who is most famous for the account of his 2-and-a-bit years of living alone in a small cabin on the edges of Walden Pond, near Concord in Massachusetts, the results of which he published in *Walden*,[4] in 1854. It's a celebration of (among other things) self-reliance, immersion in nature, and stripping back the trappings of civilised life to live more simply within the rhythms and seasons of nature, and includes the commitment to 'earning my living by my own labor only'. And for sure he grew much of his own pulses and vegetables, which he wrote about at length. What he was entirely coy about was popping back to Concord to visit friends and family on a regular basis, with his mother ensuring to supplement his modest diet with food parcels for him to take back to his cabin in the woods. She was clearly having none of this Romantic nonsense going on when her son needed a square meal.

The point of mentioning this is not to accuse him of hypocrisy (his book reads far more as a spiritual autobiography than a factual account), but to underscore this Romantic dilemma — the simultaneous immersion in nature but with just enough withdrawal from it to be actively conscious of its purifying quality on him. And what you can't escape from in *Walden* is Thoreau's forensic detailing and chronicling of the natural world around him; he'd have made a diligent climate scientist in our own era.

Before moving on from Thoreau, there's one other facet of *Walden* that's of specific interest to us, and it's to do with the type of people who came into his orbit during his time in the woods. One of the discoveries he made was of the community of outsiders who also lived on the margins of society, outside conventional society — borderland dwellers like himself. Although most people automatically accept the so-called 'social contract' — the set of literal and tacit rules that govern normal behaviour and interaction in the interests of convenience and prosperity — those constraints aren't for everyone, and those people can often end up living marginalised lives, physically separate from the mainstream. (In our era, we talk about people living 'off-grid'.) Thoreau related well to these types. In a thoughtful 2017 opinion piece in the New York Times, entitled 'At Walden, Thoreau wasn't really alone with nature' and written by John Kaag and Clancy Martin,[5] the authors list some of the oddball characters that he hung out with around the pond, and summarise it all thus:

> Part of embracing Thoreauvian wilderness is to open ourselves to individuals and groups who exist beyond the town limits. These were outsiders, unknowns, even outcasts, and Thoreau acquainted himself with them, came to understand them and spent part of his life caring for them. Thoreau entreats us to open our eyes to everyone. If he appears reclusive perhaps it is because we fail to see the significance of his companions — it is perhaps because we are not ourselves reclusive enough, or, for that matter, social enough in Thoreau's peculiarly intimate way.

Again, we're seeing that curious, reflexive from-both-sidesness in their articulation of 'not reclusive enough, or, for that matter, social enough'. This Romantic tendency has a habit of placing you *between* things, even at the very same time as you're on the edge of things. It's got something to do with the observer status, the desire to experience an intensity of sensation through the observation, instead of just plunging in headlong: living as a human feeling rather than a human being. Going back to Seth's quote that started this section, as tempting as it might be for the Romantic, it's ultimately no good being the drop of ink, dispersed into water, and losing all your identity as an ink drop. Fine, you become as one with the glass of water. But that's you, done. If you don't want that, you're going to have to retain and defend your perceptual boundaries, just as your body is systematically doing on your physical behalf, especially if you want to write about it, tell the world all about it, get it published, make a living.

Writers seem to have a particular sensitivity to this paradox. Echoes or expressions of it are to be seen in every generation, transcending literary movements. Dial right forward to our own era, and writers still feel the same quandary. Here's a section from John Banville's *Eclipse*,[6] where the narrator, Alexander Cleave, is a natural observer of events and people. At this point, he starts talking about the vagrants of the community that he lives in. Just before the quoted section below, Cleave describes the activity of following them around town as they tramp the streets, with him in slightly remote attendance:

> Along with the peculiar pleasure I derive from this furtive hobby goes a certain melancholy, due to what I think of as the Uncertainty Principle. You see, as long as I only watch them without their knowing, I am in some sense intimately in touch with them, they are in some sense *mine*, whereas if they were to become aware of me dogging their steps, that which in them is of interest to me — their lack of awareness, their freedom from self-consciousness, their wonderful, vacant ease — would instantly vanish. I may observe, but not touch.

There's the exquisite dilemma of the Romantic sensibility, still with us. You must exist on that rim of observation and resist the temptation to lose yourself in a more complete experience, or else the whole thing collapses. It's noteworthy that Banville deliberately appropriates a phrase from quantum mechanics in this passage (I assume deliberately — he's known as a writer who is highly aware of contemporary physics). The reference is to Heisenberg's Uncertainty Principle, which we've come across already — that you can theoretically know a particle's position or its speed but not both. There's an implicit, or indeed almost explicit connection being made between quantum theory and the Romantic sensibility here, with the observer's status and identity depending on not being part of the action.

In reality of course, most people with a Western mindset have no desire to lose their identity boundaries and have their essential self dispersed. It's captured by Adam Nicolson, in *Life Between the Tides*, a book we've already come across:

> All can exist only within the overarching embrace of the world-as-it-is, each life driven by the need to be, each unaware of the significance of what it is that drives them. That unknowability is everywhere here and is part of what I mean to say: to know something, a person or an animal or a place, to become intimate with it, is not to know in any conscious way, but to dissolve the boundaries. To be with anything, life must overflow its brim.

Put like that, the idea of full knowledge of someone else, or some other entity, is challenging, if not impossible. We are bound to stay within our bounds, stretching out to make whatever outward connections we can.

8. **Section summary**

a) We owe our existence to physical borders. Defending them is what our bodies are in business to do.
b) It's in our nature to combine whole-picture and small-picture attention. Denying either is to deny our humanity.
c) Our consciousness and our sense of identity is in large part due to our sense of ourselves as being distinct from others — we can't just melt into the universe and still be ourselves.
d) Especially today, with so many stacked identities, we can have multiple versions of 'being me'. All of them can be true, and they contribute part of the whole story of what it means to be you.

SECTION FIVE — BETWEEN TIMES

Time is a game played beautifully by children.

— Heraclitus

It's time to think about time. Its placement is deliberate because it bears a close relationship to the betweens of you. Time is a resource, and how we negotiate time and its boundaries is a big part of the experience of daily life. We can go further than that: everything we experience happens in and through time — it's part of who we are. But equally, let's not get too serious about it. The quote from Heraclitus is a guiding idea to this section. Time is also the facilitator of fun, and although time feels more serious as you get older and have less of it stretching ahead of you, reducing time to being a slave to your to-do list is to strip the joy out of it. Wasting time may be one of the great profligate luxuries of our era.

There are three sub-sections to cover:

1. We'll meet one of the great symbols of time from ancient mythology — the Roman god Janus.
2. Past, present, and future. This is the heart of the chapter, and we'll come across insights from famous writers as well as thinkers to explore the notion of time with an ultimate focus

on the present, which is the liminal time arena where we do our living.

3. We'll finish with a look at the pre-Industrial Revolution nighttime practice of 'two sleeps' or '*dorveille*', along with a personal experiment on time use.

As a gentle immersion into thinking about time, here is a curious fact, a little *amuse-bouche* to do with language. It turns out that three of the most commonly used nouns in English are to do with duration, with 'time' being the most frequently used noun, and 'year' (third) and 'day' (fifth) helping to demonstrate our obsession with the passage of time ('person' and 'way' prevent it from being a clean sweep of duration nouns in the top three, in case you're slightly interested, but not enough to look it up). Anyone is welcome to think that is either remarkable or unremarkable, but either way, some other peoples, such as Aboriginal Australians, don't have a single abstract noun for time, let alone have it feature on their most-used list. Therefore, at the very least, it must be acknowledged that it tells us something about our own cultural preoccupations, even if it's hard to stand outside our conditioning far enough to figure out what.

1. **Back and forth — introducing Janus**

Janus is the perfect motif to introduce a liminal outlook on time. Look at him here, pointing forward into the future and backward into the past, sitting between them both simultaneously.

He gets a bad rap in our era for the easy association of being 'two-faced', as if he was some kind of hypocrite, and for giving his name to January, that most gruelling of months. But let's not judge him that way. The Romans had him as the god of beginnings and endings, and therefore also the god of transitions. A god of transitions: this is marvellous — just what we need.

Taking our cue from the Words chapter, we should start with his name, *Ianus* in Latin. It means an arched passageway or door,

taking us straight back to the associated idea of a *limen* that we've already encountered — a threshold, also from Latin. He himself was the doorkeeper or *ianitor* (hence janitor) of the heavens. By virtue of being the god of transitions, Janus was responsible for a huge amount of heavy lifting in Roman religion — it meant he got dragged into being the god of gates, conflict, trading and exchange, bridges, passageways, time, duality. You name it, Janus had a hand in it. Whereas many Roman gods were occasionally invoked in very particular ceremonies, and for the rest of the time lounged around being fed peeled grapes on *chaise longues*, Janus was omnipresent. He'd need to start a rite off, finish it, preside over change in one, and so on. Times of the year were just as demanding — he had to be around at each seasonal transition to cast his benediction on the coming spring, summer, autumn, and winter — oh, and harvests as well. Janus was the workaholic, always-on deity. He's proof positive of one of the arguments in this book — once you start to cotton onto anything pertaining to borders and the between, it's suddenly everywhere. This was Janus's lot too: everything has its transition, so if you're the general god of transitions, then you're on duty. As a result, most Roman scholars would have it that Janus was the most important of all their gods. To add another layer of evidence, on account of Janus being the doorkeeper to the heavens, whenever a Roman was praying, whichever god they were otherwise praying to, the first prayers and offerings (such as wine, incense, or other sacrifices) went to Janus.

In a way, he can function for betweenists as a presiding muse-like presence over all this talk of borders, transitions, and liminality. To add further stature to his role, many of the depictions of Janus, like the one below, have him with a staff in one hand and a key in the other. The staff is there to guide travellers along the right path. As if he didn't have enough roles already, pretty much by definition anyone that is in transition is in motion, so he also had a pivotal role as the god of travel and travellers. And therefore the key would be necessary to open doors along the journey and to usher travellers through the portal from one place to another. The symbolism of all

this is too good to ignore, and he could have made an appearance anywhere in the book, but with his primary representation being that of straddling time, he performs a special role right here.

2. **The bendy, circular arrow of time**

Before moving on from Janus, there's one significant point to note. In these great classic representations of him, he's simultaneously looking forward into the future and backward into the past, but no part of his attention seems to be focused on the present. He'd need a third head for that, and that would certainly be more cumbersome to represent visually. But then, what is the present, and how long does it last for? At a common-sense level, it ought to feel fixed. We have these three clear and separate concepts for the kingdom of time — the past, the present, the future. They sound reassuringly boundaried, without much room for argument.

In practice though, it's anything but. Their slipperiness isn't only disconcerting — sometimes it's an opportunity for wit, such as by the American author Tim Urban, who came out with 'It's always been a dream of mine to have done a TED talk in the past.'

Of all the borders we've looked at, potentially the most elusive — and therefore hardest to capture and define — is the border between the past and the future: the very moment we happen to be in. We're going to have to come at this from more than one angle, as if it's a dimly lit museum exhibit that we keep moving around to see from different perspectives to attempt to grasp what we're looking at.

3. **The here and now — the present**

I've opened this section with an insight from one of Heraclitus's fragments that has that quality of capturing a truth with poetry and precision at the same time. The meaning is open to everyone's interpretation — but for me, it's about that ability that children have to inhabit the moment fully. They don't have a sense of 'spending' time — it's not a currency for them that needs a return. To sit with my grandsons Theo and Dylan as they get endless repeat pleasure from swings, or bubble machines, or marble runs, or books, with an absorption that is total, is to experience the pure flow of time — not in a linear, arrow-of-time sort of way, but in a circular, back-to-when-we-started-go-again sort of way. It's almost as if they have perfected the art of expanding the borders of the present to be all that there is. The past and future don't exist in those moments.

Beyond learning from children, one of the most illuminating contributions to thinking about the present that I've come across in the last decade has been the one outlined by the Israeli Nobel Prize winning psychologist Daniel Kahnemann in *Thinking, Fast and Slow*.[1] There, he outlines a distinction between what he calls 'the experiencing self' and 'the remembering self'. The experiencing self is the one that is living right here, right now. Kahnemann's construction gets some support from dictionary definitions of time. Collins, for example, defines the present as 'the period of time that we are in now and the things that are happening now', which implies the immediate past and arguably the immediate future too. However, note that their use of the word 'we' subtly expands the present away from the purely personal and into the period of time that all of us are in. The notion of the collective present is seductive, preventing it from being a self-absorbed, atomised experience of time.

For illustration, I will explore this notion of the experiencing self with a personal analysis of the precise moment I am in now — the 'experiencing me' that is typing THIS word. There's a debate to be had about whether this 'experiencing me' is also having the writing experiencing of 'Beyond learning from children…' — the sentence that opened the previous paragraph, or whether that is already consigned to the 'remembering me'. We could argue about that until the nows come home, but I'm going to make a personal judgement about how it *feels*. That 'earlier' sentence still feels like part of the 'experiencing me' because this block of time I'm in has the sensation of being one unit of 'nowness' — it has a coherence to it that feels like an unbroken string of a few minutes that are all part of the here and now. I'd even go so far as to propose that this definition of the present includes the next few minutes that still lie ahead of me, even though that's technically in the future. Why? Well, although it's a truism that we don't know what the future brings, and something disruptive could change my expectation, my conviction is that the next handful of minutes also involve me sat here at the kitchen table, writing, and so I'm calling at least the next 5 minutes as being part of my present, possibly a bit longer. However, the previous paragraph to that (the one that started with 'I've opened this section…') was written first thing this morning, at about 6 o'clock, and I can't feasibly wrap it into this expression of the experiencing me just because it happened today — too much has occurred since then, and I'm having to consciously conduct acts of recall to remember that short morning writing session. My mind is also drifting ahead to the near future, and I know that I'll be stopping this section before long to start cooking.

In summary, I'm defining the present as being *the uninterrupted focus of our experiencing self across a period of time*. In practice, this means that our conception of the present most definitely sits in a borderland. There is the overt task we are engaged in, negotiating with invading memories and future intentions, and somehow managing to have its own agenda (in my case, 'Just get some of this writing done'). Yet because this agenda is compromised by these leaks backwards and forwards in time, our notion of the present has a fuzzy set of boundaries to it.

Getting back to Kahnemann's schema, the first thing to say about it is that any events that are happening to the 'experiencing self' are over quickly. You can only experience those events in the moment, and however we define 'in the moment', we can all agree that the point will come when they are siphoned off to the 'remembering self', or in everyday language, our memory. Kahnemann has a neat way of expressing this — he says that our remembering self is essentially a storyteller. It keeps the record of the story of our life, but because the events it evokes are being remembered and then retold, it can only ever be one version of what happened to the experiencing self. That could have been conjecture, but Kahnemann was able to prove that those retold versions are inaccurate. Arguably his most vivid experiment of this involved colonoscopy patients in the '90s, who were asked to give scores for the intensity of discomfort they were feeling throughout the procedure whilst it was happening. These were a record from the experiencing self. Later on, they were asked to give another score for intensity of discomfort, but some time after the procedure was over. That later score was delivered by the remembering self. In the analysis, a startling finding came through, which was that those patients who experienced short but continually intense discomfort held onto those feelings of discomfort when they recalled and scored the event later. Whereas those patients who had significantly longer procedures, and therefore objectively far more overall discomfort, gave a more benign later score of the procedure *as long as* the discomfort dropped considerably towards the end. What was happening here was that the recalled story of the procedure ended well. I guess we should say well-ish. It was a colonoscopy after all.

Although Kahnemann doesn't specifically go on to make the point I'm adding in, it's axiomatic that the specific event — that particular colonoscopy — can only be experienced once, but it can be recalled by the remembering self any number of times, and in many different contexts, and for many different reasons. For example, it could be recalled so as to be empathetic towards someone who's anxious about going through the same procedure, to raise a laugh amongst a group of friends, or to give an account of it to your GP. The way that story gets told and the components of the event that you choose to recall and emphasise are bound to be different, because in the moment the experiencing self needs something from the remembering self that is distinct from the previous occasion the remembering self recalled the same incident. The present recreates the past and does so continually and deliberately. The past becomes whatever we need it to be — a malleable resource that we morph and shape as we see fit. Elsewhere, Kahnemann has another excellent way of phrasing this — he talks about the way that the remembering self is more interested in searching for coherence than for truth. Because it's a storyteller, the most crucial thing is for our story to *feel right* in the moment, rather than for it to *be right.*

4. Back in the days — the past

When you start to think of the past and the present in these terms, it can feel unsettling. We often have this superficial sense of the past as having fixed events and dates that aren't open to dispute — the Battle of Hastings happened in 1066, etc. But should we be unsettled by the Kahnemann thesis? Rationally, we know that our view of history is continually revised (both our own history and our shared cultural history), partly through ongoing factual discovery, but also because the past looks different both to us as individuals and to each generation as our sense of our own era evolves, and that in turn recasts the prism through which we see history. There's a great old joke from Soviet-era Eastern Europe that goes like this: under communism, the future is always certain — it's the past that keeps changing. On this theme, I find myself drawn back to considering the opening line from L.P. Hartley's classic English novel from 1953, *The Go-Between*[2] (contender for the best-ever borderland fiction title): 'The past is a foreign country: they do things differently there.' What a justly acclaimed sentence that is. It captures all these themes with breathtaking economy — the notion of the past being contemporaneous with the present, alive, not dead, still in dialogue with us now, and yet at the same time with this otherness to it. Most importantly, the past *is* a foreign country, not *was* — it's active, it's alive, it's being remade continually, just as in the communist-era joke.

The remaking of history is a phenomenon that happens in various contexts. We are all familiar with the phrase 'history belongs to the winners', which we normally think of in the context of military history or the history of nations. But it happens in the arts too. The American music historian and critic Ted Gioia's book *Music: A Subversive History*[3] is all about the way in which musical innovators, pioneers, and outliers end up being assimilated into the cultural mainstream over time, having been rejected and shunned as revolutionaries and threats when they first set out. What he demonstrates is the way in which assimilators rewrite the originals, for a whole variety of motives, but end up making songs from an earlier era more popular and palatable for a new generation. Certain genres are particularly susceptible to this treatment according to Gioia, such as folk music. If you've got a spectrum with authenticity at one end and accessibility at the other, some purists re-present their own times with highly accurate versions of previous folk classics, whereas others will opt for wholesale change, perhaps believing that it's the only way for the old standards to get listened to at all. Ironically, this particular borderland has been alive and kicking for centuries. Gioia talks about one earnest documenter of ballads in the eighteenth century called Joseph Ritson, who caused no less a celebrity than the famous Scottish novelist Sir Walter Scott to complain: 'Whenever presented with two copies of a traditional song or ballad, Ritson perversely chose the worse as the most genuine.'

Finally, this whole topic of the dynamism of history has been thrown into relief for me by an unusual but fascinating event I went to, featuring Jason Sandy, who is a mudlark based in Hammersmith in West London. If you are not familiar with mudlarks — and I confess that I hadn't been — there are several thousand of them in the London area alone, and their preoccupation is sifting through the mud, silt, and stones for historic artifacts. The River Thames is particularly good for this because it's a tidal river, meaning that at each low tide there is the possibility of a fresh discovery. They unearth bits of pottery, metal, and sometimes bone, all buried from previous eras from the city's past, which the river decides to release. The type of discovery varies according to the section of the river — sometimes reflecting the ethnicity of a location, or the particular mercantile heritage. It's yet another classic example of a liminal space, where surprise discoveries are, if not guaranteed, then at least frequent from a river in continual flux. It turns out that mudlarks have a resonant, almost lyrical phrase, describing rivers as 'where history changes twice a day'. It captures with precision and economy this idea of the past being perpetually remade. In the context of The Age of Between, this concept of the past giving itself up in a haphazard, non-predictable way is both more exhilarating and more culturally on point than the static rigour of, say, an archaeological dig, even whilst respecting the enormous discipline of that activity. It is exciting to think that the treasures you can find in the Thames involve a degree of collaboration with the river. It too has a say in what you will find and when. That really is history in the borderland.

5. What's round the corner — the future

But what of the future? In theory, there should be less to say. It hasn't happened yet. Yet in the same way that we had L.P. Hartley's literary quote about the past, we've also got a writerly quote about the future that in many ways is a mirror image of it. And that quote has also dropped into popular culture. At some point in the early 1990s, science fiction writer William Gibson became synonymous with the phrase 'The future is already here — it's just not evenly distributed yet.' Superficially, he's saying that some of the phenomena that feel part of the future for most of us, such as, say, cryogenics or space travel for consumers, are a reality for a tiny handful. Beyond that, though, there is a resonance to Hartley's phrase. Both nod to the idea of the past, present, or future being in flux and being in a dynamic relationship to each other — that there is slippage between them, porous membranes across their borders. Writers seem to be at ease drifting backwards and forwards across the border of time. We've already had one famous opening line that explicitly plays games with time, and here's another, from Gabriel Garcia Marquez's masterpiece, *One Hundred Years of Solitude*:[4]

> Many years later, as he faced the firing squad, Colonel Aureliano Buendía was to remember that distant afternoon when his father took him to discover ice.

In addition to conflating the future and the past into the same sentence, the potential role of the present is highly ambiguous. Later than when? Than now?

What we can say about the future is that it is on the other side of the border to the present, and all of us nibble off seconds, minutes, and hours of the future every day and discard them across the border of time and into the past. We're quite negligent with the future really, and that's just in minor time-wasting ways, before we even get into the whole rhetorical debate of our children's and grandchildren's future, and existential issues like climate change. If we knew for sure what was coming, we'd surely nurture the future with more care than we do. The more you think about it, the odder it is. Our experiencing self expends a truly astonishing amount of its effort bent towards some vision of the future: qualifications, saving money for a house, dream holidays, or whatnot, but for the most part when that future arrives, as it does continually, it's mostly banal. Enjoyable enough for the most part, but pretty much as ordinary as the days that are now in the past that we were then building up to.

I want to illuminate this thinking about the future by telling a story from my own day job, which happened in about 2005 but stays with me, and I believe always will. One of our large clients gave us an innovative and intriguing brief, and it went like this: 'How would our business have to change if it was modelled exclusively on our customers' use of time?' They didn't have a very big budget for this project (situation normal), so we had to come up with something quite creative within this constraint. We decided that we would run one evening workshop with three different groups of their customers, whose relationship to time would, we hypothesised, be quite different from each other. We had all three groups sitting at different tables but interacting with each other throughout the evening, completing different tasks. By way of preparation for the workshop, we asked all of them to create a pie chart dividing up a typical day into segments to demonstrate their use of time. The three groups were as follows: working mothers with children under five; young, single people in corporate roles; and finally, retired people.

The young, single people, two or three of whom arrived late, had a time-identity of being highly stressed and very short of time (perhaps it was good of them to turn up at all). When it came to sharing their pie charts, they were characterised by lots of meetings and longish working days. But in truth, the individual pie segments were quite large, such as 2 hours for a meeting. They were astonished when they looked at the pie charts for the working mothers, whose pie charts were often broken down into five-minute segments, sometimes less, to achieve a certain parenting task. For the first time, they were learning a sharp lesson about genuine time poverty.

One of the insights that started to emerge collectively as the session went on was that everybody tended to trade off money and time. If you had a decent amount of money, but a perception of very little time, then you might spend your money to buy time — taking taxis instead of taking a bus would be a classic example. The opposite was also true — if you were very short of money, even if you were also short of time, you would spend time to save money, such as going from one supermarket to another to maximise offers. A good number of people sat somewhere in the borderland of this time versus money equation. They might sometimes spend time to save money and at other times spend money to save time. Note that I've used the verb 'spend' in relation to both time and money — they are mirror resources in this context.

Turning to the retired people, they fell into one of two groups. There were those that had been fortunate enough to retire and be quite affluent and those that didn't have quite enough to get by. This second group were more similar in one respect to the younger people, in that they were still spending time to save money, just as they had been doing throughout their working lives. It was a familiar situation, and they knew how to cope with it. But the affluent retired people stood apart from everybody else in the workshop when seen through the prism of time use. They had reached the cultural nirvana that is one of the great mythic destinations of Western living, namely, to retire with plenty of time and plenty of money and still have some health and some good years ahead of them. Someone should have told them, because they didn't come across as being very happy. Indeed, in a quite poignant moment, one of them said to the room, 'I feel like I'm starting to fray. I'm having to invent things to do with my time.' It's as if at some level, he had an instinct that he needed to be short of time, even though time is supposed to be one of the great luxuries to look forward to. Once he had said that, a couple of the other affluent retired backed him up with similar accounts of their own. Having arrived at their future, and turned it into their present, it didn't have the emotional characteristics they had been expecting.*

Of course, that's the thing about the future — from our vantage point of the present, we can't honestly know what we're planning for, and therefore how to influence it. Going back to my grandfather's

* After that workshop, we became more attuned to spotting that time-vs-money equation in action. When you observe it frequently, it's hard to avoid the hypothesis that most people are at their most motivated when they are slightly short of one resource or the other and feel that they need just a bit more time or just a bit more money to be content. They can sit in the borderland between those resources and toggle from one to the other in a useful way and propel themselves forward through life. On the other hand, when they are very short of money, it's a source of despair, and people feel stuck and lose all sense of forward momentum. Likewise, in respect of time, although it's objectively a truism to say that we all have the same amount of it, it doesn't always feel that way, and when people have a self-perception of being critically short of it, it creates deep anxiety and mental health problems.

day, the decision about retirement was out of his hands, whereas now, it's our responsibility.

6. **Full circle — being present**

Having thought about both the past and the future, where does that leave the present? The concept of 'being present' — or if you prefer, 'being in the moment' — feels like one of the great memes of our era, emerging from the vogue for mindfulness. It is as if we collectively understand that pinning down the present is effortful and requires our conscious attention. Spending any amount of time Googling the notion of presence takes you across a plethora of self-help techniques, embracing yoga, automatic writing, mindful eating, a huge number of approaches to meditation, and many others. The intention here is not to critique any of these for their usefulness but to note them as a symptom of borderland living. Culturally and socially, we spend so much time raking over the mistakes of the past and getting anxious over the threats of the future that the idea of focusing on the present, like my grandchildren do, is a type of sanctuary. But it's more than that; it's about *fully inhabiting* the present rather than just drifting from the past into the future in a somewhat aimless fashion. If I can bring Janus back into play, it's almost as if he is there to represent the notion of pushing the past and the future apart and enabling the present to occupy a bigger space in the flow of time.

To bring in a third writerly quote at this point, I'm reminded of this astute observation from the nature writer Annie Dillard: 'How we spend our days is how we spend our lives.' It's a gentle but simultaneously sharp provocation. Reflecting on it in this context, she is saying that our lives comprise one present after another after another and they add up to a life. Coming back to where this section started, with Kahnemann's taxonomy, being more fully in the present is about giving more conscious space to the experiencing self.

The Dillard quote is a neat segue to an alternative synthesis of these tricky shape-shifters of past, present, and future, which brings a true betweenist solution to the conundrum of time. We met Henri Bergson earlier, and perhaps unsurprisingly, given that we are talking about the great philosopher of flow, he has a lot to say about time. He managed to elegantly side-step problems about the three domains by introducing a totally different scheme for thinking about time. In his view, there are two types of time. There is measured time, or clock time, which we know all about. Then there is 'duration', which we'll come to. But first, a few observations on clock time.

One of my favourite moments in history at school was learning that, before the coming of the railways, time was locally determined in each city. So if it was, say, 12.00 in Liverpool, it might be 12.15 in Birmingham, and the discrepancy wouldn't matter. Time was hazy, and although the timekeepers in Greenwich were meticulous, largely for the benefit of seafarers, most of the rest of the country got by on a general sense of time elapsed during the day. Brilliant — sensible, relaxed, and not strictly enforced. But once the railways came, connecting towns and cities into a synchronised sense of time became necessary, if timetables were to have any use at all. Ever since, that ascendancy of clock time has become only more critical, and more global. If we now want to have a Zoom meeting with someone in Buenos Aires, we need an international standard around literal clock time. We also need an etiquette around observing it. It turns out the former is easier to achieve than the latter, but that's another story.

But in modern life, we have gone beyond simple clock time now, and as Michael Foley implies in his book, Bergson would be horrified by the emergence of the 'quantified self', the obsession with performance data in every metric of our life. I remember early in my career in retail, a grizzled veteran senior director barking back at my gentle objection to filling in a time sheet with 'What gets measured, gets done.' The implication was that I was a callow young individual who could only find motivation through managerial surveillance. I filled it in, albeit with an unknown and unknowable impact on my future productivity, or indeed my past productivity for that matter. What can be said conclusively is that the time spent filling it in was detrimental to my productivity in the present.

Meanwhile, Bergson's alternative version of time stands in direct opposition to clock time and is something he called 'duration'. If that comes across as suspiciously insubstantial and somehow elusive, then that is the point. It's rather as if Bergson hopes that we'll somehow just 'get' duration, rather than him having to spell it out for us. But in fact, we can get it, and in fairness, he does help us out somewhat. The core idea almost has a Buddhist feel to it — it's experienced more in the letting go of a concept of time than in the attempt to define it. Duration is borderless — it doesn't seek to demarcate past, present, and future, so much as exist in the flow of experience. Foley quotes Bergson's metaphor of choice in communicating the essence of this, likening it to a person listening to a melody.

> Real duration is what we have always known as time, but time perceived as indivisible. I do not deny that time implies succession. But I cannot admit that succession is presented to consciousness with the distinction of a before and after set side by side. When we listen to a melody we have the purest impression of succession we could possibly have… and yet it is the very continuity of the melody and the impossibility of breaking it up which makes that impression upon us.

I had this passage in mind when I wrote a few pages ago about the 'experiencing me' sitting in a short spool of time that, from a clock time perspective, included the past, present, and future, but which to me felt like a coherent block of 'duration'. I like to think that Bergson would have been a protagonist for the idea of being fully present. When the strict marking of the boundaries of time melts away, the opportunity to have a more profound encounter with your own experiencing self is something worth… I was going to say striving for, but that is almost certainly the wrong choice of verb. Maybe it's 'submitting to'.

7. Between sleeps — dorveille

> Midnight. Rise and shine… Carney knew crime's hours when he saw them — dorvay was crooked heaven, when the straight world slept and the bent got to work… In-between things: night and day, rest and duty, the no-good and the up-and-up. Pick up a crowbar, you know the in-between is where all the shit goes down. He upheld the misspelling in his thoughts, in keeping with his loyalty to his mistakes.
> — Colson Whitehead, *Harlem Shuffle*[5]

I'm indebted to American Pulitzer Prize winning novelist Colson Whitehead for bringing back to mind a curiosity that I'd once heard about but then promptly forgotten. But any meditation on notions of the betweens of time would be just that bit poorer for not dwelling for a while on dorveille, or to give it its prosaic scientific term, biphasic sleep.

I'm even more indebted to the research of A. Roger Ekirch,[6] an American history professor, who's done extensive study into the sleep patterns of previous eras. According to him, dividing the nighttime's sleep into two halves was pretty much the norm in pre-industrial times. Two things changed. One was the Industrial Revolution, which reconfigured the working day such that elongating the night became impossible. And alongside industrialisation came the invention of the light bulb, which enabled people to cheat the first few hours of night before going to bed.

But prior to that, the routine was to have a 'first sleep' of around 4 hours, and then an hour or two of wakefulness, followed by the 'morning sleep' into dawn. This middle period of being awake had a distinctive quality to it. For one thing, the quality of wakefulness was not the same as being wide awake, or even the tiredness before sleep that we're all familiar with. It had a more fluid, betweenish quality to it. There's a clue in the name: dorveille comes from a medieval French word that simply translates as sleep-wake (another lovely oxymoron to relish there), which captures that in-between state perfectly. Robert Moss, the author of *A Secret History of Dreaming*,[7] gives some of the background in an illuminating 2017 blog post, firstly by quoting from the work of a French historian, Michel Stanesco, describing dorveille as 'a sort of second state where the protagonist, half sleeping, moves in an inherently ambiguous universe, between the near and the far, the strange and the ordinary, the mysterious and the familiar'. It's also captured very nicely in a line from a poem by George Szirtes,[8] called 'Naples Yellow', in which he describes this indeterminate nighttime period as:

> It's the time of night
> when minds move sideways out of symmetry.

This would all make (some sort of) sense. We're talking about the middle of the night after all. Ekirch, in his compendious study into the history of sleep, *At Night's Close: A History of Nighttime*, talks about the discoveries he made following a chance finding in London's Public Record Office whilst looking at legal proceedings. In the way that court witnesses talked about crime events occurring after 'first sleep', it occurred to him that this was taken to be normal, as we might talk about waking at dawn as normal. Further research led him to realise that it was commonplace for people to wake naturally after a few hours of deep sleep. In Britain, this time of night was known as 'the watch', but he discovered other phrases in other countries, including France, Italy, and the American colonies.

So, what to do at this time of night, in this state of semi-wakefulness? Well, the answer is that it was an incredible range of things. For many, it was a typical set of chores, such as they might do during the day, but in addition, there were a set of other, more distinctive activities, which included sex (hard to find the privacy for at any other time of day), and then the more consciousness slipping activities alluded to in the Stanesco quote above. For example, people's ability to capture dreams was far more vivid during dorveille, and those with a creative disposition found that their fluency was heightened during this period. It was common for people to discover in the morning that they had accomplished things that surprised them and that they had forgotten they'd done. Going back to *Harlem Shuffle*, in that book, the main character, Ray Carney, is a man that is trying to lead an honest life as a furniture retailer, but by dint of his location, the family he's been born into, and the times he's in (the book is set in the late '50s), it's pretty much impossible for him to do that. Dorveille, or *dorvay* as it's consistently spelled by Whitehead, comes to symbolise that blurred time of night, when the boundaries between legal and illegal interweave, and it becomes harder to know what's right and wrong. In another fabulous short passage, Whitehead implies that once the spirit of dorveille gets into your system, it starts to shape your worldview.

> The circulation of envelopes. It reminded Carney of his idea about churn, the movement of merchandise — cabinet TVs, easy chairs, stones, furs, watches — in and out of people's hands and lives, between buyers, dealers, and the next buyer after that. Like an illustration in a National Geographic story about the global weather, showing the invisible jet stream and deep-fathom currents that determine the personality of the world. If you took a step back, if you were keyed in, you might observe these secret forces in action, how it all worked. If you were keyed in.

Circulation, churn, currents. Synonyms for flux, in rhythm to the way things shape-shift at night, with dreams coming into ascendancy, and the fixed, rigid world losing its prominence. It also puts me in mind of the folklore phrase of 'the witching hour' — that non-specific time in the middle of the night when the powers of magic are at their height.

In the context of thinking about duration and flow, and a new way of experiencing time and the present, it felt like all this needed some personal investigation. Although I've had a lifelong tendency to be a light and occasional non-sleeper, I've never flirted with this type of structured biphasic approach. Now, it so happens that there are contemporary dorveille practitioners, but not ones that are commuting into London for an office job in an agency. Therefore, I waited for a time away from work to try this out, and, on sabbatical, and finding myself alone for a few weeks in a beach house on the south coast, I set my alarm for 1 a.m. each night, with the aim of wandering around outside for up to an hour, and then trying out some writing, given that I was most interested in dorveille's impact on my creativity.

For the record, I made a point of going to bed much earlier than normal, no later than 9 p.m. Each night, I found myself startled by the alarm and not at all happy and excited about the opportunity that stretched ahead. Having said that, awakening too soon from deep sleep certainly gives a strong feel for the sideways disorientation that George Szirtes describes. It was odd. The house I was staying in backed right onto a stony beach, with only a public promenade to separate the end of the garden from the shingle. It was unlit, and, with deep cloud cover most nights, I had a proper experience of dark ahead of me, with only the breaking surf providing any sensation of light. On coming back to the house, I'd immediately capture what I'd experienced, in the form of automatic writing, where you just allow impressions to pour out of you without allowing your pen to stop on the page. I've included one night's output as an example below. For useful context, the house is directly between Worthing to the west and Brighton to the east, in the coastal town of Lancing. (In retrospect, I now realise that the name Lancing is a bit too sharp and forensic for writing a book on this topic. I should have been staying further west in Wittering.) I've left the spelling mistake of 'looom' as I wrote it — I think my imagination was responsible for the spelling of that word.

> Lightless, wind-rage. No companions on the promenade. Breakers break, waves give and take, belching shells, removing sand as tax. Gulls — where are they? Expect a bit more from them. Grasses yield to gales, but don't snap. Bending is strength. And everywhere pebbles, stones. Will this be sand in a billion years? Peer right, see pier. Peer left, Brighton darkens. Look back to house. Steps beckon. Warm bed cooling. Eyelids heavy as groyne boulders, fighting buffets of wind. Houses looom over me, menace of cotton mills, glooming, looming, gloaming. Feeble rectangle of orange reading light pulls me back. Gravity, levity, words play, words splay, split, divide, bounce off stones, fly away, out of reach, beyond mind, beyond mine. Sleep two. To dream.

What do I conclude from this time-slip experiment? What it helped me connect to was Anil Seth's notion of the 'controlled hallucination', the idea of the brain throwing out its usual quota of 'best guesses', with the aim of those guesses being a match to the incoming sensory signals. However, perhaps due to a combination of the lack of a full night's sleep, the quality of light at night, and the lack of other people and social constraints, a kind of mind-slip zone was created in which my imagination was looser, less rule-bound than usual. The result was something more mentally freewheeling, more liquid.

8. **Section summary**

a) In our current world, clock time and the associated measurement of everything that is part of the 'quantified self' are all-pervasive.
b) However, that obsession prevents us from managing to 'inhabit the moment', as we are so often encouraged to do.
c) Children have a lot to reteach us about how to 'be in the present'.

d) Embracing the concept of 'duration' can give us a new way of thinking about time, allowing the immediate past, present, and immediate future to slip together into one unit.
e) Dorveille may not be a practical reality for modern living, but it's a provocation for rethinking our hard-wired approaches to time use and looking for more creative ways of experiencing the flow of time.

SECTION SIX — BETWEEN PEOPLE

> We cannot live only for ourselves. A thousand fibres connect us with our fellow men.
>
> — Herman Melville

Back in the Words section, we saw how the word 'between' often has this physical, spatial quality. It can also carry out that role in terms of objects or even mathematical concepts (Archimedes arguably came out with the most foundational 'between' quote of all time with 'The shortest distance between two points is a straight line'), but arguably it's most at home when it's illustrating people in relationship with each other. In that role, it's often quite intimate, almost conspiratorial — the whispered 'between you and me'.

This section is all about the space between people. We'll see this space from a variety of perspectives — rather like a very small twist on a kaleidoscope, it doesn't take much of an adjustment to see quite different pictures emerging. We'll start with personal interactions — what happens between two people — and then gradually move out into broader contexts, such as political affiliation.

We'll begin by returning to the idea of being boundaried. If we're thinking about what happens between people, then what are the edges that define those interactions? That will take us towards the idea of collaboration — the constructive working together in the interests of a shared goal. We'll then consider a concept called transactive memory — how memories build between people. And because that topic introduces some doubt about the changing nature of memory, and how conditional and mutable it is, it leads into thinking about notions of truth, and therefore truth, lies, half-truths, and white lies. Almost inevitably, that discussion brings us onto politics and those ever-widening borderlands caused by increasing polarisation, with perhaps also some recent evidence of an appetite for a consensual middle ground again. Because nothing stands still.

1. Good fences make good neighbours

In the opening chapter on words, we looked briefly at the contemporary rise of the notion of 'being boundaried', including some of the phrases that have become associated with that concept, like 'they're always invading my personal space'.

My first rich immersion into this theme came from talking to Rob Poynton, the writer and facilitator who has brought improvisation into the business sphere. He spends a lot of his time running sessions where people transact with each other in ways that arise organically from the group. He describes his role as to 'hold the space between them'. One thing that he has increasingly realised is the need for people to have respect for their own boundaries as well as those of other people if the sessions are going to work. I was initially surprised by this. For one thing, his principles for improvisation begin with the deceptively simple 'letting go', which suggests fluidity and openness, rather than the implied sensation of something static and defined that comes with any type of boundary. But he has a beguiling piece of wisdom around this, in the form of a Robert Frost phrase: 'Good fences make good neighbours.'

His point is that a wholesome respect for your own boundaries as well as other people's is a precursor to successful interaction with those around you. So ultimately there is no contradiction between good personal boundaries and being able to let go and be a fluent improviser. The two things go hand in hand. He emphatically agrees with the insight provided earlier by Anil Seth's work, that boundaries are essential to living systems, and his perspective on that is that without boundaries, it's not possible for us to have a sense of identity. As he said to me when we met, 'It's not the right question to ask whether boundaries or borders are good or bad. It's a question of what kind of borders? I'm interested in the ones that are enriching.'

Having listened to Rob, as a facilitator in improvisation, I was keen to understand the notion of being boundaried from a different type of professional facilitator, and I got a complementary perspective when I caught up with Cherry Potter, a Brighton-based psychotherapist. In addition to seeing patients on a one-to-one basis, she also runs 'stranger groups', whereby a group of either six or seven people agree to meeting together once a week. Each person stays in the group for as long as the group is useful to them in working through whatever issues have brought them there in the first place. This can represent a commitment of years in some cases. Cherry tends to use the image of 'conductor' to describe her role and, like Rob Poynton, uses the specific phrase of 'holding the space' to explain one of her most important primary responsibilities. Some of that is physical — the ambience of the place they meet — but some of it is emotional, meaning that she creates a safe environment for people to let their guard down, to reuse that phrase we had earlier. As the name suggests, the distinctive thing about a stranger group is that none of the members of the group knew each other prior to being introduced into the group by Cherry. Therefore, another of her responsibilities is to try to anticipate the likely impact on the group dynamics of any person that she considers bringing into the group if a member leaves.

In terms of boundaries, the most fascinating thing about the working of the group is one of the critical rules, and that is that group members agree to not meet each other outside of the group itself. In a real sense, despite getting to know intimate details of each other's lives in terms of what is shared in the group, they remain strangers. They agree not to share addresses, phone numbers, etc., and in the event of ever bumping into each other in the street, they can do nothing more than make a tiny acknowledgement, like a nod of the head. It's a non-negotiable strict boundary, but its role is to help create a wall around the group, within which there is equality and safety. The space inside the group is bound to be liminal to a tremendous degree, and people need high degrees of trust to be able to share effectively with each other, which means that the corresponding boundary that surrounds it needs to be secure and reliable. It's a perfect illustration of Rob Poynton's maxim that good fences make good neighbours.

2. **Two heads are more creative than one**

A while back, I was at a book launch in the London Review Bookshop near the British Museum, listening to the charismatic mythologist Martin Shaw read from his then latest book. He's in the habit of landing astonishing insights in only four or five words, which suggests he's mulled and whittled them over decades. One of his short thought-bombs was 'intelligence happens between people'. It's the sort of phrase that, when you hear it, gives voice to something you've instinctively always felt but never had the words line up in the right order to express it. He wasn't denying the intelligence that people have as individuals, but it's not the type of intelligence that excites him. Later, after being released from the spell of his delivery, I realised that he was reframing something that we generally call collaboration. Now, collaboration is a critical skill, and indeed a vital borderland concept, but as a word, it's so ubiquitous as to have its interesting edges smoothed away to blandness through overuse. But we mustn't allow that to happen, and mulling on 'intelligence between people' creates a new way to see a familiar process. By way of example, and speaking personally, for the longest time, this book was a private project that I worried away at in quiet moments, allowing the ideas to percolate slowly. It was my wife, Elen, who said to me, 'You can't write this book on your own.' Sadly, she wasn't offering to ghostwrite it for me, although she'd have done a brilliant job of it. She meant that many of the best ideas were squirrelled away inside people that I'd never even met, or people I did know but didn't know they had an exciting thought about borders rattling around in their heads. She was right, and once I decided to go public with it, I found myself having multiple conversations with people that provided new angles on the entire topic, and there was an acceleration in both ideas and output. One instance of this was a conversation with my colleague Natasha Ward on a train journey to meet with a client. I'd just announced to everyone at work that I was taking a sabbatical break to concentrate on writing, and she asked me what I was writing about. As soon as I mentioned the topic of borders, she immediately said to me: 'You'll have already thought about Janus, won't you?' I hadn't at all, but there he was, plain as day, and in an instant, I realised that he had a role to play.

At a far higher level of endeavour than me and this book, there has been a longstanding tendency to propagate the idea of the lone genius at work. We all know the roll call of European white men that get trotted out here — Leonardo Da Vinci, Galileo, Mozart, Newton, Shakespeare, Einstein, and so on. But as Rob Poynton says in *Do/Improvise*:[1]

> Ask most people to conjure up an idea of someone creative and it's likely they will come up with a version of the eccentric inventor or artist in his garret. The image is of a lone individual, of rare talent, engaged in a tortuous process of creation, with inspiration occurring in blinding flashes.

> There are two striking features of this image. First, it is not a very accurate depiction of how creativity occurs, either in the arts or in science (or, for that matter, in business). Secondly, it depicts creative people as 'other'. They are disconnected and separate.

He's right — it's easy to lose sight of collaboration and shared work being a crucial part of creativity and good work in general. You'd probably be surprised to discover how many novels are co-written by more than one person, given the fact that none of those co-written novels advertise the fact on their covers. Publishers have historically been reticent about them — for some reason, there's an uneasy sense that readers will shy away from stories written by more than one person. It's not easy to fathom why this would be the case. Music fans don't resist songs with multiple writing credits. Indeed, the most famous song writing credit of them all, Lennon and McCartney, was mostly a myth in that they generally wrote alone. TV watchers know all about the writing room phenomenon and recognise that it leads to better watching, and all art lovers in the Renaissance would have been very aware that paintings that emerged from, say, Titian or Veronese were actually coming from their studios and were in large part worked on by students. (I was part of a team of 15 writers that co-wrote a novel, which, to the best of our knowledge, was a record. In our case, the level of co-writing was overt, and part of the point of writing it at all was to see if it could be done. It turned out to be a genuinely harmonious experience.)

If the idea of the lone genius was ever true, and it probably never was, it's certainly not true any longer. There are increasing rumblings each year that the idea of giving Nobel prizes in science to an individual practitioner makes no sense at all. It's becoming impossible to make meaningful developments in science other than through teams of people working together. And in the realm of engineering, the sheer level of complexity and specialisation has got us to the point that there isn't any single individual on

Earth that fully understands all that's involved in getting a modern aircraft into the sky — it can only happen through collaboration of multiple talents.

And it is in this experience of collaboration where intelligence happening between people comes to life. There's a well-loved — but still worth retelling — story of the writing of 'Hey Jude', which John Lennon always thought of as Paul McCartney's best-ever song. Although it's common knowledge that Lennon and McCartney wrote separately, nearly all the Beatles' output that came from either of them had a joint writing credit, and possibly with good reason, because the input of the other one was often critical, if only in a small way. 'Hey Jude' is a case in point. In *Revolution in the Head*,[2] author Ian MacDonald tells the story of how McCartney initially composed much of the song in his head whilst driving.

> Demo-ing it on piano, he took the tape to Lennon, apologising for the lyric as the first words that had come into his head. His partner would have none of this, dismissing McCartney's embarrassment over the line 'the movement you need is on your shoulder', and declaring Hey Jude all but finished as it stood.

In other accounts of this conversation between them that I've read elsewhere, McCartney claimed to have been startled by Lennon's reaction, but the moment he was able to see the line through Lennon's eyes, it was transformed for him from the filler line that he had it down as. It's a small story of collaboration, but an iconic one. And in fact, it's hard to disagree with Lennon. The line is elusive in a brilliant way — that sense of meaning withheld or a fraction out of reach which so much great writing has, even when it's inadvertent at a conscious level, as it was in this case.

I'll conclude this section by returning to Rob Poynton. A large part of his work is about the facilitation of collaboration and using simple techniques to open up the space between people. In this way, it's a working embodiment of Martin Shaw's way of putting it. In a conversation we had, he told me about one of his colleagues who self-describes herself as a 'half-a-sentence-person'. The idea is that she'll put a half-formed idea out into the space between her and someone else and invite them to build on it. His implication was that she could easily have the ingenuity to complete her own thoughts, but in a spirit of both generosity and intellectual adventure, she's more interested in seeing how another person develops the thought in a way that wouldn't occur to her. It's this kind of collaborative exploration of the borderlands of ideas that produces better work in everyday contexts.

Speaking to Rob Poynton took me back to one of the classic texts on improvisation: *Impro* by Keith Johnstone, published way back in 1979.[3] I've read it three times, especially the heart of the book where he talks about the basic techniques of offers: accepting and blocking. But I'd forgotten how that section starts.

> There are people who prefer to say, 'Yes' and there are people who prefer to say 'No'. Those who say 'Yes' are rewarded by the adventures they have, and those who say 'No' are rewarded by the safety they attain. There are far more 'No' sayers around than 'Yes' sayers but you can train one type to behave like the other.

The reward of safety is linked to its opposite, which in this case is a fear of loss of control, which can lead to other fears, such as looking stupid, drying up, and so on. The formal techniques of improvisation create a safe space because you're not obliged to be original, or clever, or creative, or funny. What you do need to do is obey the rules and allow the content to generate itself. There's an echo of Cherry Potter's hard-boundary rule. Obey that, and meaningful conversation at a deep level can happen. Obey the improv rules, and meaningful creative content can emerge. So much of Johnstone's training of students was helping them find ways to say 'yes' to offers, and learn to defy the instinct to say 'no'. What helped was students experiencing for themselves the deflation and loss of energy when the first block in an improvised scene killed off a promising dialogue. This would often happen through fear (loss of control, or anxiety about where the content was going, or feeling stupid). A good improvisation requires either both participants to be 'yes' sayers, or if there *is* going to be blocking, then it's coded into the rules of that session. Johnstone's use of the word 'adventures' feels well chosen. This extends beyond acting — there's a thrill in everyday life when two people are chasing an idea and saying 'yes' to each other's contribution. It's a mental adventure that amplifies the net amount of creativity than either could achieve on their own.

I have one final observation on these 'rules', in whatever context. When you've got some measure of obedience to a code in a group context, at some unstated level, people are putting their ego to one side. Implicitly, the rules of the group are bigger than any one individual, rather like we saw in those anthropological initiation rites earlier on. It's not that people are serving the rules, but the objectives of the group are achieved by people observing the rules. Earlier in the book, in the Words section, we looked at some of the common phrases and proverbs of the borderlands, and we can bring another one in here. You often hear people saying, 'He thinks the rules don't apply to him.' It's a borderland phrase because it's about crossing the line, transgressing. By contrast, the best collaborations involve qualities like respect, listening, observance, and some humility. To rephrase Martin Shaw a touch, it's a case of 'emotional intelligence happening between people'.

3. **A memory shared is a memory doubled**

It's not only intelligence that can happen between people. It's also possible to build and sustain memories between people too. This can be true in work, family, and friendship groups as shared memories become part of the fabric of the web of relationships. Although that sounds obvious, there's nuance and subtlety to this commonplace observation. In the mid-'80s, an American social psychologist called Daniel Wegner proposed a new idea that he dubbed 'transactive memory'. It's a concept that, once heard, most people would understand intuitively as making common sense, but he was the first to codify it in a structured way. We're considering it here because it's an example of unconscious collaboration between people.

Simply put, the theory says that when people are in continual proximity to each other, they build up a store of shared memory that is common to the couple or group. So far, so obvious. But there's more to it than that, because the members of the group don't all store all the knowledge — they learn that some members of the group will lean towards some 'memory expertise' amongst the full set of stored knowledge. In a work-based group this might be, say, technical expertise, and other members will work together (or transact, hence the name) to extract the appropriate memory from the person that holds it.

Again, that might feel reasonably straightforward, based on job titles and a clear division of responsibilities and skills in a team, but less expected is that a similar thing happens in couples that live together, but in subliminal fashion. We're all used to the idea of dividing domestic tasks according to acknowledged skills (the money tasks, the planning tasks, the social tasks, the DIY tasks, etc.), but it's less overt that couples unconsciously tend to allocate aspects of memories between each other as well — one person remembering the context that sat around the memory, the other having a better grip on the events themselves. That's fine if the couple stay together — memories can be reconstructed between each other. But following separation, or when one of them dies, it becomes far harder to retrieve the whole memory when you've got used to delegating part of it to your partner, without even realising that this was what you were doing.

I experienced a personal version of this when my mother died. As part of the process, my brother, sister, and I had to go through her house, making decisions on all her belongings, and inevitably, many things, especially documents and photographs, sparked memories and conversations between us. Occasionally, I'd have no recall of some story they told, and they had their versions of that too. But typically, we'd all remember a story, but in a partial way. Sometimes, that would make sense, because we'd all had separate roles in the story. There were other times in our reminiscences, though, when it was more startling than that. I'd realise there was more texture to a memory that we were all present at, because I now had their aspect of it as well. The memory was being recreated and increased. It was exciting, and enriching, to have memories added to like this, but also a bit troubling — I was forced to confront either how editorial my memory must have been, or that I hadn't been able to empathise and internalise how that event had seemed to them. Had I, at some level, *chosen* to remember some aspect of a memory and not others? Or was the explanation more banal than that, such as simply forgetting part of the story because I hadn't found it that interesting? Or perhaps it didn't quite seem to fit the narrative of the story. It feels impossible to get to the bottom of all that. What I do know is this: our mother died in late 2016, and all those shared memory conversations happened in the spring of 2017. But now, if I try to recall some of those expanded memories of our mother that we recreated between us, I can tell it's mostly just my memories that come back, not the extended ones that involve Nick and Sarah-Jo's extra memories. It's not because my memories are in any way superior or more accurate than theirs are/were. On the contrary, I'm left with a very sharp sense of the exact opposite. I was often left thinking that their residual grip on events we all took part in was in some sense better than mine. It's simply that my memories had become chemically hardwired into my neural networks through internal repetition and recall, but I was hearing their version just the once. There was an imbalance in the weight of the shared memory, and their versions faded.

I can also see another version of transactive memory in action at my workplace. We started our business in 2002, and there are now 17 of us, of whom three are part of the original team. Inevitably, the other 14 have all arrived at different times, including two or three in the last year. What that means is that when nostalgic memories are being recalled, new joiners are hearing things they weren't originally part of. However, some of those tales have become part of the mythology of the business, and I've heard people who have been with us for, say, 7 or 8 years, tell famous stories to new joiners that happened ten or 12 years ago, i.e., before they themselves joined. Although they weren't there, they've heard some of those stories so often that it almost feels as if they had been. The fact that they are part of the shared folklore is the key thing.

There's an excellent creative meditation on shared memory, conceived and directed by the Canadian filmmaker Sarah Polley, in 2012. Called *Stories We Tell*, it's a personal documentary film that features all the members of her family, close family friends, and a few other characters whose relationship to the family isn't clear in the first half hour or so. All of them are recreating memories of her mother Diane, who died of cancer aged 42 when Polley, who was the youngest sibling of five, was only 11. Everyone gets to tell their story, other than Polley herself, but central to the film is Michael, her father, who had originally been an actor and would-be writer, until he felt an obligation to earn a more reliable income to support the family. We see him writing his own contribution to the film, and, in addition, the professional apparatus of the film is laid bare as we watch the lights and recording equipment set up to capture each person's memories. Occasionally, we'll hear Polley ask someone to rerecord a sentence, thereby making a wry observation on the performative nature of any recall that you say out loud.

All these interviews are intercut from the beginning with home videos from when Diane was still alive, and the first part of the film is gently benign. There is an occasionally artful bit of editing, where one opinion or memory of Diane is immediately contradicted by the next voice, but that raises a smile more than anything else. But then there is a major twist halfway through, which changes the entire pace and direction of the film, and some of the contributions suddenly change in intensity, deepening the philosophical nature of the project, as the film starts to turn into a discourse on the reliability of memory and who gets to have the right to tell stories.

And although Polley herself *doesn't* get to tell her version of the story in the film, she is the editor, as more than one character points out, so that gives her a strong measure of control. One of the continual themes, coming from nearly every character, is that of truth. In their own ways, nearly all of them comment on the importance of getting at the truth, which feels clear to each of them, but when the stories are all refracted through personal perspective, can that truth be any more than the sum of the total contributions? There isn't one truth; there are eight truths, or 12, depending on how many people have a stake in the story. One major character tries to make a case for the versions of truth to be weighted according to how close they were to the centre of the story, which was a clear pitch for his own version to be given greater prominence.

Speaking later to *The New Yorker* about the experience of making the film, Sarah Polley said:

> "You know, making 'Stories We Tell' was so interesting because people remember things differently. They get the events that are life-changing right, but all the details around those things, even when they're *not* traumatic, are wildly inconsistent. We can agree that my mom died. But I don't think we can agree what happened that night, afterward. We were shattered, so our memory is shattered, too. It's not a great barometer by which to figure out the truth."

To add to that, what I have held back so far is the fact that the 'home videos' I alluded to are reconstructed, and therefore acted by non-family members. It's incredibly convincing footage, yet part of the layer of artifice of the film, adding substantially to the meta question of 'What is the truth?'

I'm left wondering if there is, perhaps, an answer to that question, it being another echo of Martin Shaw's formulation that 'intelligence happens between people' and the theory of transactive memory. Maybe truth also 'happens between people', and of course 'memories happen between people'. If the relationships are harmonious, then those memories and versions of the truth can be consensual. It's only when they're not that shared memories can become a battleground for purposes of control or succeeding in winning arguments or setting personal agendas.

4. **Truth and lies**

> What is the nature of the border between truth and lies? It is permeable and blurred because it is planted thick with rumour, confabulation, misunderstanding and twisted tales.
> — Hilary Mantel, *Bring up the Bodies*

In contrast to the highly equivocal perspective offered by Hilary Mantel, consider this from St Augustine, from his book *De Mendacio* (*On Lying*): 'Every lie is a sin.' (Given the emphatic nature of this assertion, you've got to give him credit for stringing the topic out for a full 108 pages.) Well, easy for him to say. Maybe times were less ambiguous in the fourth century. And you can see why he'd say that, because even in our secular age, in which alarming notions of sin and its hellish consequences have greyed out into the realm of simple wrongdoing, there is still a reflex to think of lying as a moral absolute. We tell our children to 'always tell the truth'. I can hear that parental voice still: 'It's worse to do something naughty and then lie about it than just do the naughty thing.' And there's the clue, of course. The childhood lie is about self-preservation, sometimes about transferring blame or a flat rejection of culpability — 'I didn't do it,' or 'It wasn't me.' In this type of scenario, what parents are objecting to is not so much the lie itself as the motive behind it — the attempt to deny responsibility. In moments like this, the situation feels entirely black and white.

Social lying

And yet, there is a huge grey area, and adults emphatically believe in lying, whatever we tell our children to the contrary.

American psychology professor Robert Feldman, author of *The Liar in Your Life*,[4] has conducted extensive research on this topic and has concluded that, in conversation, the typical adult lies an astonishing three times every 10 minutes. We can probably take a generous view of myths we tell children, such as (spoiler alert) Father Christmas, the Easter bunny, and the tooth fairy, as part of preserving 'the magic of childhood', but what about the whole territory of white lies? Whoever first said that 'a white lie is aversion of the truth' did more than come up with a smart pun. Many a child has been comforted with lines like, 'Don't worry, darling. Thumper has gone to heaven.' When in reality the guileless rabbit has disappeared down the gullet of an urban fox, and nowhere else. The defence to this is self-evident: it's about the protection of innocence, shielding children from the merciless laws of nature for just that bit longer. And perhaps there's an extra dimension to this as well. We've already looked at the domain of limbo in the liminality section. What if these parents have the same reflex as so many leading religions, to hold out to their children the comfort of the notion of not being separated from their pets by death, but that death is simply a temporary boundary that will be dissolved in time?

What the existence of the white lie hints at is the notion that a 'good' motivation transforms a lie into something else. It's still not factually accurate, but it could be morally positive. If you're out shopping with a friend and they try some jeans on and say, 'How do I look in these?' you may be faced with a moral choice — if you don't think they look good. If you sense that they want you to say they look great, you might agree, in the interests of friendship. And you might rationalise that to yourself by thinking, *Well, it's only my opinion — it's not a fact*, or just consider that supporting your friend's confidence is the greater moral decision, especially if you believed they were pretty committed to buying them anyway. What purpose would have been served by an answer that was more honest to your own opinion? We've clearly got two overlapping lines in this scenario. St Augustine's unequivocal moral absolute truth line, which would have your friend having their feelings hurt, and then the contemporary line that's overwritten it, which we might call the kind line. In the case of the white lie, we prefer the kind line, in the interests of caring about continuing friendships. In a way, the kind line doesn't belong anywhere between or to either side of the truth or lie lines. It sits in a different paradigm altogether.

This perspective has been given a recent academic gloss by two American researchers, Prof. Maurice Schweitzer and Emma Levine.[5] They argue that throughout philosophical history, pure honesty and benevolence have been fused together in our understanding of truth and falsehood. They believe it is helpful to disentangle the two concepts and think of a lie as being either pro-social or pro-self. If the intention behind a lie is pro-social, then perhaps the lie can even build trust, whereas honesty at all costs can erode trust and be seen as immoral. Emotional intelligence is frequently deployed in moments like this to navigate our way around human relationships.

The white lie is a cousin to the half-truth, and they both hinge on questions of motivation. In 2023, the National Theatre in London staged a new play called *Dr Semmelweis*, based on the true life story of the Hungarian physician Ignaz Semmelweis. Whilst working in Vienna in a maternity unit, he discovered the link between antiseptic hand washing and reduced child mortality. Although he was able to use statistics to demonstrate the validity of his approach, he clashed strongly with medical orthodox opinion at the time, which was offended by his implied criticism of their standards. In the stage version, Semmelweis has several lower-ranking supporters, who are close enough to the situation to see that his new methods are working. What they have, which Semmelweis doesn't, is the emotional intelligence, or perhaps even just sufficient smarts to understand how to work the system. By contrast, Semmelweis is an uncompromising truth-teller, and lacks the subtlety to make his case. For him, truth is a moral absolute. At one point, one of his supporters tries to persuade him to moderate his language, by saying that 'A half-truth is still halfway to the whole truth.' Semmelweis cannot accept this and continues to attack authority head-on, as a moral crusade, to no effect. A classic conundrum. Slyer, more sophisticated and nuanced approaches, perhaps with some flattery involved (which as we all know gets you everywhere), could have been the way forward here in order to save the lives of the babies and their mothers that were at stake. As the phrase goes, the ends would have justified the means.

I'm closing this section with a saying that one of my colleagues occasionally uses. She will say, 'If I think I can get away with it, I'll always tell the truth.' It's a brilliant linguistic construction, very knowing, and aware of the gnarly borderland between honesty as a virtue on the one hand, and getting along with people on the other, which is also a critical life skill.

Lies as social cohesion

Now individual motivation around half-truths and white lies is one thing, but this type of thinking easily ladders up into the public sphere. There's a famous example from twentieth-century British legal history. In 1974, six men were incarcerated for an atrocity in Birmingham, where bombs exploded in two pubs on the same night, killing 21 people and injuring nearly 200. Ultimately, the Birmingham Six had their convictions quashed in 1991, and were to go on to get substantial, seven-figure compensation a decade later. But prior to that, in 1980, they brought a case against the police which eventually went to appeal, and was ultimately thrown out by the most senior law lord, the then Master of the Rolls, Lord Denning, using a startling piece of logic, reproduced here:

> Just consider the course of events if their action were to proceed to trial. If the six men failed it would mean that much time and money and worry would have been expended by many people to no good purpose. If they won, it would mean that the police were guilty of perjury; that they were guilty of violence and threats; that the confessions were involuntary and improperly admitted in evidence; and that

> the convictions were erroneous. That was such an appalling vista that every sensible person would say, 'It cannot be right that these actions should go any further.'

In other words, he was saying that the issue of the public's confidence in the police took precedence over the actual facts of whether the men had committed the crime or not. Many years ago, quite close to the events in question, I debated this judgement with a group of law students and discovered that we were arguing from inside entirely different paradigms of belief. They thought my (then) black and white perspective of natural justice (they'd either committed the crime or they hadn't, and if they hadn't, then justice could only be served by them being exonerated) was quaint, if not downright naïve. But what's instructive about that story is the realisation of which side we were all invested in. The law students were invested, like Lord Denning, in the perceived integrity of the law, whereas I was invested in a soup of notions of natural justice, innocence or guilt as absolutes, along with fairness to the individual. I think I assumed at the time that their belief was self-serving and careerist, but in hindsight, I can see that they had a more sophisticated position — along the lines that public faith in the law is an essential piece of cohesion that helps to hold society together. I still wouldn't buy into that, and in fact it feels to me that the orthodox position has moved as well over the decades, towards a belief that institutions are stronger when they are transparently held to account. But the point is, we were having an argument in an ethical borderland but where both parties were starting from opposite sides and struggling to appreciate each other's position. Or rather, I didn't appreciate theirs — they were better thinkers than I was.

Truth withheld

While still in the realm of twilight-truth, there is also the genre of the truth withheld. In the infamous Spycatcher trial in 1986, the Cabinet Secretary Sir Robert Armstrong coined his notorious phrase, 'being economical with the truth', when asked under cross-examination to define the difference between the truth and a misleading impression. By leaving the explicit truth unsaid, we allow an alternative impression of the truth to hover. This is another everyday tactic in the personal realm as well. Children often call things as they see them and have complex parental conversations as a result. ('I know Uncle John is fat, but it's not kind to say so out loud.' 'But you always tell me to say the truth…') What children go on to learn is that there is an entire etiquette around not passing any comment at all in social situations, and this is analogous to being economical with the truth. It's that notion of 'pro-social' that we just encountered — the necessary skill that makes social living tolerable and sustainable.

Truthiness — the truth you want

Adjacent to the truth withheld is a fellow-traveller — the truth you want, rather than the actual truth that is. In 2005, the American comedian Stephen Colbert coined the word 'truthiness' in one of his satirical sketches to precisely describe this phenomenon. George W. Bush had started to become renowned for coming out with statements that he *felt* to be true, but which lacked demonstrable backup in terms of facts. What Colbert had understood was that leaders like Bush had mastered the rhetorical device of expressing their point of view with enough conviction that the emotion was seen as an analogue for the facts. Obviously, there's nothing new here — mendacious political leaders have been doing this for centuries. But in an era of mass communications, such proclamations of 'truthiness' can spread virally, because emotion travels more quickly than rational statistics.

More recently, truthiness has been added to with the subtle introduction of 'my truth' and 'your truth'. It's likely that Oprah Winfrey has contributed to the popularisation of this phrase, as it's one of her trademark exhortations to her guests. In one of her most celebrated interviews, she famously said to Meghan Markle, or the Duchess of Sussex if you prefer, 'How do you feel about the Palace hearing you speak your truth today?' It's a tiny phrase that is full of insight into the times we are living through. There's an implication that 'your truth' has just as much validity as 'the truth', maybe more. Because no one can deny the way you see the world, right? So '*your* truth' can't be questioned, but '*the* truth' is debatable. The argument goes that we've gone past the point where 'the truth' is possible, or maybe for some people even desirable, any longer. There's a strong echo here to the phrase that I mentioned from the statistician David in the Between Ideas section — 'Uncertainty is a personal relationship with the world.' The notion of 'my truth' and 'your truth' is just a way of expressing that in everyday language.

And no meditation on this topic is complete without bringing Donald Trump and Boris Johnson onto the stage. They both went on to perfect the art of emotional assertion that Bush Jr started to burnish in his time in office. Where typical democratic leaders may privately acknowledge inconvenient truths but attempt to swerve past them in public, and totalitarian leaders simply suppress the facts, Trump and Johnson became world-class purveyors of truthiness, and maybe with the benefit of hindsight, Dubya starts to look like a paragon of restraint… What this meant in practice was using their personal charisma and force of conviction to recreate the version of truth that suited their belief systems. In a highly insightful blog post on the BBC website, written in May 2021, the BBC's then political editor Laura Kuenssberg managed to get a variety of people close to Johnson to talk off the record about his relationship to the truth, including some second-hand reporting of Johnson's own attitudes in this area.[6] One of these sources, talking about Johnson's cultivated habit of selective memory, recalls him saying, 'I choose to remember certain things or not remember others.' Another is quoted as saying, 'Is there wilful lying? I would struggle to point to a direct example. Does he recreate the truth to suit him? Yes.' Tucked away in Kuenssberg's article is one fascinating contradiction. Set amongst a long list of his creative interpretations of events, comes an insight from a pollster, saying that despite all this, Johnson conveys a sense of authenticity to the electorate, in the sense that what you see is what you get. Trump is like this too. His untruths are so flagrant as to render him ironically trustworthy to his base. It's as if both men are saying a version of 'Judge me whatever way you want, but not on my relationship to the truth.' As a tactic, it makes them curiously bullet-proof. It's essentially impossible to call them out as liars, because all of that is factored into their reputation already, and in essence is now discounted. It's a fantastic entanglement, and tremendously modern. It puts me in mind of the jaundiced Russian saying, 'He lies like an eye-witness.' It's as if notions of objective truth are now so elusive as to not be valued, whereas the higher-order quality is to appear authentic, which can be judged without recourse to fact checking.

In pondering tactics like that, what we're seeing is a border of a different sort. If you've got factual truth on one side and falsehood on the other, the borderland here comprises partly the appearance of authenticity, but also the art of assertion. And when assertion is deployed with a mixture of wit, confidence, and passion, it starts to carve out a territory for itself that overwhelms factual truth, because to a certain, increasingly large audience, it's simply more attractive. For one thing, assertion is likely to come along with, say, storytelling or the invocation of a sense of pride and identity, and to be delivered with bravado. What you're ultimately getting is colour, flavour, and texture. It adds up to entertainment, and if you've got no strong expectations from politicians in any case, entertainment is as good a measuring stick as anything else. It's just altogether more interesting. In addition, what comes with all that is a far greater speed in the communication of those types of stories through social media than can be achieved by the purveyors of earnest policy and statistically driven political positions. I was chatting to an American friend of mine, a lifelong Democrat, six months into the first Trump presidency, and he said, 'Martin, I hate to say this, but I've never been more fascinated by what's going on in the world of politics.'

The implication is that we should be careful what we wish for. In the recent past in the UK, the British population have lived through two sincere if dull Prime Ministers, Gordon Brown and Theresa May, both of whom demonstrated high levels of personal integrity in their conduct, but neither of whom succeeded in their first general election as prime minister. Gordon Brown lost, and Theresa May ended up leading a hung parliament, despite taking what looked like an impregnable lead in the polls into the election campaign. They were superseded by David Cameron and Boris Johnson respectively. The pre-political careers of these two are instructive — corporate affairs and journalism, both involved in the varnished presentation of stories with a specific agenda for public consumption.

As an interesting footnote to this whole topic of fake news, it's tempting to think that we're witnessing something new here. But we're not. This was demonstrated when reading a book that has superficially nothing to do with borders or truth and lies. In Gordon Kerr's *A Short History of Coffee*,[7] there's a passage talking about the rise of coffee shops in London in the seventeenth century, and the way they became a hotbed of political dissent, to such a degree that there was eventually a royal proclamation in June 1672, which included the statement in its long-winded title 'Restrain the Spreading of False News, and Licentious Talking of Matters of State and Government.' Note the use of the phrase 'false news', so close to the 'fake news' of our own times. The detail goes on to accuse plotters of 'speaking evil of things they know not', amongst other presumed misdemeanours.

It's a reminder that for as long as we've had political parties, each side is coming from an entirely different paradigm of how they perceive the world, or indeed their leaders. It's become a frequently expressed view about Trump that his supporters take him seriously, but not literally, whereas his opponents take him literally, but not seriously. It's a very concise formulation, exquisitely mirrored, and demonstrating the almost impossible division around one controversial character. For liberals who are obsessed and still wedded to notions of accuracy, objectively derived true facts, and notions of verifiability, it's inconceivable and confounding that his supporters can't 'see through' Trump's easy relationship with 'the truth'. It makes it impossible for them to take him seriously. But to his supporters, they aren't taking all his statements at face value: they know full well that it's not all fact checked and a lot of it is improvised and off the cuff. But that's understood, and what they are responding to is disruption and energy and making things happen. So they can take that seriously, without being bothered by literal accuracy.

Corporate truthiness

This twilight world of white lies, personal truth and silent discretion leads us inexorably into the realm of corporate truthfulness. One of the great overused words of our age is transparency. If you'd been bussed in from the 1970s, you could be forgiven for thinking that modern institutional life has been overtaken by a truth crusade, based on the volume of mentions of transparency in corporate discourse. It's another occasion when the Google Ngram Viewer is helpful — transparency is one of those words where usage has exponentially rocketed from about 1990 onwards, after having remained at a steady state for the best part of a century. It's a word that speaks to an idea, and that idea is having a cultural moment. In reality, this transparency has been forced upon corporations. Prior to the internet, they were far more able to control the narrative that surrounded their businesses, and it was the work of dedicated investigative journalists to dig deeper into the murkier underbelly of corporate life. It was routine for ordinary customers to be ripped off, with businesses knowing that they had every chance of either getting away with it entirely or for any exposure to be limited in its damage. Nowadays, what with the digital flotilla of review sites and forums, it's far easier for the public to hold companies to account. Many businesses that are essentially reputable, seeing the direction of travel, have decided to get ahead of this and turn transparency into a virtue.

And yet be in no doubt that businesses, especially large ones, still spend a good part of their existence dwelling in ethical borderlands. We all understand this, and the public have developed good instincts in decoding modern marketing. For instance, we never expect a company to tell us the whole truth about what goes on behind its closed doors. Nor do we expect them, any more than we expect it of political parties, to do anything other than present the best version of themselves to the world. We know full well that their public utterances, as experienced by the public through advertising or other forms of marketing collateral, are designed to paint the most positive picture — to describe their best self, if you will — and that it's our job to filter what we hear through our own prior experience of such claims.

Any slip from that expectation can be disastrous. Back in 1991, Gerald Ratner, the founder of the jewellery business that bore his name, admitted in a speech to the Institute of Directors that some of his products were 'total crap'. Two years later, after a calamitous slide, the brand name disappeared from view. Honesty had not been his friend. Although that incident is not in the forefront of the public's mind now, it's still a case study that businesspeople get to hear about.

More recently, there have been other examples of self-inflicted egregious corporate behaviour, although not involving such ill-advised examples of truth telling. Think back to, say, the Volkswagen emissions scandal, which came to light in 2015; the horsemeat affair that caught out a good number of UK supermarkets; and the financial skulduggery that brought down the Patisserie Valerie chain in 2018. Without question, there will be others to come, but the type of moral borderlands I've got in mind are less about grand deceptions and actual fraud so much as everyday executive choices about areas such as claims, the framing of apologies, the presentation of facts, what to put in and leave out of communication and so on. Many of these are banal. We're all used to price promotions such as 'up to 50% off', and know how to manage our expectations there, but other choices that get made are tiny but still significant instances of a business positioning itself in an ambiguous territory, either by accident or design, or most likely some muddle of them both. Take an example faced by many commuters on almost a weekly basis — a delayed train, accompanied by a prerecorded announcement apologising 'for any inconvenience caused'. The key borderland word here is 'any'. Because in the black and white world, of course it's inconvenient! When has a passenger been *convenienced* by a train delay? But because of the phrasing of the announcement, with this injection of the word 'any', the train operator doesn't accept the premise that we are *necessarily* inconvenienced. The apology only operates conditionally, in a scenario in which the passenger happens to be inconvenienced. Otherwise, no apology necessary. (For comparison, this formulation belongs in a very similar camp to the infamous 'expressions of regret' of politicians, in which they apologise 'for any confusion /misperception/offence caused to the public'. Notice they're not apologising for what they did or said, but only for its potential impact. The implication is that it's your fault for being confused or offended, not theirs for causing it.) By this point, the train announcement cliché is so familiar to travellers as to pass without notice, but imagine a scenario where a visitor to your home broke a beautiful vase, and immediately said, 'I apologise for any distress this breakage may have caused.' You'd be outraged at their attempt to transfer the responsibility to your reaction rather than their action.

And yet, despite the patent absurdity of the use of the word 'any', at some point, some action or small set of actions was taken by some train operator that resulted in that form of words being publicly used, and then taken up by other operators. Because it's the way in businesses, someone would have written it in response to an obvious communication need ('We have to have a standard announcement for train delays…'), and it went through an approvals process. But the suspicion is that you'd never get to the bottom of how a decision like this was made. It's too small a decision to be workshopped, or researched, and yet it happened. The real likelihood is that it emerges in some barely visible way from an organisation's culture. Over time, middle and junior managers, at least ones with a well-developed corporate antenna, absorb the unwritten priorities of their business. Stories are heard about risk-averse decisions influenced by lawyers; they get involved in damage limitation exercises; they might get media training about how to present their company's position in the best light. As cultures develop, sculpted by experiences like these, an organisational preservation instinct kicks in, and almost unconsciously, a word like 'any' can slip unnoticed into an apology announcement. It's what happens when reputation management becomes an increasingly important part of the overall business agenda, leading to company cultures that begin to exist in a grey area between not lying and not truth telling.

In any consideration of this topic, I'm always reminded of a quite brilliant, skewering Leo Cullum cartoon. It features a (male) executive sitting at a typical corporate desk, with a standing (female) junior employee looking somewhat befuddled. The executive says, 'Honesty is the best policy, Fernbaugh, it's just not company policy.'

If we lived in a godlier era, you'd hear more heads of corporate communication invoking Jesus for moral direction around this vexed issue of corporate honesty. For in Matthew Ch. 10 v. 16, he says, 'I am sending you out like sheep among wolves. Therefore, be as shrewd as snakes and as innocent as doves.' There's an ethical borderland for you. Imagine navigating your way around that.

In an ironic echo of the Cullum cartoon, one of my co-founders, the late, great Wendy Gordon, used to have a wry take on business ethics: 'There's always more than one version of integrity in any situation.' Beyond the wit, the serious point Wendy was making is that if you're advising a client about a potential course of action, even when that decision is based on evidence, there are choices, each of which could be legitimate. It's a matter of judgement. To help with that judgement, you might have a moral compass. For example, we have one in our business — we say that we'll only make recommendations that are simultaneously in *our clients'* commercial interests and *their customers'* human interests, but even that principle has lots of complexity to it, especially when future conditions are unknowable, as they always are.

I happen to think it's a good principle, in that you can weigh potential recommendations against the statement and evaluate whether they stand up. If they do, then you can infer that the recommendation, and the business decisions that flow from it, sit in the middle ground of fair transaction between a business and its customers.

The out-and-out con

Let's return to where this all started, and St Augustine's emphatic opinion about lying and sin. Because truth and lies is such a huge borderland topic, it's useful to explore the edges of it with reference to good old-fashioned deceit. Russian-born writer on psychology, Maria Konnikova, author of *The Confidence Game*,[8] looks at cons and deceits from multiple angles. One of the points she makes is that con artists (and she does use the word 'artist' deliberately, due to the levels of skill and artifice involved) can only exist because most people are trusting. She makes the point that, from an evolutionary perspective, we are better off trusting people — there are many studies that correlate higher levels of generalised trust with being successful in life. Over the long term, it's a good strategy. But what this all does is to open up a space within which con artists can do their work. They rely on most of us having this orientation towards being trusting, which can easily tip over into gullibility. Her take on why this might be, and how con artists exploit it, is insightful.

> For our minds are built for stories. We crave them, and, when there aren't ready ones available, we create them ... Human beings don't like to exist in a state of uncertainty or ambiguity when something doesn't make sense, we want to supply the missing link ... The confidence artist is only too happy to comply — and the well-crafted narrative is his absolute forte.

She goes on to say:

> Cons thrive in times of transition and fast change, when new things are happening and old ways of looking at the world no longer suffice … Transition is the confidence game's great ally, because transition breeds uncertainty. There's nothing a con artist likes better than exploiting the sense of unease we feel when it appears that the world as we know it is about to change.

It's a salutary point. In the Age of Between, the conditions of uncertainty are perfect for con artists, snake oil salesmen, and conspiracy theorists to flourish. We've had these conditions before, but never so easily fuelled by mass communications as we have today. The point about the ability of con artists to create satisfying narratives that we want to believe is well made. I'll leave you to judge if there's an obvious segue to be made to our next section, on the borderlands of politics.

5. **Polarisation — the death of the middle ground**

> Understanding that we exist in relationship with our political institutions, that they are changed by us and we are changed by them, is the key to this story. We don't just use politics for our own ends. Politics uses us for its own ends.
> — Ezra Klein

With truth and lies, the borderland appears to be getting increasingly congested. There are fewer absolute truths and absolute untruths that everyone accepts. But in the political sphere, the opposite is happening. The borderlands are starting to empty, as voters start to get forced out to the partisan edges by strong centripetal forces that they can't fight against, even assuming they want to. It must be the case that the lack of agreed sources of truth increases polarisation — in the same way that individuals can now have 'my truth', political tribes can have 'our truth', coming from 'our sources of truth'.

Ezra Klein, whose quote opens this chapter, has written a detailed analysis of this in an American context in *Why We're Polarized.*[9] It's worth staying with the USA for now because this is a case study where polarisation is strongly advanced. But other countries are not far behind, and the direction of travel is similar in most democracies. He demonstrates through use of extensive historical data that Democrat and Republican voters used to overlap in their attitudes and beliefs, to the point where there were very large areas of agreement between them, with some skewing towards liberal and conservative positions at the margins. In fact, seen through the prism of the stark division we see in American political life now, it's startling to be reminded that it was Abraham Lincoln's Republican party that was responsible for the abolition of slavery, and not the Democratic party, which had strong roots in the slave-owning deep South.

Klein sees a lot of feeds into why this is so, but one contributing reason is that because of the nature of modern communications, we end up in a self-fulfilling reinforcement loop where increasing polarisation risks becoming inevitable. His thinking brought to mind an illustrative example I heard in a radio news report about 18 months after the end of the pandemic, in which a man spoke of his brother, a highly educated man who'd had various scientifically based reservations about the decision to go into lockdown, and around the speed of the vaccine rollout. This person joined an online community of people with the same disquiet, and in what felt like no time at all, had bought into a wide variety of other contrarian issues and conspiracy theories, such as believing that 9/11 was a hoax, and even to the point of believing that the Earth was flat. To his family, this set of new beliefs was utterly incredible in relation to the man they'd known up until then. But the point was that within his new community, these yoked beliefs came as a job lot — it ended up being harder to exist only as someone who was only an anti-Covid vaxxer on clinical trial grounds. There wasn't a tribe for that position.

With accounts like that in mind, Klein's analysis seems especially compelling when he talks about the overlay between personal identity and political identity and the way in which personal identities can easily become subsumed by, or at least hard to distinguish from, political identities. He gives one potent example of this in the case of American football, which used to be a unifying aspect of American life that sat outside political alignment. But when Colin Kaepernick, and then other players, started to kneel during the playing of the national anthem during the 2016 season, it set off a chain reaction that ended up with the NFL losing a significant amount of affiliation amongst Republican voters, at least at that point in time.**

However, this process started earlier, with stacked behaviours and preferences starting to be perceived as *de facto* proof of political sympathies, because of the presumed identities they were evidence of, even when in theory those behaviours had nothing to do with politics. Klein brilliantly points to a campaign ad in the 2004 election, where an elderly white couple is stopped on the street and asked about the then Democratic presidential candidate, Howard Dean, and his plan to raise taxes.

> "What do I think?" the man replies. "Well, I think Howard Dean should take his tax-hiking, government-expanding, latte-drinking, sushi-eating, Volvo-driving, *New York Times*-reading-" Then his wife cuts in: "Body-piercing, Hollywood-loving, left-wing freak show back to Vermont where it belongs."

** It's worth noting that President Trump became the first serving president to attend the NFL Superbowl in 2025. It will be interesting to see if this creates a tidal change in the political spectrum that sits around American football. If it does, then it will be further evidence for the flux and flow of political forces. Nothing is forever.

Woe betide you if you're a Republican who likes sushi and lattes. It starts to look like a guilty secret you don't admit to amongst your political bedfellows. And remember, that was 2004. Behaviours that were once simply a matter of taste and preference are now so loaded with symbolism that they need to be carefully curated for what they say about your political identity.

For all that, Klein's analysis of the increasing polarisation of American political identity made for depressing reading, a question that lingers upon reading his book is 'How come this hasn't happened before?' Plenty of writers, including a good number of anthropologists and behavioural scientists, have documented human herd behaviour many times, and so the polarisation that he documents doesn't strike as a revelation. James Clear, who writes about behaviour and decision-making, is very good at articulating the borderland between the need for truth and accuracy and the need to belong. In his article 'Why facts don't change our minds',[10] which is hosted on his own website, he writes this:

> Humans need a reasonably accurate view of the world in order to survive. If your model of reality is wildly different from the actual world, then you struggle to take effective actions each day.
>
> However, truth and accuracy are not the only things that matter to the human mind. Humans also seem to have a deep desire to belong.

He goes on to make the point that when those things come into conflict, the need to belong can easily win out, and partly for longstanding evolutionary reasons. He quotes from his own bestseller, *Atomic Habits*:

> Humans are herd animals. We want to fit in, to bond with others, and to earn the respect and approval of our peers. Such inclinations are essential to our survival. For most of our

> evolutionary history, our ancestors lived in tribes. Becoming separated from the tribe – or worse, being cast out – was a death sentence.

The use of the phrase 'death sentence' is sobering. It took me to memories of watching wildlife documentaries, and remembering the way that older males, previously in a leadership position, are finally cast out of the pack, ending up in a situation of grave jeopardy, leading to their demise. It's a grim prospect, and the isolation that follows from that is unbearable. Coming back to a human setting, you can see how the alternative to that isolation — fitting in and conforming your opinions and beliefs to those that are around you, feels not only comforting, but even essential.

This cohering around a group ethos can happen at many levels of nested identities. You can fit right into your immediate set of friends, your sports team, your city, your political party, your country. Many, perhaps most, humans have a tremendous gift for it — it's that herd instinct. To state the obvious, you are significantly more likely to be successful in life by finding your place within social norms, despite some measure of compromise involved, than striking out alone, going off grid, and surviving by just your own wits and skills.

For all that I've known this to be true for ages, during the writing of this, I've still struggled with the arbitrariness of it. To take national identity for example, why should someone living in Carlisle, right up by the Scottish border, share common cause with someone 450 miles away in Truro near the tip of Cornwall, and not with someone half an hour over the Scottish border in, say, Lockerbie. Mulling this over, I had an insightful conversation with Tim Marshall, author of several bestselling books on geopolitics. He summed it all up with precision, in a way that left me wondering why it had been such a puzzle. 'With national identity issues, it's easy to forget the importance of what you're not. Being not-Scottish is easier and quicker to figure out than 'What does it mean to be English?' He's entirely right of course. Whatever else you disagree about, you can quickly agree on your not-identity. Once you start, it's hard to stop — you're also not-French, not-American, not-German...

When I was growing up, the Second World War had only finished some 30 years or so previously, and it was common to hear older people that had lived through it talking wistfully about how cohesive the country had been then, compared to how fractured it now felt (the 1970s, rather than today). That felt bizarre to listen to at the time — how could they feel nostalgic for the war? — but I get it now. They had a common enemy, and the force of unity against that enemy was far more powerful than local issues that divided them. It was possible for the entire nation to feel unified because the scale of the threat was existential to everyone.

Ezra Klein also talks about this phenomenon in relation to political parties. At one point, he quotes evidence from a Pew Research Center poll in 2016 that showed the significance of something that he terms 'negative partisanship'. In other words, and most dramatically amongst Republican voters, voting intentions were twice as strongly correlated to negative views of the Democrats than to positive views of their own Republican party. In other words, fear of otherness was demonstrated to be more powerful than affiliation to your own side. And amongst the current rise of populist parties across the developed world, whipping up antagonism against immigrants or asylum seekers has proved to be a very reliable way of creating tribal identity. As depressing as this feels, it's also a reality of human nature, and not something we're likely to wash out of our genetic inheritance any time soon.

To compound all this, there is the issue of the amplification of strong opinion in the digital sphere. This has been documented endlessly, so it doesn't need more commentary here. Suffice to say, you have more chance of building an online presence and cultivating a following through powerful opinions, forcefully expressed. As the social media commentator Marianna Spring said on the BBC podcast 'Americast', 'It's very hard to have a nuanced conversation online.' She's right. I've yet to see the X (tweet as was) that says, 'Once again, struggling to make my mind up about the

Online Safety Bill. Feel pulled in both directions.' And let's say you did see an X like that, what are the chances of that being re-Xed thousands of times? The reality is that people with mild opinions are less likely to take to social media to express that moderate, lightly held point of view in the first place. I'm rather taken with the fantasy of becoming such a contributor — the pure eccentricity of holding that position appeals: 'Feeling ever so slightly put out by the PM's comments at Prime Minister's Question Time this lunchtime.' Because what we have instead is an abandoned space in the political discourse, even if that mildness might well be the dominant opinion. Klein brought me up sharp when he says in his book, 'It's easy to be in the middle of a muddle; it's harder to be in the middle of a chasm.' True — there's no foothold in a vacuum.

6. **Rebirth of the middle ground**

And yet, for all the evidence of polarisation, and the role of digital media in accelerating it, there is still truth in the old cliché of nature abhorring a vacuum. At the time of writing, it's been fascinating to see the rise and rise of the UK political podcast, *The Rest is Politics*, featuring former political adversaries from the left and right: Alistair Campbell, the ex-chief spin doctor for Tony Blair; and Rory Stewart, who held a variety of ministerial positions in the Conservative governments of David Cameron and Theresa May. Admittedly, neither of them were ever on the outer fringes of their parties — both were moderates. Nevertheless, I'm not alone in finding this interesting. Listenership to their podcast has taken off, and their spin-off books have gone straight to the top of the bestseller charts. Their brand of courteous, intelligent, nuanced political debate happening in the centre ground seems to be filling a need that many members of the public have. Campbell and Stewart have a particular mantra that has caught my attention because it's an oxymoron — they talk about agreeably disagreeing. This notion of respectful listening to someone who comes from a different political tradition and weighing the value of what they have to say seems to have become curiously addictive. You'd think that our appetites would have become so coarsened by the incessant diet of combative rhetoric that we've been served up through polarised media over many years that we'd find this all too banal — but apparently not. Their agreeable disagreement would be more impressive if the distance between the two of them were greater than it now is, but it's a start. As things stand, *The Rest is Politics* is something of a poster child for how the abandoned liminal space of politics, which is in danger of looking like scorched earth, can be reclaimed and inhabited once more. I realise this is a UK example, where polarisation is not as advanced as it is in the US, but if polarisation can spread, so perhaps can nuanced, intelligent debate.

7. Section summary

a) Boundaries can be a force for good in relationships, building trust, safety, and the conditions within which trust, collaboration, creativity, and good work can flourish.
b) Some borders or borderlands are subliminal and therefore invisible, such as cultural rules or the ways in which collective memory is built up. In cases of misunderstanding or hurt, these underpinnings need to be brought to the surface to be understood.
c) The lack of agreed benchmarks of truth and the polarisation in politics are linked phenomena. Conditions are created where it's easier to insert a feeling of truth that appeals to your tribe, in place of actual truth that everyone abides by.

SECTION SEVEN — BETWEEN STORIES

There are only two stories: man goes on a journey and a stranger comes to town.

— Leo Tolstoy

We've already seen how one very simple idea — liminality — has taken root and spread. Story is another supremely simple concept. And of course, stories have been with us for even longer, perhaps for as long as we've had language. As with liminality, it's the simplicity that gives them flexibility and a universal quality that means we can respond to endless variations on a basic theme. And stories don't discriminate — they work for all purposes, be they entertainment, instruction, or duplicity.

The reason stories are getting their own section is that storytellers (and in fact artists of many kinds) are far more at home in liminal spaces than the rest of us. They need to be — inhabiting borderlands is part of their day job. There's a case to be made that in any list of people that like the borderlands, writers are close to the top, although I'll allow that cartographers have also got a good claim.

There's no mystery to the classic story structure. We have a central character (hero) and their opposite (antagonist, anti-hero).

There is some opening scenario, which establishes the want, need, or lack that the hero has, shortly followed by an inciting incident of some description that will typically involve the anti-hero and set off a chain of events (the plot). Importantly, that set of events involves a journey of some description. The hero doesn't solve their problem on the sofa. It's a quest. Somewhere within this journey is the period of transformation, or liminal space, somewhere that represents the unknown, a place outside the hero's comfort zone or knowledge. It can, and often is, represented symbolically by woods, or a sea voyage, or, in more recent times, by a road trip. (We'll look at woods and water separately when we think about the betweens of nature.) The transformation itself is the result of choices that are made by the main character, after they've come through some set of tests or challenges, often within this liminal space. The final homecoming or resolution doesn't happen until this crucial part of the story is complete. As the mid-twentieth-century American crime novelist Mickey Spillane put it with definitive finality: 'No one ever read a book to get to the middle.'

As short as this description of the classic story structure is, it can be simplified further. Hero faces a problem and goes on a journey in which they face tests and decisions, including some point of greatest crisis at the furthest point out. After facing that issue, they return. Or as the author and broadcaster John Yorke summarises it even more pithily in his book *Into the Woods*:[1] journey there, journey back.

If that feels perfunctory, look again at the quote at the top of this section. It seems like the people that really know their story stuff see it in very simple terms indeed. In conversation with John Yorke, I had the chance to ask him what he made of the Tolstoy take on stories. He thought about it briefly, before nailing it with: 'Well, they're basically the same story, aren't they? Just with the perspective flipped round. At heart, every story is a grail quest.' Incidentally, in the Between People section, we considered tribe identity in passing, when thinking about the issue of polarised politics. I'm reminded of that when thinking about the stranger coming to town. The reason this is such a recurrent story is precisely because the solidity of local identity is threatened by the encroachment of the stranger. It strikes at the root of what it means to be a social animal — our collective identity is in jeopardy. The history of storytelling demonstrates that we are prepared to engage with this basic story arc time after time, and never tire of it.

Now to bring liminal spaces and borders back into view. Within this simple narrative structure, there is plenty of scope for exploration. You've got the opening conflict between the hero and antagonist — plenty of boundary crossing going on there. You've got the journey itself with all those thresholds being crossed. There's the moment of greatest jeopardy and the transformation that goes with it, all of which resonates with, for example, traditional initiation rituals. The degree of change, drama, conflict, and transformation that is going on during the average story is so extensive that a condition of liminality is pretty much the default setting for storytelling. It brings to mind one of my favourite storytelling observations of all, from the master of espionage fiction, John le Carré, who said, 'The cat sat on the mat is not a story. But the cat sat on the dog's mat is the start of a story.' Brilliant. There's no drama or conflict of any sort in watching a cat on a mat. But when the cat sits on the dog's mat, you've got the conditions for a story to begin. You have a hero and antagonist; you have some desire, in the cat wanting the mat; some conflict, in that the cat has overstepped a boundary and started a turf war; and then decisions that must get made by both parties. We'll learn a lot about both the cat and the dog by what happens next. And to bring Tolstoy's thought in here, and then John Yorke's twist on it, if we see this drama from the cat's perspective, then it's 'man (cat) goes on a journey'. If we see it from the dog's perspective, it's 'stranger comes to town'. And of course, we're seeing the same event happen, so Yorke is right: it's just a question of who's telling it, who is inviting us to identify with their narrative.

In the rest of this section, I'm going to introduce a smorgasbord of borderland observations from diverse writers. I've got a hunch that if you trawled long and hard enough, you'd discover that virtually all writers have got a published point of view on crossing borders or liminal spaces — it's hard to see how they wouldn't. Collectively, these reflections demonstrate that borderland thinking is fundamental to the storytelling craft.

1. **Truth and lies and, oh, art**

> We've got truth and lies and then there's this little space, the edge, in the middle. That liminal space, that's art.
> — Mac Barnett

By way of segueing from the last section, we'll start with a rumination on truth and lies in fiction. A while back, I happened across an entertaining TED talk from 2014 by an American children's author called Mac Barnett. He opens it by saying, 'My job is that I lie to children, but they are honest lies.' He had me with the oxymoron.

His talk reflects on the nature of truth and lies in art, including a reference to Pablo Picasso, before saying the quote above, accompanied by a Venn diagram, where he has truth and lies on either side, and then art in the middle. He introduces it as a joke, but there's an insight here, and it's one that a children's author is more likely to perceive. As he points out, children know that characters in books don't *really* exist. But they simultaneously know that they do. Their imaginative realm doesn't need to have those things separated into buckets of truth and lies. It's just one big, magical, playful space of wonder and what-iffery which doesn't need to be classified according to its truth or otherwise. In fact, Barnett then goes one stage further and, in my view, gets to the nub of it when he says, 'We know these characters aren't real, but we have real feelings about them.'

And that is the joy of stories. The stories have their liminal space, as part of the hero's journey, but the reader has theirs too, in the transformative space between story (and by extension author) and reader. Barnett references the English poet Samuel Taylor Coleridge, who first coined the phrase 'the willing suspension of disbelief'. And it's that state of suspension of disbelief (or belief) that cracks open the liminal state and allows any number of emotions or qualities to come in, such as wonder, affinity, joy, pain, and so on.

2. **Fact and fiction**

> Facts and alternative facts, truth and verisimilitude, knowledge and information, art and lies: what could be more timely or topical than to discuss where the boundaries lie? Is there a firm divide between myth and history, fiction and fact: or do we move back and forth on a line between, our position indeterminate and always shifting?
> — Hilary Mantel

In storytelling, there is a such a strong overlap between truth and lies and fact and fiction that they could almost be thought of as synonyms; however, in a technical sense, the factual basis is critical in certain instances. For writers of historical fiction, this border between fiction and the historical record is precisely the membrane that gives dramatic tension to their work. It's not too strong to say that there is even an *obligation* to establish a position on this border. These thoughts by Hilary Mantel (from an *Observer* newspaper article in 2017) were written just before she delivered the annual Reith lectures of that year. In writing her celebrated trilogy of *Wolf Hall*, *Bring up the Bodies*, and *The Mirror and the Light* (although this concluding volume had yet to be published at that point), she thought deeply about the nature of historical accuracy in relation to her source material. In the first of her lectures, she went on to make many points about the nature of memory, and the past, the historical record, and therefore about telling stories of the past:

> As soon as we die, we enter into fiction. Just ask two different family members to tell you about someone recently gone, and you will see what I mean. Once we can no longer speak for ourselves, we are interpreted.

And also:

> History is not the past — it is the method we have evolved of organising our ignorance of the past. It's the record of what's left on the record.

In her experience, no storytellers were subject to so much scrutiny as historical novelists. Perhaps because the evidence is so partial and incomplete, she was subjected to continual questioning about whether her stories were 'real'. As if that were answerable. After much reflection, she came to this position:

> In time I understood one thing — that you don't become a novelist to become a spinner of entertaining lies: you become a novelist so you can tell the truth.

She was referring to the inner life of her characters. She had access to certain facts about their life from the historical record, but not to their inner motivations — those she had to feel, interpret, and search for coherence, moving back and forth along the line she talks about in the opening quote.

Curiously, historians are often given more licence, despite the certain reality that some are bound to be more rigorous than others, and all will come from one interpretative stance or another. It could be that this licence goes right back to the very first historian whose work has come down to us — Herodotus, an ancient Greek from the fifth century BCE. He has been known as the Father of History and then again also the Father of Lies, which is quite the spectrum of opinion. One excellent perspective on him as a historian has been provided by Irene Vallejo, in her excellent history on books as physical artefacts, *Papyrus*.[2] She wrote:

It's clear that Herodotus thinks legends, oracles, fantastic tales, and divine interventions should feature alongside documented facts. He lived in a world where a king's nightmare, caused by indigestion, might be interpreted as a message from the gods and change the course of an empire or the strategy of a war. The borders between the rational and the irrational were diffuse.

3. **Truth plus**

> The difference between fiction and reality is that fiction has to make sense.
> — Tom Clancy

Many writers adopt a highly assertive stance in relation to questions of truth in fiction. They take the position that life is unruly or even meaningless, but by contrast literature, or fiction, is sense-making and has the capacity to capture a deeper essence about life than a literal account of the details of life can achieve. Writers of different genres and from different times end up saying very similar things in their own way. In addition to thriller writer Tom Clancy, quoted above, reflect on these four:

> It is only through fiction that fact can be made instructive or even intelligible, because the writer rescues them from the unintelligible chaos of their actual occurrence and arranges them into works of art.
> — George Bernard Shaw, early twentieth-century dramatist

> When you're in the middle of a story, it isn't a story at all, but a confusion, a wreckage of shattered glass or splintered wood. It's only afterward it becomes a story at all, when you're telling it.
> — Margaret Atwood, Booker Prize winning novelist (quoted from *Alias Grace*)

> People who don't like my work say the connections are too arbitrary. But that's how life is.
> — Paul Auster, American novelist

> I want to convey something that is truer than truth about our common humanity.
> — Isabel Allende, Chilean novelist

Truer than truth. That's not mincing words. These are writers that are aware of the borderland that exists between fiction and reality but believe in the redeeming ability of the storyteller's art: first, to make sense of it; and second, to create meaning, truth, and art out of it.

I have one more quote in this vein, but it's said of a writer rather than by him. It was said of the novelist and travel writer Bruce Chatwin, by his biographer Nicholas Shakespeare. Chatwin's most famous book is *In Patagonia*,[3] a travel book published in 1977, and it's controversial because of the degree of licence he allowed himself in the accuracy of his accounts. Some of his writing takes tremendous liberties, to the point where some of the people he met took public issue with his content and flatly contradicted his telling of the tale. But Shakespeare takes a different stance, and presumably one that Chatwin himself would have agreed with. There is an echo of the Allende quote here:

> Chatwin tells not a half truth, but a truth and a half. As in fiction, you lie to tell a greater truth.

That's properly doubling down and here we are, circling back to truth and lies again. It's a writerly obsession, and it's bringing back to my mind David Bodanis's observation about Einstein from earlier in the book — that notion of surfing the line between supple and stubborn. If we substitute truth and lies for supple and stubborn, then that idea of surfing, the balancing point where you just about stay on board, is a good image to consider the writer's attitude to reality and the fictional representation of it.

4. **Fiction and reality borders — to what end?**

So far, all these examples have demonstrated a couple of things: that writers have a keen awareness of the borderlands between fact, truth, and reality, on the one hand, and lies, fiction, and drama, on the other; and that the storyteller's art is about finding a human truth that rises above the literalism of human experience. But what is that truth, and how do borders of one sort or another help to illuminate human truths? Consider these two contributions.

> Borders may appear in many guises: psychological; racial; sexual; sociological; professional; as well as geographical. Paradoxically, the border may be at once what provides us with some security about our identity, demarcating ourselves from others, while also being the barrier that prevents us from developing new capacities or trying on new identities. Theatre processes, on the other hand, depend upon the willingness of the actor to cross borders not only to impersonate the dress, manner and speech of another but also to achieve, temporarily, the ultimate expression of border-crossing, empathy.
> — Prof. Tim Prentki (Emeritus Professor of Theatre for Development)[4]

> What if, the girl says. Instead of saying, this border divides these places. We said, this border unites these places, this border holds together these two really interesting different places. What if we declared border crossings places where, listen, when you cross them, you yourself become doubly possible.
> — Ali Smith[5]

Both quotes appear on the website of the theatre company Border Crossings, founded by Michael Walling in 1995. Everything that Border Crossings do is in the endeavour of cultural exchange, and working across borders, in terms of language, cultures, nations, and indeed art forms. What's brilliant about the quotes is the acknowledgement of complexity. What they haven't put up on their site are idealistic quotes about dissolved boundaries and ensuing harmony. Instead, these quotes speak to the role that borders have in establishing identity in the first instance. It's that point that unless you have some awareness of the non-you, then who is the you? But neither quote stops there. Both go on to assert that it's in the crossing of the border, the willingness to explore what lies beyond, that the real magic happens. In novelist Ali Smith's hands, the idea of becoming doubly possible is seductive. You're not experiencing loss through stepping across the threshold. It's all additive. And Tim Prentki's angle is the great gain of empathy. Through the medium of storytelling, in this case theatre, the inevitable playing with the identities and mindsets of others, it's possible to get closer to true insight of other people, other cultures.

To underscore Michael Walling's vision, there's a neat anecdote in Mike Parker's book on the England–Wales border, *All the Wide Border*.[6] At one point, he's referring to a conversation he had with a man called Mark Jickells, who has an unparalleled knowledge of the River Wye and all its tributaries, and he writes this:

> Mark's main concern is the health of his beloved Wye, and he fears that the "human ego" of different administrations and authorities is making that worse. All the same, he has always been drawn to the border, both for the sense of conflict and uncertainty that it holds, but also for its joys: "Borders are the point at which hands are shaken, hugs are made. It's the crossing point, the bridge."

This idea of the simultaneous challenge and opportunity that borders provide lies at the heart of their unease and attraction.

5. Between the author and the reader

Although most writers are happy to settle for the borderland of fiction and reality being enough for them to explore, some writers need more than that. During the twentieth century, with the rise of post-modernism and meta-fiction, some writers played with the blurring of boundaries between the author and reader, and the uncertain role of the narrator. It leads to novels that do an equivalent of breaking the fourth wall in theatre or TV — making overt reference to the presence of the viewer. Whereas regular novels, including literary fiction, set up an imagined reality *within* the context of the story, post-modern meta-fiction strays beyond that. The results tend to be playful, confusing, startling. These authors do not want you to suspend disbelief and 'lose yourself in a good book'. They want you to think and be confronted with questions about the acts of reading and writing that often turn back on themselves. Here is a typical meditation on those blurred lines, and the nature of the reading experience, from Italo Calvino's 1979 masterpiece, *If on a Winter's Night a Traveller*.[7] In the lead-up to the section quoted below, the main character thinks he's about to visit a publisher with a female character that he's become infatuated with. The point of the visit is to get to the bottom of a mix-up that has led to sections of several manuscripts being randomly bound together. This mix-up impacts on the book they are both coincidentally reading, which, like we the readers, is also *If on a Winter's Night a Traveller*. She starts to explain why she's not coming on the planned visit:

> "Why don't you want to come?"
> "On principle."
> "What do you mean?"
> "There's a boundary line: on one side are those who make books, on the other those that read them. I want to remain one of those who read them, so I take care always to stay on my side of the line. Otherwise, the unsullied pleasure of reading ends, or at least is transformed into something else, which is not what I want. This boundary line is tentative, it tends to get erased: the world of those who deal with books professionally is more and more crowded and tends to become

> one with readers. Of course, readers are also growing more numerous, but it would seem that those who use books to produce other books are increasing more than those who just like to read books and nothing else. I know that if I cross that line even as an exception, by chance, I risk being mixed up in this advancing tide; that's why I refuse to set foot inside a publishing house, even for a few minutes."
>
> "What about me then?"
>
> "I don't know about you. Decide for yourself. Everybody reacts in a different way."

It's fabulously nod-and-a-wink stuff. There's a wistful tone to the point of view, the belief that there is some state of pure pleasure from reading that demands you keep your distance from both the art of writing (how stories are made) and the craft of publishing (how books are made), and that once you cross that line into some post-Edenic knowledge of the industry, your reading pleasure is bound to drop. Calvino himself would have been alive to the irony in this character's perspective, given that the book is in part about the illusory boundaries between authors, narrators, and readers. As a sidenote, it's worth pointing out that it was prescient of Calvino to have this insight into the self-referential nature of the world of books, reading, and book production back in the '70s, a trend that has only accelerated since. As a sidenote to the sidenote (post-modernism is like a virus — it's catching), if you can perceive an authorial voice speaking in that long quote, rather than just a character's (let alone the narrator, whoever that might be), it might well be because Calvino himself had a senior editorial position in a publishing house…

I said at the top of this section on Calvino that this post-modernist surge was a twentieth-century phenomenon, and indeed it was. But in the interests of accuracy, it's important to mention that one of the first meta-novels was also one of the first novels. Laurence Sterne's *Tristram Shandy* was published in sections between 1759 and 1767,[8] in the first great flowering of British fiction. It's a comic novel that plays endless games the reader is drawn into. Superficially, the point of the book is to tell the life story of Tristram Shandy in autobiographical form. However, Shandy, as narrator, is unable to resist rambling distractions and digressions, and as a reader, it's disconcerting to realise, for example, that you're 15 pages into a think piece on noses, and as you flick forward, you discover you've got more than 40 pages of the same still to come. The reader is frequently directly addressed, often with apparent instructions on what to make of the reading experience. It's playful stuff and sits well outside the mainstream of the time. The key point here is that fiction was a very young art form at this stage — it was highly malleable, with no blueprint laid down by custom and practice.

In our era, we've got hundreds of years of precedent, but it's not choking the template. The inventiveness keeps on tumbling, and the simplicity of the basic story structure shows no sign of being exhausted. One compelling hypothesis as to why this is the case must surely be the liminal space that sits at the heart of every story. Like people, stories are always between.

6. The sting in the tale

There can be no question that storytelling has come roaring into the cultural mainstream in the last 20 years or so. I've already referred to Google Ngram Viewer in relation to 'liminality' and 'transparency', and 'storytelling' is another word that has seen a vertiginous climb in usage over the last 20 years. Whenever this happens, it tells us that we're dealing with a cultural phenomenon.

In earlier decades, before story and storytelling became ubiquitous cultural memes, the word 'story' was confined to its fictional realm to a far greater extent than it is now. It was almost technical, very closely connected to books and literature. Somewhere along the line, storytelling as an art form developed a significantly greater degree of self-confidence and succeeded in permeating popular culture. As ever with these accelerated cultural events, there's never just one influence, but a weaving together of several threads. A few of them must include the following: the rise of excellent long-form TV drama and wide awareness of the writers' room phenomena raising interest in storytelling as a commercial activity; the role of social media in helping everyone tell a version of the story of their own lives (including the overt use of the word 'story' as a feature in Instagram and TikTok); the annexation of storytelling by business and brands, as a more emotive way of establishing connection with customers; the adaptation of stories into powerful and transmissible packets for a digital age; and potentially the complexity and abstraction of modern life giving storytelling a simplifying, sense-making role. Whatever the tapestry of factors, once you're attuned to it, you hear it everywhere, even down to TV news anchors introducing a report by saying, 'So and so has the story,' which would surely have sounded flaky in a previous era.

It's all come together to a point where storytelling is so prevalent in contemporary life that the edges between fiction and reality get harder to discern, and I mean in the real world, not just in books. Much as I love the Tom Clancy quote, its sharp distinction between fiction and reality starts to make it feel like a quote of its time (it's from the mid-1990s). From about 2016 or so, I had been starting to become aware of a certain mistrust in storytelling, partly because of its use in the political arena. Certain practitioners, like the Brexit camp in the UK led by Boris Johnson, clearly understood the power of story at a profound level and realised that it created emotional connection with the public in a way that analysis and rationality never do. These thoughts, which I'd been feeling somewhat nebulously, coalesced when reading a *New Yorker* article in July 2023, written by Parul Sehgal and titled 'The Tyranny of the Tale', which takes aim at story and narrative. Early in the article, Sehgal quotes the literary critic Peter Brooks from his book *Seduced by Story*,[9] who uses the phrase, 'a narrative takeover of reality' to describe the ascendancy of narrative in modern public life, and goes on to say that this takeover is like 'an evocation and understanding of the world which was purely narrative, which could not see that living and telling might be different things'. That's a haunting idea — the blurring together of living and telling into one entity to the point where real life and narrative fuse. You can see the role of social media — it's commodified storytelling into a skill that anyone can have, mining their own autobiography as easy source material. The blurring is due to its recursive nature — you publish that 'story' and then start to live towards the version you've put out. The role of editor is crucial. We all know that a huge amount of the content of our life — getting up, having breakfast, cleaning our teeth, setting up direct debits for garden waste collection — has no drama to it, no conflict that can be coerced into narrative. But that's OK, because all those parts never feature in our published 'story', which exists as a series of beautiful, inspirational, soulful, funny, self-deprecating, maybe outsized posts of which the connecting thread is a highly filtered version of ourselves. No wonder the playwright Simon McBurney came out with his wry observation: 'We confuse our lives with the story of our lives.' These days, they merge into each other.

So where are those edges? The same borderline of fiction and reality that has long preoccupied fiction writers now preoccupies everyone who narrates a version of their own life. Where is the real personal identity? In the lived life, which only one person gets to experience from the inside? Or the public life, which is the version that is put out for mass consumption? Or, dare I say it, does it exist somewhere between?

7. **Section summary**

a) Storytellers have a relish for liminal spaces and borderlands — they can't tell stories without them.
b) There can be an extra dimension to the liminality — it's not just the liminal space *in* the story. There are often also those *between* the writer and their characters, or their source material, and also *between* the writer and the reader. This means that liminal issues of truth and lies, and fiction and reality are always part of the storytelling discourse.

c) Because stories are about conflict, testing, decisions, quests, and change, crossing borders and going into liminal spaces are adventures that can lead to growth and development, and towards the resolution of the story.
d) Now that everyone can be the narrator of their own story, and storytelling is ubiquitous in culture, there is a risk of a backlash against the idea of story if it comes to be seen as a mechanism for emotional manipulation.

SECTION EIGHT — BETWEEN PLACES

Wool-gatheringly, the clouds migrate:
No checkpoint checks their tenuous flight.
— From 'Postcard from Berlin' by Derek Mahon, *The Hunt by Night*[1]

This couplet from a stunning poem by Irish poet Derek Mahon is the literal inspiration for this book, the spark that took my general interest in borders into a more fully formed idea of writing about them. It contains such a deceptive insight that it stopped me in my tracks when I first read it. Ever since we've had national boundaries, people have remarked on the ability of birds to defy borders through the simple act of flight, and Mahon points out here that clouds have this attribute too. The insight is that geographic borders are for the most part political, frequently the result of war, imperialism, or some other destructive human activity. Over time, the original tentative national border line, which historically was sometimes as brutal as a straight line drawn on a map by an administrator, can be strengthened on the inside of the border by other human constructs, some of which are physical, such as checkpoints, barriers, or military presence; others of which are cultural, such as language, educational curriculums, official histories, national anthems or football teams; and still others are administrative, such as statute law, political parties, and taxation. In his 1983 book on the rise of nationalism, Benedict Anderson calls them 'imagined communities',[2] to get at this idea that nation states are not real, in the way a stone, tree, or, indeed, a cloud is real, but are brought into being by people.

Clouds, meanwhile, are free to float above these borders (in fact they have no choice). The revelation that was fresh to me, although it's hardly a secret, is that precisely because they are man-made, in as much as they exist at all, geographic borders only truly exist at ground level or on maps. For sure, geographers think of a conceptual plane that exists below and above ground level, and that allows for concepts such as, say, 'British airspace', which are enforceable if you happen to have a fleet of fighter planes to hand, but for all that, wherever there is an unpoliced geographical border, you can just step right over it, and keep going. You might well not even know you've crossed it. In that moment, the border has no meaningful existence. Nothing changes for the walker, and the deeper reality of this 'line' being a human invention is reinforced. That doesn't stop certain borders, even when they are not policed, having a profound resonance, and somewhere there is or was a photograph of me at Gretna Green with one foot in England and another in Scotland, a moment that I found quite thrilling, although there's a hint of embarrassment in admitting to this. The point is that the, er, frisson can only exist in the context of all those centuries of Anglo-Scottish wars, jokes, rivalries, and whatnot, contributing to the idea that having a foot in either country amounts to something. It's no accident that there's no equivalent picture of me with one foot in, say, Huntingdonshire and the other in Cambridgeshire. Even I draw the line somewhere (it becomes hard to avoid these figures of speech…)

Earlier on, I mentioned a conversation I had with Tim Marshall, one of the most authoritative commentators on geopolitics and author of several bestsellers, including *Worth Dying For*, *Prisoners of Geography* and *The Power of Geography*. We were talking about borders in the context of national identity, which is of central interest here. Tim has a well-defined set of factors in respect of the forces at work in creating identity.

1. **Geography**. Nations or regions are fundamentally defined by the geographical facts they can't escape from. They have no choice but to confront or exploit their geography as a primary reality of their nationhood. By way of example, Saudi Arabia has no rivers whatsoever — hard to imagine when you live in a country with hundreds of them. Greece has thousands of islands, which means it's obliged to have a larger navy than a country of its size would normally have. And so on.
2. **History**. The history layers on top of geography and is embedded in cultural identity. For example, it's seared into the Ukrainian people that Stalin's regime starved literally millions of Ukrainians to death in the Holodomor genocide of 1932–1933 in its unyielding drive to introduce collectivism into agriculture. This historical event receives almost no mention in current Western media, but it has a profound impact on Ukrainian resistance in the conflict that started in 2014 and was still ongoing at the time of writing, with no end in sight.
3. **Politics**. Certain decisions can be made for either politically expedient reasons or due to the personalities of the people that came to power. These decisions weren't inevitable, weren't forced on the players through geography or even history, but they happened anyway. But those decisions have a long reverberation, go on to have historical significance, and can impact on the identity of a people. The decision of the UK government to stage a referendum on membership of the EU comes to mind as a recent example — this is likely to be a shaping factor for the UK for years to come.
4. **Language**. Language is often the glue that binds a group of people together. For all that minority languages have been dying out at an alarming rate all over the globe, it's just as true that some lesser-spoken languages have made a strong

comeback. The renaissance of Welsh has been a case in point. And if you take a region like the Basque region, which straddles southern France and Northern Spain, the absolute uniqueness of Euskara (some of which we saw when talking about oxymorons), which bears no relation to any other language on Earth, forges a fierce sense of identity.

5. **Psychology**. Tim Marshall accepts that the impact of collective psychology is hard to prove, and is somewhat elusive, but still believes that it's part of the mix. He may feel more diffident about this than I do, because his realm of geopolitics benefits from a demonstrable audit trail, but in the realm of betweenity, the bar of belief is a bit lower. So, when he talks about there having been 'an idea' about Germany for several centuries before it came to pass, or that the USA was uniquely founded on a guiding philosophy that makes it a far more homogenous nation than any country with a 3000-mile reach has any right to be, it has the ring of truth. As it happens, I did find some corroborating support for this thought, by comparing the American experience to that of the Austrian Empire in the nineteenth century. The version of the USA that we all know is the result of 100% immigration. The classic, and very liminal, metaphor for this was 'the melting pot', the mythic idea that the nation's ideology was founded on a set of high-minded principles and inalienable rights (as long as you weren't a Native American, in which case nothing in the constitution applied to you). The concept that this myth facilitated was the idea that people of all nations could come together and forge a new collective identity in this emergent nation. There is widespread scepticism about the legitimacy of the melting pot as a metaphor, but myths are like that — they often become part of the narrative idea, regardless of the evidence to the contrary.

In Europe, meanwhile, there had been centuries of jealousies, warfare, broken and remade alliances, shifting borders, and rises and falls in status, caused by swings in relative economic and military strength. Countries in the middle of Europe were especially muddled by all of this, compared to edge nations, such as Portugal, Britain, and Russia, which retained a sense of relative cohesion, with their settled and common languages forming a lot of the glue. This is all documented in a famous work of historical scholarship by Paul Kennedy, *The Rise and Fall of Great Powers.*[3] At one point, he quotes another historian, Anthony Sked, from a chapter he contributed to *Europe's Balance of Power, 1815–1848*:

> By contrast the Austrian emperor ruled an ethnic mishmash that must have made him groan every time he thought about it. He and eight million of his subjects were German, but twice as many were Slavs of one sort or another (Czechs, Slovaks, Poles, Ruthenians, Slovenes, Croats and Serbs), five million were Hungarians, five million Italians and two million Romanians. What sort of nation did that make?

The answer is none at all.

This section on geographic betweenity does some zooming out and zooming in. The zooming out starts from the position that most national borders reflect conflict, or at the very least difference, even when they separate now friendly nations. Already in this book, we've seen how borderlands can create the conditions for either collaboration or conflict between people, but geographic borders reveal that at scale. And the zooming-in part shows how some of these dramas happen at a local scale, and how land can be both a scarce resource and a transitional space that is forever going through transformation. The stories and examples in this section demonstrate many human qualities, attitudes, or activities like mistrust, negotiation, compromise, sacrifice, how we deal with complexity, adventure, courage, identity, our relationship to land, even eccentricity, all woven around different border scenarios. Borders are like an intensifier of our humanity, and because borders are human constructs, they hold up a mirror to what we are like and what we need, or think we need, showing us at our best and at our worst.

Above all, after spending a lot of time thinking about, reading about, and crossing borders, the thought that comes back to me most often about physical borders is that they matter to people, and can matter surprisingly quickly after they've been defined. And yet it's amazing how often they are treated as tradable commodities. The feeling is that we don't know what we're dealing with, what we're unleashing. I'll conclude this introduction to physical borders with a brilliant paragraph from Lewis Baston's *Borderlines: A History of Europe Told from the Edges.*[4] It's the start of a chapter where he's introducing the gothic nature of borderlands, called 'The occult romance of Lower Silesia'.

> Border zones are uncanny. A straight border, separating radically different places either side of an artificial line, is a strange mirror with a brutal past. A fuzzy border can be destabilising in a more subtle way; one can be unsure about where one belongs as the borderland throws up middle options to what one lazily considers a binary distinction. Areas where borders have changed have another layer of mystery about them. People live among ever-present rescues of the lost tribe who occupied the buildings and the land before them, constantly coming across their ghostly legacy. The people who have been displaced, and their children, live with an idea of home that no longer exists. The reality of border life blurs into the literature of horror, the imagining of the Other on the far side of the line.

1. Measure for measures

Before we get onto the border stories themselves, there's a bit of business to deal with first, and that is the not-so-small matter of measuring borders. It's illuminating in its own right, as a means of throwing light on the arbitrary, almost illusory nature of mankind's relationship with physical borders.

In principle, it ought to be a matter of objective fact about how long a border is between two nations, and indeed any casual internet search will reveal with absolute conviction how long the borders are between countries, but as with all things borderish, it isn't that simple. Although it may be a bit of a stretch to claim this, there is a good argument for saying that, indirectly, the measurement of borders contributed some thinking to chaos theory in mathematics and science, which is a fair indication that there's more to measuring borders than just, well, measuring.

The story starts with the British mathematician Lewis Fry Richardson, who discovered a curiosity in 1951, namely that at that time, Spain and Portugal gave dramatically different accounts of the length of their borders. The Portuguese reported it as being 987 km long, whereas the Spanish had it down as 1214 km, which is a difference of 227 km. Quite a discrepancy over 1214 km, and even more so over 987 km. For betweenists, this level of indeterminateness is something to relish, but it won't be to everyone's taste. It's not that they disagreed about where the border was, but simply how long it was. Mathematically, you're far less likely to have this type of disagreement over a very straight border. For example, the longest land border in the world is the one between the USA and Canada, weighing in at a mighty 8891 km, and large portions of that are dead straight, making it simple to decide on. But when a border is squiggly (this may not be the formal term that cartographers use), the way to figure out the length is to break the border down into sections and measure each section. And deciding on how many sections involves some discretion, but in principle you're making a judgement about how straight a given section of border is and measuring that. And then you decide on the next straight section and measure that, until you've covered the whole distance. In essence, the fussier, or perhaps more granular you are, the more sections you'll decide to measure. We can allow that this is tricky — let's say that there is a section of river as part of the border, and it curves; then how detailed do you get in defining a 'straight' section of that curve, when there's nothing straight at all? In practice, the more sections a cartographer decides there are, the longer their measurement of the total distance will be. This does match common sense, because if they decide to cut corners, literally and metaphorically, and have a section between two points that ignores part of a curve, their estimate will be lower than the 'real' distance, whatever that is. Coming back to the Spanish and Portuguese curiosity, we can reasonably infer that the Portuguese took a less-mathematically disciplined approach to measuring the border, whereas the Spanish were more rigorous. To be fair to the Portuguese, they weren't alone in being less systematic than a border sharing neighbour. Richardson found that most countries that shared a border in that era came up with different lengths as well.

Now, I mentioned in the previous paragraph that much of this ought to sound like common sense, and indeed common sense might lead to the assumption that if it were ever possible to do some 1:1 mapping and measure the actual landscape itself rather than a good map of it, we'd end up with an unarguable, definitive measurement. But not so. In point of mathematical fact, what happens is that you disappear down a rabbit hole, and mad things start to happen. The more forensic the measuring becomes, and the more account is taken of each individual landform along the border, this leads to a greater number of straight-line sections to be measured. Once this happens, from a mathematical perspective, the closer the measurement of that border will start to approach infinity, as a version of an infinite regression starts to take hold. If you struggle to make sense of this, you might want to take a quick look at the Norwegian coastline and think about how you might take account of the fjords. Anyway, Fry's work was so startling that it led to an entire branch of mathematics that we now know as fractal geometry, and which lives in the popular imagination through the quite beautiful computer-generated visualisations that are the result of plotting out Mandelbrot sets. When you look at those, like the example below, and zoom in on the infinite regression that they represent, you start to conceptualise how the measured length of a border can end up being longer than the border itself.

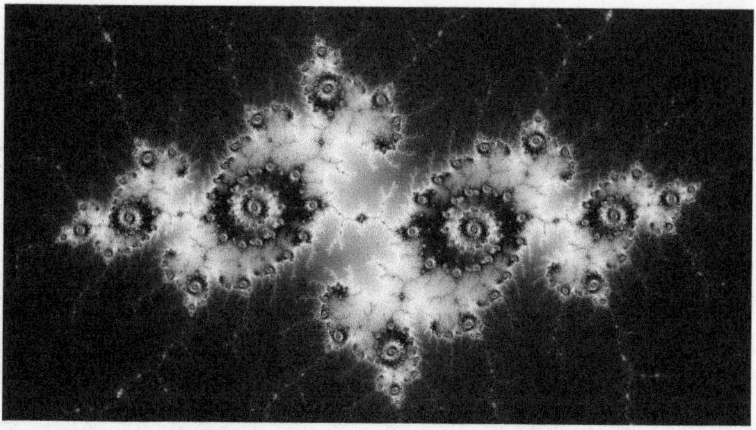

And all of this simply because measuring a border is a tricky thing to do.

2. **An oasis of stability**

In a book that is almost entirely about flux, conditions of change, and indeterminacy, about now you might be craving a touchstone of rigid stability. You've come this far; you have earned one.

It's 8 September 1278. Something extraordinary in the history of the world is happening, even though, over 700 years later, virtually no one on Earth will have any sense of it. Two parties are signing a *pareage*, a medieval French term to describe a joint sovereignty agreement. It will demarcate a border, and in doing so they will create the tiny nation of Andorra, demurely snuggled away in the Pyrenees between France and Spain. For the record, the parties concerned are the Count of Foix from southern France, and the Bishop of Urgell, in Catalonia. Unbeknownst to them, they have just instituted the 70-mile land border that has gone on to become the most enduring, unchanged border on Earth.

The *pareage* was written in Latin, and here is a facsimile of it, stored in the Library of Congress in the United States.

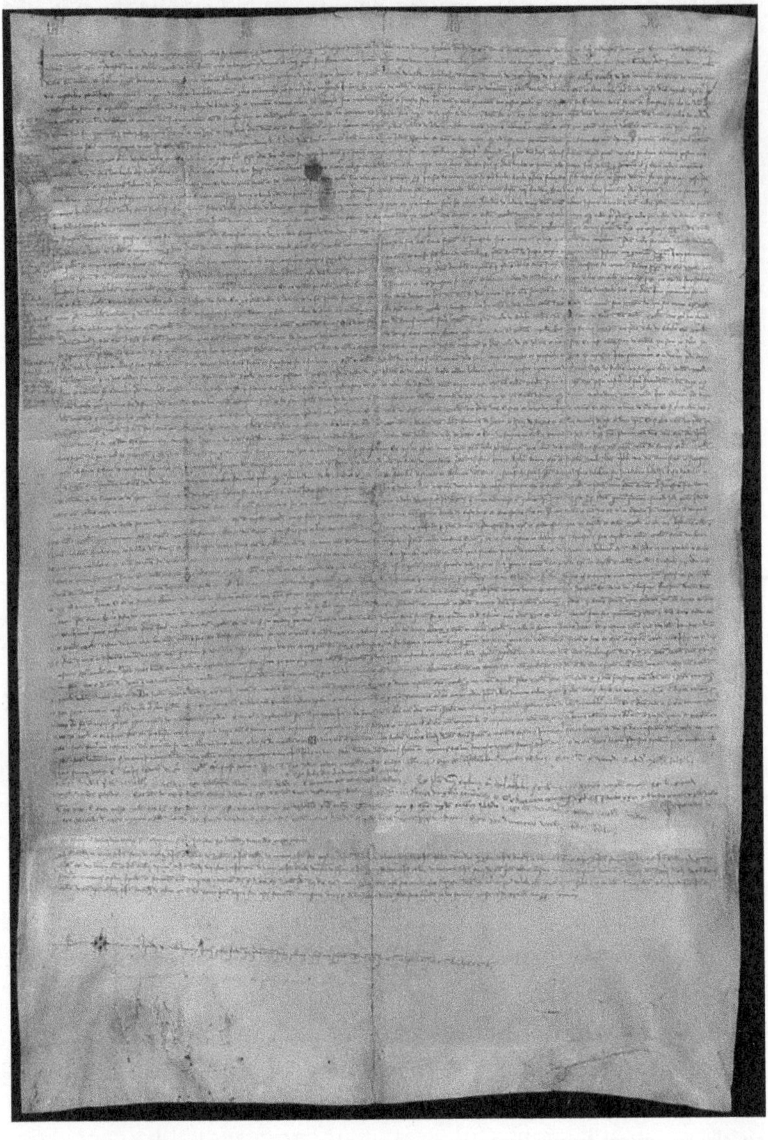

It is a 750-year-old formal written agreement to establish a nation state and agree its borders. At the time that it was signed, the notion of ratified border agreements was exceptionally rare. Whereas in the last 150 years, the creation of national borders and treaties between both parties to ratify them has become epidemic. There are currently over 310 international land borders between countries and counting, adding up to over 240,000 km. In the last 15 to 20 years, there has been a small oasis of calm where new border changes are concerned, but we shouldn't fool ourselves. If we take a perspective starting from the mid-nineteenth century, then the hiatus in border churn we're in now is probably just a pausing for breath.

So, because we've already spent so much time washing around in unstable, intermediate spaces, let's devote a few moments to celebrate this record-breaking stable nation. Certain island nations could claim longer identities as a nation, but that's quite easy compared to the jeopardy and effort of sustaining a continuous land border. We should therefore allow Andorra its moment in the sun, the international poster boy for national border steadfastness.

This needs some digging into, in case there's something to learn, border-wise. Deliciously, at least for our purposes, the land and people that inhabited the Andorran valleys in the medieval period existed in an uneasy buffer zone between the Frankish empire to the north, and the Muslim empire of Al-Andalus to the south. It's believed that Charlemagne gave the Andorran people a charter to exist as an independent entity in return for their role in acting as a kind of garrison to hold the line against the encroaching Muslim empire. And it was precisely because Andorra's borderland status was of equal strategic interest to Catalonia and the French aristocracy that its position was solidified by treaty in 1278. And thereby we have this rather sweet irony: the most enduring land border the world has yet known came into existence because of shifting territorial border disputes.

Having stumbled on this agreeable curiosity, I assumed that researching the history of Andorra would unearth layers of turbulence, with a fragile land border surviving against impossible odds, but that's not been the case at all. Pretty much every account of Andorra's key moments relates to the granting of some local autonomy in the early fifteenth century, followed by over five centuries of essentially feudal law, until a local government was set up in the 1990s, albeit still under the honorary 'rule' of the two co-princes, one of whom is still the present Bishop of Urgell and the other is the President of France — currently Emmanuel Macron, at the time of writing. That's some story of permanence, and its uniqueness is underscored by Andorra being the only example anywhere in the world of a country that is governed as a co-principality.

In summary, we have a tale of borderland ironies — a state that was conceived in instability to manage a disputatious borderland, and that has been governed by two other parties rather than free to govern itself, ends up being an icon of stability. Such is the *Alice in Wonderland*ish quality of the liminal world.

3. **Bordering on insanity**

Having discovered the story of Andorra, there was a natural curiosity to discover the other end of the border time capsule — those international borders that had most recently changed. The accolade of most-recent border change is always bound to be a temporary honour, given that another one is certain to come along in a year or two. Because we typically think of border changes in the context of conflict, warfare, and human tragedy, low-key new border arrangements tend to fly under the radar, attracting almost no publicity, except between the nations concerned. But it's surprising how often they crop up.

The most recent was an agreement between Denmark and Canada over a tiny, disputed island called Hans Island in a channel between Canadian territory and Greenland. You could walk across this island in a lazy 15 minutes. It sits in the dead centre of the channel, and both countries had claimed full ownership of this small, uninhabited outcrop. From the point that this became a formal dispute between the two nations, it took fully 17 years for them to find a harmonious solution, finally coming up with the ingenious idea of sharing the island, resulting in an agreement in 2022 where Canada took ownership of 40% of it and Denmark the other 60%, and thereby creating the world's fourth shortest land border, at just over 1000 m.

As in this case, it's not uncommon for border changes to occur between friendly nations, and prior to the Hans Island agreement, one of the most recent realignments was between Belgium and the Netherlands, using their collective will to resolve a small but niggling hangover of illogicality in a part of their border area. There's a section of their 450-km border that has historically been demarcated by the river Meuse. To make navigation for shipping easier, the Meuse was straightened in 1961. This was a solid, practical decision, but with an unanticipated consequence. Because what *didn't* happen at the same time was a simultaneous alignment of the border along the newly straightened river. As a result, the two nations were left with nearly 16.5 hectares of Dutch territory on the new Belgian side of the river, and three hectares of Belgian territory on the new Dutch side. Initially, the anomaly was considered neither here nor there (so to speak), but in both cases, they became small lawless parcels of land dominated by drug trafficking, because due to border technicalities, it was more trouble than it was worth for police to get the permissions necessary to cross the river and manage their respective spaces. Finally, though, when a headless corpse was discovered in Belgian territory on the Dutch side of the river, both sets of authorities realised that events had gone too far, and it provoked a desire on both sides to sort the situation out, which they did in a cordial fashion, even though the Netherlands did slightly better out of the bargain. Both governments are understandably proud of this piece of collaborative administration, and a couple of years before the new borders came into force, the then Belgian Foreign Minister, one Didier Reynders, announced that this 'agreement shows that borders can be exchanged peacefully'.

Which would be all well and good, except that it conveniently overlooks the fact that were you to drive an hour and a half further along the border on the Dutch side until you got to the province of Aachen, you'd encounter the picturesque town of Baarle-Nassau, which boasts a defensible claim to having the most ludicrous border scenario anywhere on Earth, again with neighbour Belgium. The situation dates back to the medieval era, and relates to a series of land disputes, swaps, and treaties between the Dukes of Brabant and Lords of Breda. The situation became so convoluted that legislators tried and failed to sort it out for 800 years, before giving up all pretence of an elegant solution in 1995, and now justifying the situation on the basis that it's turned into a lucrative tourist attraction (a true modern way to resolve a liminal conundrum). To the best of my knowledge, Mr Reynders has been entirely silent on the matter. It's almost as if we're dealing with a politician who is very quick to trumpet successes, whilst burying failures. Imagine.

OK, are you ready for this? We'll start gently. Firstly, I called it Baarle-Nassau, being the Dutch name for the town, but the Belgians call the same place Baarle-Hertog. And in case you're wondering why they bother having their own name for a smallish Dutch town of only 7000 people, it's because there is a portion of Belgian territory inside the town. Well, you might be thinking, it's not that far from the border, it's not too surprising that they might have a Belgian enclave inside the town — some historical residue. And that would also be fair enough if there was just the one enclave, but in fact there are 26 separate parcels of land that collectively go to make up Baarle-Hertog, fully under the control of Belgian law (for the sticklers out there, 22 of these are inside the municipality of Baarle-Nassau, and the other four are in adjacent areas). That would be mad enough, but to make matters substantially more complex, there are also seven Dutch enclaves inside the Belgian enclaves. At which point, you need visual help, although I'd be the first to concede that the simplest available diagram is still a headscratcher. Nevertheless, in the map below, H stands for Hertog (Belgian), and N for Nassau (Dutch).

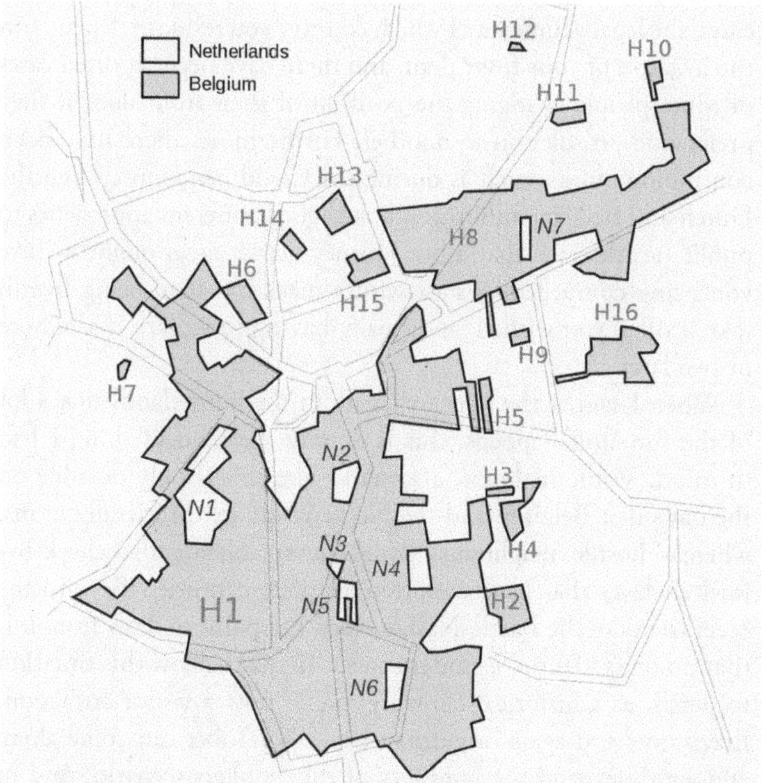

It's mad in a good way. Personally, I'm particularly drawn to some of the crazy fingers of land, such as in H16, and the insanely small Dutch sliver between H5 and H1. Are they really telling us that even that anomaly couldn't have been rectified? What exactly do the Dutch plan to do with that bit of territory? Don't get me wrong, I'm glad they didn't sort it out, but seriously. Kafka wouldn't have dared dream this one up, and it's superb to know that the medieval period was into post-modernism centuries before we put a name to it.

There are many curiosities that have arisen as a result. A good number of residents have a border going straight through their property, meaning that they can, say, go to sleep in Belgium but come downstairs to have their breakfast in the Netherlands. In such cases, the legal definition of which country you reside in depends on the location of your front door, and there have been reported cases of some people changing the position of their front door if they prefer one jurisdiction to another. Furthermore, there have been continuing quirks, such as during the Covid pandemic, when the Dutch and Belgian authorities took slightly different approaches to public health, such that a bus journey across town might involve you being compelled to start with a mask on, then being free to take it off if you wished, and finally having to replace it a minute or two later.

When I said at the outset that it's in the borderlands that a lot of the fun stuff happens, this is exactly the kind of thing I had in mind. Without doubt, a scenario like this is only possible on the basis that Belgium and the Netherlands are on friendly terms, whereas hostile neighbours could never tolerate the cheek-by-jowl enclaves that have coexisted all these centuries. Beyond the eccentricity of the Baarle-Nassau story, the point to draw from it is that no one's identity is under threat. They can allow this situation to persist as a historical curiosity that is now a visitor attraction. Every now and again, a journalist or a YouTuber can come along and gently expand the notoriety of this bonkers scenario. And in the same way, the land swap in 2016 put nothing at risk in terms of identity — Belgium and the Netherlands are countries of broadly equal status, both under the higher jurisdiction of the EU. They have nothing to fear from each other, and both gain from a minor sense of otherness at each other's expense.

4. **Borders as a matter of life and death**

Not all borders in Europe are so benign. As already mentioned, since the spring of 2022, the border between Ukraine and Russia, in addition to being Europe's longest, has become its most contested, most volatile, and, of course, most tragic. At the time of writing, it's impossible to say whether or when that border will end up being redrawn. I'm going to leave that border alone, mostly because books don't do current affairs well, and that is properly the domain of journalism. All I will say about it here is that everyone who has been attentive to the Ukraine–Russia war is likely to have had a visceral reaction to events on that border during 2022 and beyond. They will have watched and heard about people sacrificing their lives for concepts of nationhood and collective identity, and whatever the outcome ends up being, the peace treaty, however bitterly agreed to, will include an agreement about borders — they will be the visible imprint on maps and atlases of everything that has gone on.

Now, having read that, there's a case for pausing at this point and checking out any of the time-lapse videos on YouTube that show Europe's border changes over the centuries. It takes between 3 and 11 minutes to watch 1000 years of shape-shifting (there are both slow and speeded up versions). It's worth taking note of certain countries, especially Poland, and imagining the heartache, tragedy, and sacrifice that has been undertaken in the defence of national borders. As the years flick past, each border change taking about a second, it's sobering to realise that most of them have entailed some equivalent measure of personal cost, upheaval, death, and state-sponsored aggression to that we witnessed in just one such case, starting in 2022. And to what end? Because one unavoidable insight is the realisation that many of those desperately hard-won border changes last a matter of a few years, perhaps decades, other than in those countries that are lucky enough to be posted around the edge of the continent, such as Spain and Portugal, and even they are stable only on a relative scale. By way of further underscoring this, without in any way wishing to diminish or deny Ukraine's sense of national identity, which had been building up with increasing force throughout the nineteenth century, it doesn't actually appear on European maps as a nation in its own right until 1918, and then only briefly, before being subsumed again by Russia, until the break-up of the Soviet Union after the tumultuous events that followed the fall of the Berlin Wall in 1989. The point is that it doesn't take that long as an independent nation for its borders to be felt to be worth defending, including paying the ultimate price.

5. **Border as ideological divide**

But leaving the Russia–Ukraine border to one side for now, another Russian border that has had its full level of symbolic power, as well as incident, has been that between Russia and Finland. Whereas in the case of the Russia–Ukraine border, part of Russia's argument is that, at least in eastern Ukraine, there are ethnic Russians speaking Russian, there is nothing like as much blurring in the case of Russia and Finland, or at least not since Stalin cleared all ethnic Finns out of Russia between the First and Second World Wars. To cut a long story short, the current 1340-km border between the two countries is fully ratified and uncontested. This was done in 1975, although in practice it had been settled by 1947, after Finland had reluctantly ceded some of its former land to the Russians after military skirmishes between them during the Winter War, which the Russians opportunistically started in 1939 whilst everyone else was preoccupied with the Second World War.

During the years of the Cold War, this border represented the western edge of the Iron Curtain (how about that for a border metaphor), and still represents the most high-profile border, as well as the longest, in the entire European Union. In that era, the border region also represented a stark disparity in prosperity between the two adjacent nations. The economic asymmetry was mirrored by the level of defence of the border by both nations. There was a tacit presumption that all the attempted flows of people and goods would go from Russia to Finland, rather than vice versa. As a result, whereas the widest border region on the Finnish side has never been more than 3 km, on the Russian side, even today, it extends no less than 20 km from the actual border, and at one time was as wide as 200 km. Measures included wide sand traps, high fencing, and a significant border force in terms of personnel.

Having said that, after the era of Russian glasnost (a Russian word that translates best as openness) led by Mikhail Gorbachev, there was something of a thawing of tensions between Finland and Russia, resulting in a more relaxed approach to the border itself. At certain points, such as in forested areas, you could see the close adjacency of a tall Finnish blue-and-white striped post, an equivalent Russian red-and-green striped post, with the exact borderline between them marked by a smaller white post.

But even so, for obvious reasons of proximity, the Finnish have always been on the alert in respect of perceived Russian threat. One statistic makes the point. Including reservists, Finland is in the top ten of all nations in the world in relation to the proportion of its population that is on active military duty at any given time, with the highest ratio amongst all European nations. In practice, this means that Finns are far more sensitive to any hint of Russian military intent, even when it's not aimed at them. I had a chastening experience reading an academic paper by Jussi Laine, from the University of Eastern Finland, written in 2015.[5] Laine makes the point that the border has been a kind of weathervane of levels of tension over the decades, with less than a million people per annum making the crossing during Cold War years, rising to over 13 million in 2013, and then dropping again sharply in the immediate aftermath of Russian's Crimean incursion in 2014. And whilst much of western Europe absorbed the Crimean story quite quickly, and moved on, Finns were far more clear-eyed about what it represented. Laine quotes the Finnish Foreign Ministry from a 2015 review as follows:

> Russia, through its actions in Ukraine, has breached international law and the fundamental principles of European security, which include inter alia the right of states to independently take decisions regarding their own security policy guidelines. While Russia's precise goals and intentions are unknown, great-power posturing and spheres-of-influence thinking seem to be guiding its actions.

It's a salutary lesson, and a reminder of Tim Marshall's contention that nothing concentrates the mind at a national level quite like your own immediate geography. To underscore the point that all border stories are dynamic and restless, by the start of 2023, the physical border situation between the two nations shifted again, with the Finns this time initiating a more physical barrier at the borderline. The beginnings of this can be traced back to 2015, shortly after the Crimean incursion by Russia. In response to this move, Finland, as evidenced above by its closer eye on Russian activity than other European states, reduced some of its historic bilateral co-operation with Russia. In response to *that*, Russia took advantage of the relatively relaxed border arrangements that then existed. By this stage, other than formal road crossing points, as already mentioned, a fair amount of the actual border was not heavily defended by either side. Russia instigated a provocative act, by ushering thousands of migrants across the northern border into Finland from countries like Afghanistan and Iraq. What they were trying to do — and succeeded in doing — was to bring Finland back into line on bilateral arrangements. The flow of migrants came to an abrupt halt. Learning a lesson from this, and after the stepping-up of Russian aggression in Ukraine following the invasion of eastern Ukraine in 2022, Finland decided to take its border security into its own hands and started constructing a more robust physical barrier in especially sensitive areas, such as the far north and the south-east.

The ultimate border crossing

Before moving on, no time spent discussing the Russia–Finland border is quite complete without reference to one of the great bits of espionage derring-do of recent decades: the tale of Oleg Gordievsky's exfiltration in 1985 from the then Soviet Union in the boot of a Ford Sierra. The reason for mentioning it here is because it is a prime example of the way in which borders can be a focal point for bravery, adventure, and ingenuity, all happening within the context of tension and a conflict between ideologies. The story is told by Ben McIntyre in his book *The Spy and the Traitor*.[6] Reading it now feels like a tale from a quaint old-fashioned era, with signals being communicated through the visible eating of chocolate bars and the holding of Safeway bags at predetermined spots in Moscow. Even knowing the outcome, it's hard not to be gripped by the tension of the escape, what with the sheer unlikelihood of the enterprise, and with both Gordievsky and the British embassy team being tracked by KGB officers for weeks in the run up to the attempt. When they finally got to the border territory, there was a 20-km stretch of land on the Russian side, leading up to the crossing point near Vyborg in Russia and Vaalimaa on the Finnish side.

There were no fewer than five separate border checkpoints to go through, three of them being Russian and two Finnish, with the potential for catastrophe at each one, because had they been exposed by the Finnish border guards, Gordievsky would certainly have been turned back to the Russian authorities. The British had to get Gordievsky all the way through Finland up to the far northern border with Norway before he could be considered safe.

To spell it out, the level of excitement and adrenalin is heightened because of the painful crawl through the borderland territory and the fact that his exfiltration has him breaching the border whilst hidden in the Sierra. There is already symbolic power in the Russia–Finland border, with this being the literal frontier between ideologies, but then the execution of this plan concentrates and distils that symbolism through everything that the border represents.

6. Conceiving of nations

So how did we get to this point, where we have so much invested in our sense of national identity? One thing that didn't happen after the creation of Andorra was a great rush of treaties and well-defined nation states. That took centuries to happen. Two types of alternative structure stood in the way of that, one being organised religion and the other being monarchies or dynasties of one sort or another. I've made brief reference to Benedict Anderson's *Imagined Communities* already, but there he outlines how both of those structures did a sufficient job in creating cohesion, meaning there was no strong need for any other way of ordering things. In the case of religion, there were the three powerful traditions of Christendom, Islam, and Buddhism, each generating an impressive geographical reach that encompassed a swathe of what we would now think of as quite disparate nations. Partly they would achieve this through events like pilgrimages, activities that would help to deepen a feeling of belonging and affinity to a unifying religious idea.

And in the case of monarchical dynasties, in those times there were divinely ordained sovereigns, who ruled people as subjects, rather than citizens. Sovereignty had a gravitational orientation, with the court around the king being the centre point, and the influence of that sovereignty weakening with geographical distance. Anderson expresses this in a way that is very useful for our exploration of liminality:

> But in the older imagining, where states were defined by centres, borders were porous and indistinct, sovereignties faded imperceptibly into one another.

During the early modern period, there was a very gradual loss of influence in both religions and monarchies. Some of that loss of influence was twinned — the erosion of the notion of the divine right of kings for example. It's too simplistic to pin the rise of the nation state entirely at the door of these two dominant constructs fading away, but there is a correlation.

The new factor that Anderson identifies that helped to fan the flames of embryonic nationalism was literacy. Whereas both religious and dynastic structures were 'top-down', literacy opened the way to more democratised organisation. Nation states have a concept of citizenship rather than subjectship. In addition, education and wide access to print — not only through books but, importantly, to newspapers — spread affiliation to a sense of place. What went hand in hand with this was the switch towards making local languages the language of politics and the court, rather than, say, Latin. With all these trends in place, borders started to organise people that were linked through language and communication. People's sense of shared identity started to be shaped by the type of information they got access to. On first encounter, I found this idea of the influence of print journalism to be quite flimsy, especially at a time when that medium is falling away. But then I got to thinking about this in my own case, growing up in the north-east Midlands. In terms of news, I'd get to hear through regional television news about what was going on in places like Worcester, which is a full 130 km away from where I lived in a south westerly direction, but I felt connected to it via news. Conversely, I'd never hear about Lincoln, which is only 50 km away and for which I had no feeling at all. The simple fact of being at the edge of a TV region distorted my sense of my locality.

Scaled up to whole nations, these types of forces can create cohesion, even if it's sometimes an uneasy one. Indonesia is perhaps the most startling global illustration of this point, comprising a massive 17,000 individual islands, having the fourth-largest population in the world, and the fourteenth-largest land mass, across a huge east to west reach of over 5000 km. With a substantial array of ethnicities, religions, and literally hundreds of linguistic groups, there should be no way that it holds together as a single nation. For example, people to the far west of the country in Sumatra have far more in common ethnically and linguistically with people in Malaysia than they do with their fellow citizens far to the east. And even a cursory look at the map of Indonesia throws up the impact of colonialism, by looking at the clean slice taken to the island of Papua to the east, which was claimed by the Dutch in 1828 as part of their Dutch East Indies. The story of the twentieth century was a merry-go-round of changes of control and turn-taking, influenced by two world wars, and international decisions imposed by the League of Nations through countries like the United Kingdom, The Netherlands, and Japan, who, in their colonial 'wisdom' clearly felt that these were issues that needed to be resolved by them.

Meanwhile, inside Indonesia, some of the modern tools of nation building were being deployed to create a degree of cohesion.

For instance, there was a decisive role for education, including a standardised model of primary schooling that was mandated and stencilled from Jakarta (then called Batavia) which had the impact of imprinting some element of consistency around what was taught and therefore assimilated from a young age. Ironically, this programme was launched by the Dutch colonial masters, and one of its impacts was to foment an embryonic independence movement, kickstarted by the younger crop of new local leaders that emerged from this new educational thrust.

The struggle for independence first took shape in resistance against the Dutch, and then against the Japanese, who took advantage of Dutch distraction in the Second World War to invade, and then the Dutch again once the Japanese left after the war. These struggles did wonders to create a common purpose, and therefore a sense of identity. The Dutch were finally defeated and ceded full independence to the newly created state of Indonesia between 1949 and 1950.

Overall, a remarkable feat of nation building has been pulled off, although of course, no one has seen the end game for Indonesia (or any current nation for that matter), so the jury is out as to how enduring this will be. I'm not the judge of that, but I will say this: it tends to be the case that the type of common cause that can expel an invading or colonising force and create a sense of shared identity has a sell-by date. I've been told by people older than me that Great Britain (England, Scotland, and Wales), felt very unified after the Second World War finished, but roll forward a few decades, and the strength of independence movements in Wales and especially Scotland has enormous energy. When you spend time looking at the ebb and flow of nations and their borders, you realise how vulnerable these borders are. Don't be fooled by checkpoints, barbed wire fencing, and armed guards. If anything, the presence of those things is evidence of how frail they are. Because borders are human constructs, once they've outlived their usefulness, no one will fight for them. You rarely if ever hear the case being made to restore the border between the old West and East Germanies.

7. **Don't forgive us our trespass; we've done nothing wrong**

Two of the last three topics to look at in this Between Places section reside within the United Kingdom rather than on the international stage. The first of them takes its cue from this observation about borders being artificial human constructs imposed on land and relocates that back to the domestic sphere. For inside those national borders are countless (perhaps literally) lines and boundaries that demarcate property rights and land use. The laws that relate to all of this are so historic and embedded that they can feel natural and beyond enquiry. As far as the UK is concerned, the country's relationship with land law didn't get going until the Norman Conquest, when William the Conqueror first started to exercise power. His mechanism for this was to import a quantity of French barons, and in the act of doing this, allocate parcels of land to them. Succeeding centuries involved ever-increasing quantities of property and land laws being passed, which always went in favour of land holders, as opposed to being rights of access to peasant farmers. This process was accelerated by a stream of Enclosure Acts, the first of which was in the thirteenth century, but they got going in earnest from the late eighteenth century onwards, all of which had the effect of concentrating land ownership into the hands of existing landowners. The tenant farmers who had previously had rights to dwell upon and work the land, even when ultimately owned by a local lord, were typically displaced by enclosure, and had little alternative than to drift towards the cities, thereby helping to fuel the Industrial Revolution by supplying a workforce.

But this drift towards ever-tighter rights to land isn't inevitable. Most indigenous people's attitude to land differs to that of Westerners. There's a skewering observation on this by an Aboriginal elder, Tom Dystra, who compares the Aboriginal approach in Australia to the white settlers who came later. 'We endeavour to live *with* the land. They seemed to live *off* the land.' Rarely has a simple change in preposition felt so insightful. For the first time, for me at least, the phrase living off the land comes with a realisation of being above it, as in, disconnected from it. You can't be 'off the land' and be rooted to it at the same time. By contrast, the phrase 'living with the land' brings us right back to a concept from earlier in the book, namely that of collaboration. It's an outlook that is hard to adopt and maintain when your primary philosophical perspective to land is one of possession and ownership as opposed to stewardship.

But even back in the UK, the law, like everything else, can also exist in a transitional space. Nothing is for ever. One further impact of the Enclosure Acts led to workers being denied access to areas that had once been common land, which in turn meant that urban dwellers had no recreational rights to land outside their bleak industrial towns and cities. This resentment came to a head in the 1930s, leading to a mass rambler protest in 1932 on Kinder Scout in north Derbyshire, now part of the Peak District National Park, but then owned by the Duke of Devonshire. Four hundred ramblers took part in a deliberate act of trespass. The Duke sent his groundkeepers out, armed with sticks, whereas the ramblers were armed only with indignation. Several of the trespassers were arrested and received prison sentences, no doubt intended to be in part a deterrent warning as to future consequences for similar protests. But as so often happens, the opposite transpired, and the harshness of the treatment for the simple act of walking brought a wave of sentiment behind the ramblers' cause. Since then, a certain amount has changed across the United Kingdom, or at least a lot has in Scotland, where radical access to land was provided for in the Land Reform Act of 2003. Those freedoms are enshrined in law by a very simple and human transaction — that walkers, canoeists, and cyclists respect the interests of other people, care for the environment, and take responsibility for their own actions. The simple, grown-up dignity of the way this is expressed feels like a Western equivalent to living with the land.***

*** Some of the gains in access that have been made since the Kinder Trespass event are celebrated on the Ramblers website. I couldn't help but smile that these gains are described on the site as 'great strides'.

8. **Suburbs — expanding borders**

This is my city. You cannot see past the edges it doesn't have.
— Tom Chivers, talking about London.[7]

By no means are all our geographic borders and borderlands so full of real, emotional, imagined, or quirky significance as the ones we've been looking at so far. Some are so banal and humdrum that we don't even see them.

Nowadays, we accept urban sprawl as a reality, a basic truth about how the built environment works (or doesn't work). The suburbs, which were initially made possible by the growth of the railways, and then even more so by the ubiquity of cars, mean that city centres and the countryside often have miles of separation, with a large smudge of building leaching into the beginning of rural land. But look at this — Van Gogh's 'Factories at Clichy', from 1887.

There's no knowing reference to the pun, but I choose to believe it was deliberate and put there to be enjoyed quietly by those of us with a relish for that kind of thing.

I remember seeing this in a Van Gogh exhibition and experiencing a strong sense of surprise. Where were the suburbs? In our time, the expansion of city limits is relentless — we have these enormous indeterminate zones of sprawl, which tend to represent the largest physical part of an urban area. It was startling to reflect on Van Gogh's picture and see the lack of any middle ground here: a modest wall demarcating an unambiguous division between industrial development and fields and farms.

Reflecting on the picture with the benefit of historical perspective, you just know, without visiting or needing to do any research, that those fields aren't there any longer. It's not how it goes. But it's also not as simple as being a case of the countryside surrendering to development and the expansion of cities. These large suburban areas are themselves transitional. It was spelt out in a book called *Edgelands*,[8] written by the poets Paul Farley and Michael Symmons Roberts, in 2011. They both have suburban northern roots, and set about looking more into these nebulous zones, which had already been coined edgelands by the geographer Marion Shoard. They make any number of insightful comments about edgelands, but in their set up introduction, they make this statement to set the scene:

> If parts of remote rural Britain feel timeless (though this feeling is, of course, illusory) then the edgelands feel anything but. Revisit an edgelands site you haven't visited for six months, and likely as not there will be a Victorian factory knocked down, a business park newly built, a section of waste ground cleared and landscaped, a pre-war warehouse abandoned and opened to the elements. Such are the constantly shifting sands of edgelands that any writing about these landscapes is a snapshot. There is no definitive description of the edgelands of Swindon or Wolverhampton, only an attempt to celebrate and evoke them at one particular time.

It's so true. Like the authors, I grew up in a similar landscape. At the time, I thought it was a discrete village on the banks of the river Trent, just outside Nottingham. But with the more detached view of an adult, I can see that it was part of the city's edgelands, forming one link of an almost continual ribbon of small towns to link up with Derby, 15 miles to the west. Farley and Symmons, later in the same passage, use the image of 'connective tissue', conjuring up the inevitable development that happens along these infrastructure routes, but because that development has no real soul or substance to it, other than the temporary utility of whatever is built there, it can easily get grubbed up and reused. This is in sharp contrast to more well-loved and iconic aspects of city centres that confer identity and purpose on buildings and sculptures, and which often have a fair sprinkling of listed building status protecting them. Speaking for my own neighbourhood, the Chilwell Ordnance Depot felt like a fixed and necessary part of the immediate area I grew up in, but lo and behold, one year when I revisited as an adult, it was no longer there. There's no physical commemorative plaque that I've been able to find that details the former history of the site. You have to know it was there and use Google if you want any information about its prior existence. Even the folk memory of the depot will be receding. What has taken its place is the inevitable edge-of-town retail park. For now. Until, that is, retail parks cease to have any economic viability, which can only be a matter of time.

9. **Borders at sea**

> Borders are fictitious enough at the best of times, but this one, where tidal flats become sky, wrapped in fogs and rippled by watery hazes, is pure make believe.

This opinion is voiced by Mike Parker in *All the Wide Border*, his book on the England–Wales border, which we've come across before. He's referring to the notional sea border shown on British Ordnance Survey maps, which separates England and Wales in the estuary of the River Dee.

Parker's perspective sets the tone very well for this final section on between places, as we turn our attention to the even more liminal issue of borders at sea. This book started with a poetic rumination about sea borders, but here we look at them from a more technical perspective.

We'll start with a recent story, an outcome of the Russian invasion of Ukraine, which shows how the impact of such action ripples out to other borders beyond the one under immediate dispute. Before telling that story, though, here is a quote from the Canadian-American economist, Alex Tabarrok, who, writing in *The Atlantic* in 2015, said: 'Closed borders are one of the world's greatest moral failings, but the opening of borders is the world's greatest economic opportunity.' Tabarrok's use of the word 'moral' leaps out of the phrase — the inference is that nations should be capable of conducting trade despite their differences. And that when it happens, the act of trading is not only mutually beneficial economically but, moreover, those shared commercial interests can lead to greater cooperation and therefore tolerance.

An interesting example of that is the case of bilateral fishing arrangements between Norway and Russia, who share both a land border and a sea border up beyond the Arctic Circle in the Barents Sea. Despite differences of opinion about how the sea should be 'owned' between them (it's not a major surprise to discover that both nations had claims over the same stretches of water), they managed to sign a workable treaty in 2010. This treaty laid the foundations for an ongoing commercial relationship around fishing rights, despite mistrust on both sides. The Barents Sea happens to have some of the last remaining major stocks of cod anywhere in the world, but the cod, being no respecter of international border treaties, have their spawning grounds on the Russian side of the sea, but migrate to maturity on the Norwegian side. Without agreement, there could have been a scenario where the Russians ended up fishing the cod when young, denying the Norwegians any fish, but killing off the benefit of the fish to both nations. Therefore, they managed to negotiate a situation where Russia didn't fish the young cod, but where Norway gave Russian trawlers rights to their territorial waters and the catches of the respective nations were respected and managed. So far, so good. But the Ukraine invasion changed all that, even though it happened 1000 miles further south. The trade between the two nations started to tail off, with access to Norwegian ports being frozen. In a remote area where few other economic avenues are viable, the loss of cooperative relationships with Russia has the potential to be existential for a fragile region like the far north of Norway and brings the significance of Tabarrok's quote into view. It's a demonstration of the tentative nature of these types of arrangement, and how they sit in a transactional space that holds for as long as it holds.

This story sits within a wider context. Since 1994, all global waters have come under the jurisdiction of the ponderously named United Nations Convention on the Law of the Sea (UNCLOS). Getting to it was a Herculean task, involving the drafting of 320 articles and associated annexes. There was a 9-year process of getting to the Convention, between 1973 and 1982, and then a 12-year gap before it came into force. Saying that gives the impression that it was binding, whereas in fact it relied (and still does) on individual countries ratifying it. As an act of pragmatism, it was also built on top of previous laws and historic practices. Perhaps because of this, but also partly because of the odd configuration of nations, UNCLOS is insanely complex. Therefore, examining it feels like a case study in how borders in our age come to look increasingly blurred and fractal.

Let's nibble away at it. In the simplest terms, UNCLOS states that there are three tiers to the territorial waters of any nation lucky enough to have a sea border. Firstly, there is a baseline. It's more complex than this, but let's simplify by saying that this is, in effect, the coastline. Beyond this, there are the territorial waters. These extend 12 nautical miles from the baseline, which is 22 km. Inside these limits, the nation concerned has sovereignty. It can effectively do whatever it wants — set whatever laws it wants and access the resources of that stretch of sea as they see fit. It's almost as if these territorial waters are an extension of their land. The qualifier of 'almost' is necessary, because this being about sea borders, there are special cases. One such example is the case of 'innocent passage', where ships of all states are allowed to traverse through a country's territorial waters if they have no other option to complete their journey.

Now, beyond the boundary of the territorial waters comes a region that is a further 12 nautical miles out, meaning 24 nautical miles in total from the baseline, and this is called the contiguous zone. UNCLOS has a majestically obscure definition of this zone, which is reproduced in full here to demonstrate the sheer indeterminacy of the law relating to sea borders:

> In a zone contiguous to its territorial sea, described as the contiguous zone, the coastal State may exercise the control necessary to:
> (a) prevent infringement of its customs, fiscal, immigration or sanitary laws and regulations within its territory or territorial sea;
> (b) punish infringement of the above laws and regulations committed within its territory or territorial sea.

The immediate thought on reading that was to wonder how such an infringement would be dealt with, followed by the adjacent thought of what UNCLOS advises a coastal state to do if it believes it's suffered such an infringement. And having worked my way through the entirety of UNCLOS, I was none the wiser. They are ultimately no more than the written words that the UN could get the majority of nations to agree to.

But we're not done with these sea borders. Beyond the contiguous zone comes the exclusive economic zone, which, if the coastal state is lucky enough to have sufficient unbroken sea to a neighbouring country, can extend up to a maximum of 200 nautical miles, or just over 370 km, as long as this wouldn't create an overlap with a neighbour. The idea here is that a coastal nation has rights to manage the zone for its economic value, including mining, exploiting fish stocks, exploration, and so on. What it can't do is to control the passage of international shipping, which have rights of passage within this area. One conceptual way of thinking of it is that the coastal state has control of everything under the surface, but not the surface itself.

It doesn't take a lot of imagination to realise that there are many parts of the world where this mammoth UNCLOS agreement has its challenges. The South China Sea is one such, where tensions run very high, with many nations competing over highly strategic and disputed territorial waters. And even in a stretch of water with only two claimants, relations can break down to an almost warlike level. One such situation is in the Aegean, where tension exists due to the presence of literally thousands of Greek islands, many of which are within spitting distance of the Turkish coast, including some significant sized places, such as Lesbos in the north, down to Rhodes in the south. They sit there like sentries, extending Greece's territorial claim over the Aegean far away from its mainland, leaving Turkey with a thin strip of coastline to call its own. In fact, whereas the standard UNCLOS convention is for a 12-km delimitation of its territorial waters, in the Aegean, it remains at 6 km, which was a convention from earlier on in the twentieth century, making the Turkish 'allowance' very meagre. It's not hard to see how this would look from their vantage point. Recalling that UNCLOS must be ratified by each individual state, it's perhaps not entirely astonishing to discover that Turkey is not a signatory. Needless to say, it all looks very different to Greece. Thousands of islands, each with its 6-nautical-mile territorial ring around it, means that in practice large swathes of the Aegean Sea fall under Greek maritime sovereignty, especially given the extreme proximity of some of the larger islands already mentioned.

The situation is complicated by the way that airspace works, and then again, how it works uniquely in the Aegean. In principle, any nation with a coastline can draw a vertical line up from the edge of their territorial waters (i.e., normally 12 nautical miles), and enjoy sovereignty over all the air above that is on their side of that line. Of course, civil aircraft are allowed to come and go to enable international travel, but there's no equivalent of the 'innocent passage' in the air that exists at sea. What *this* means is that military aircraft are strictly not allowed to impinge on the airspace of another country, and this tends to be hotly defended. In the case of the Aegean, Turkish and Greek fighter jets are continually sparring with each other and have been for decades. It's another reason why the stakes are so high. For instance, behind that fortress of Greek islands that are right up close and personal to Turkey, there is a portion of empty sea. Turkey claims that this is part of the natural continental shelf that extends from its coastline, and that a median line should be drawn down the middle of the Aegean to account for that. This would enable its air force to operate over parts of the Aegean and keep the pressure on Greece.

If at this point, the thought occurs, *Hang on a minute. Aren't Greece and Turkey both members of NATO and therefore supposed to be signatories to some higher purpose?* you'd be correct. In fact, they both joined in the same year (1952, for the record), and yes, what this whole story demonstrates is that issues of land borders, sea borders, and international alliances also involve nested identities, like a set of (Dis-) United Nations nested dolls. There can exist a profound local enmity that goes back centuries — or even a millennium, as in this case, back to the rise of the Ottoman empire. And even while nations are pointing military hardware at their nearest neighbour, they can simultaneously be profoundly on their side against even greater existential aggressors, which brings them into alliance.

Maybe what the world needs now is a literal alien invasion, to bring us all to our senses and start to find common cause with those billions of people we need to share a planet with.

10. Section summary

a) With the possible exception of island nations, there's nothing intrinsic about the shape and territory of most countries — they are the result of human activity and man-made borders.

b) Borders are very malleable — over extended time, they change more often than they don't, and yet people can quickly become hugely attached to them and be prepared to fight and die for them. Of all the stacked identities we can have, national affinity can be one of the most emotive in driving belonging, partly because it defines people by what they're not.
c) Even friendly neighbours, with nothing to fear from each other, can find the issue of dealing with border anomalies a headache. Border cans get kicked down the street.

SECTION NINE — THE BETWEENS OF NATURE

I have for some time been imagining such [landscape] transitions as 'border crossings' … They exist even in familiar landscapes: there when you cross a certain watershed, tree line or snow line, or enter rain, storm or mist, or pass from boulder clay onto sand, or chalk onto greenstone. Such moments are rites of passage that reconfigure local geographies.

…

Landscape is still often understood as a noun connecting fixity, scenery, an immobile painterly decorum. I prefer to think of the word as a noun containing a hidden verb: landscape scapes, it is dynamic and commotion causing, it sculpts and shapes us not only over the courses of our lives but also instant by instant, incident by incident. I prefer to take landscape as a collective term for the temperature and pressure of the air, the fall of light and its rebounds, the textures and surfaces of rock, soil and building, the sounds (cricket screech, bird cry, wind through trees), the scents (pine resin, hot stone, crushed thyme) and the uncountable other transitory phenomena and

atmospheres that together comprise the bristling presence of a particular place at a particular moment.
— Robert McFarlane, *The Old Ways*[1]

In the last section on between places, I made the point that birds and clouds have a shared ability to ignore borders. Not all of nature is so lucky. The anthropologist Mary-Ann Ochota produced a three-part podcast for the BBC's World Service series *The Compass*, in which she walked along sections of the old Iron Curtain, meeting various people and considering the human and ecological aspects of its existence and its dismantling.

Although we're all familiar with the Berlin Wall as the great visible symbol of the Iron Curtain, there was just as definitive a physical barrier in the rest of Germany. It took quite a few years for it to be built after the creation of East Germany, but once the trickle of defectors turned into a flood, and hundreds of thousands of people had moved to West Germany, the building of the barrier accelerated, accompanied by mines to increase the deterrence. Although the barrier is no longer there, its imprint is still visible decades later. Ochota accompanied some people on a history walk along the route of the old border. She learned that not only did the barrier keep people out, but it also kept animals out. The numbers of many species diminished, as their habitual routes were blocked. After the dismantling, some species, such as wolves and wild boars, repopulated the forests very quickly, but others, notably red deer and European wildcats, would not travel across the border space, even though they were now free to do so. Some naturalists are keeping a statistical record of the gradual increase in the movement of these species across the border, and although it's climbing, it's still quite tentative.

Nevertheless, there is encouragement in the gradual reclamation by nature of what was a desolate and hostile space, and the experience of walking the border route moves one of Ochota's contributors to say, 'Borders divide, but nature connects.'

That insight comes to mind when reading the two resonant quotes from Robert McFarlane, one of the pre-eminent nature writers of the twenty-first century so far. He has an uncanny sensitivity to the liminality of nature. As he points out, the natural world is full of transitions, and nature's borders are never abstract. At the outset of this book, I described them as unequivocal physical facts, like the border between life and death. A beach represents an unarguable junction between sea and land — it doesn't need to be negotiated and ratified through treaty. It just is. Likewise, the tree line — the line in a high altitude or latitude that demarcates the point beyond which trees can't grow. But as we've already come to realise, nothing about borders is ever quite that cut and dried. Nature's borders may not be abstract, but they are in a continual state of flux. Taking just those two examples, beaches evolve continually through erosion and the formation of new landforms caused by longshore drift and the action of waves and estuaries. And for all that the tree line looks very severe from a distance, get up close and you realise that the 'line' is more of a zone, characterised by a gradual thinning out of the trees, together with a weakened condition of the most exposed of them, which tend to be weedier and more stunted in their growth. Eventually, there are no trees, but in the same way that a beach is a transitional space, so is the tree line.

Ecologists have a technical term for these zones of transition: ecotones. It lacks the poetry that McFarlane brings to bear with his 'border crossings', but it refers to the same idea. An ecotone is an area of land which, due to its characteristics (e.g., soil, climate) can support within it all the types of fauna and flora that are found on either side, meaning that the area of the ecotone is richer. Indeed, some species may only exist in the ecotone area. As a result, they are areas of great biodiversity, and many scientists are making the case that conservation efforts put into ecotones are especially fruitful and, in an era of limited resources, should be prioritised. To give a slightly more poetic, less technical gloss on ecotones, here's a lovely brief phrase from Beatrice Forshall's *The Book of Vanishing Species*:[2] 'Mangroves are places of exchange.' She makes a very passionate case for defending the vital role that mangroves play in supporting delicate coastal ecotones.

There is one other important aspect to nature's borders to point out. It's the way that we humans perceive them. It's not enough for them to just, well, be. We can't resist interpreting them, mining them for their metaphorical potential, seeing our own dramas reflected back at us through them. There's even an echo of this truth in the roots of the word. The 'eco' part comes from the Greek 'oikos' or 'home', and the 'tone' part comes from 'tonus' or 'tension'. So, we have 'a home in tension', a dynamic equilibrium. I find myself drifting off into analogous thoughts about cities and other human ecotones, buzzy environments of rich diversity where the flux is the point. I introduced James Crawford's *The Edge of the Plain* earlier. At one point, he interviews an ecologist called Laiken Jordahl, who works close to the American border with Mexico. Crawford quotes Jordahl, who begins by talking about naturally occurring ecotones and then extrapolates from them to the human implication:

> "From a conservation perspective, borders *are* natural. There are so many naturally occurring collisions of ecosystems, lines where communities overlap and intersect."
>
> The irony, Laiken said, is that, in ecology, it is usually at these borderlines that you find the most beauty and biodiversity.
>
> "And I think that's very applicable to humans as well. I think the border, in so many ways, *is* one of the most beautiful versions of America. These amazing communities all across the borderlands with these incredibly rich histories. These places of cultural exchange and opportunity. This is the culture that I think we need to be uplifting, preserving as a source of national pride."

Well said. Unlike us humans, nature doesn't fear its borders. It doesn't have to defend them with passport controls, treaties, and so on.

There's no suspicion or threat, no preference for keeping people in or out. To anthropomorphise for a moment, it's as if nature has more confidence in its transitional zones than we do. The permeability is the point, rather than an anxiety. As we often witness, natural borders frequently become a battleground for political borders. What might start as a border of convenience to define a state and its territory, such as a river, becomes a matter for international treaty and dispute, and if we're lucky, sometimes cooperation.

The borders of nature, on the other hand, allow us to think of borders in a different way. These liminal physical spaces can be used by us as liminal mental and metaphorical spaces, where we can create and transform and think in more creative ways. I want to use this final section to show examples of that exploration, and to point a way forward for us to see less anxiety and threat in uncertainty, but rather to see it as a wellspring for constructive energy. Rather late in the day, it occurred to me that our well-known phrase 'Is the glass half-full or half-empty?' is a classic borderland saying. Nature will tell us that it's half-full. Most of the natural things we'll look at are visible in the landscape or seascape, but we'll start with a liminal time of day, caused by the natural spin of the Earth.

1. The zone of twilight

We looked at the word twilight in the Words section, but now it's time to think about it in the hands of artists. One thing you realise early when you start to think about the symbolic power of natural phenomena is that they can not only symbolise more than one idea, but also more than one *liminal* idea. In the case of twilight, my mind first slips towards notions of the unexplained and mysterious, which I'll come to; but before that, twilight can also represent melancholy, in the specific sense of the end of vitality and that transitional state into old age. A luminous example of this is Joan Didion's *Blue Nights*,[3] published in 2011. Blue nights are those evenings after the summer solstice, when, as she says, 'you find yourself swimming in the color blue: the actual light is blue, and over the course of an hour or so this blue deepens'. She makes the point that the French use the same phrase, '*l'heure bleue*', whilst the British refer to 'the gloaming'. What comes with it, in that autumnal time of year, is the sense of chill, the end of summer, and the approach of winter, all presaged by a twilight signal from a specific time of year.

> This book is called "Blue Nights" because at the time I began it I found my mind turning increasingly to illness, to the end of promise, the dwindling of the days, the inevitability of the fading, the dying of the brightness. Blue nights are the opposite of the dying of the brightness, but they are also its warning.

Her book goes on to examine that time of life with searing honesty and courage, and the clarity of that symbolic use of twilight remains for the whole reading experience.

And now, to demonstrate the wild flexibility of twilight as an image, comes a complete tonal shift. As a teenager, I was gripped by repeats of the early '60s American cult series *The Twilight Zone*, created by Rod Serling. Here's the way each episode started, (cue spooky music and abstract smoky visuals on screen, followed after a second or two by this voiceover, delivered in a sonorous, authoritative American accent):

> There is a fifth dimension, beyond that which is known to man. It is a dimension which is as vast as space and as timeless as infinity. It is the middle ground between light and shadow, between science and superstition, and it lies between the pit of man's fears and the summit of his knowledge. This is the dimension of imagination. It is an area which we call *The Twilight Zone.*

(And the title starts to cohere onto the screen.) Mulling on this all over again, it really is a fantastic intro in the context of this book.

It's hardly a surprise that I became a betweenity geek. Having this seep into my subconscious once a week for however many series there were, over a period of impressionable years, was bound to skew my outlook on life.

The episodes themselves were a mash-up of SF, horror, the supernatural, and the inexplicable. It's a territory that every generation feels the need to explore for itself through the medium of TV. Later, there was a UK series, Roald Dahl's *Tales of the Unexpected*, which was more grounded in everyday reality than *The Twilight Zone* but still teased the viewer with indeterminate conclusions that were left open to interpretation. Later still came American series such as the landmark *Twin Peaks*, from David Lynch; closely followed by *The X Files*, with the FBI's Mulder and Scully investigating all manner of supernatural goings on; all the way up to the much more recent *Stranger Things*, featuring a dimension called The Upside Down, which is normally hidden from humanity, but which got opened following work in a secret scientific facility. Sometimes these series double down on the liminality, and there's a case in point with *The X Files*, because the lead characters are characterised from opposite temperamental sides of the twilight divide. In a neat reversal of orthodox expectations, Scully, the female, is the rationalist, a medical doctor by training, whilst the male character, Mulder, is a true believer in all things supernatural, meaning that the liminal space is not just the territory of the plot, but the emotional space between the characters.

No account like this can be considered complete without a mention of Stephanie Meyer's *Twilight* saga, and the huge film franchise it spawned. When thinking about the original novel that started it all off, I think about the cover art, with its held apple, and the quote from Genesis 2:17 that Meyer uses at the front of the book — 'But you must not eat from the tree of the knowledge of good and evil, for when you eat from it you will certainly die.' It's a powerful thought to leave suspended over a whole novel saga, with the entirety of all the books being acted out under the murky umbrella of that liminal idea.

Often, twilight is used by creatives not as an entire organising idea for a project, but just as a mechanism to make one point. Here's an example of what I mean, taken from a 2022 Norwegian novel by Lars Mytting called *The Reindeer Hunters*.[4] At the point of this short extract, set in the early seventeenth century, we are being introduced to two sisters, who are conjoined twins (the lack of a physical boundary between them is symbolically important too). Just prior to this extract, we are introduced to the sisters' routine daylight tasks, and the account of what they do is delivered in a straight, matter-of-fact tone. Then, with the introduction of twilight, we shift into a nebulous mood.

> The girls were taught the rarest methods of plant-dyeing, and then in the half-light they were shown — so it was said — weaves from pre-Christian times, pictures that depicted ancient Norse legends through mysterious symbols and the figures of shape-shifters and creatures that were half beast and half human.

Even the confidence of the narrative tone becomes more provisional at twilight ('so it was said') along with the symbolism and presence of chimeras.

All these books, films, and TV series play with the borderland between what we believe we know about the everyday and what is mysterious and elusive. Although *The Twilight Zone* was formative for me, this intoxicating, heady brew gets retold continually and never tires. One out-and-out gift for creatives that twilight confers as an image is the idea of having a foot in two camps. Daytime is unambiguous; nighttime is also well-defined (albeit that it brings its own liminality), but twilight is all about not being one thing or the other. It's a time of surprises, of transition, of potential transformation. And because, unlike dawn, twilight slips towards night rather than day, there is more potential threat: the ambiguity holds more jeopardy. Twilight gives us the opportunity to explore that transgressive space whilst we still have a foothold in the world of day. It's a version of that Romantic tease we considered earlier: the opportunity to almost surrender to the unknown whilst remaining on the cusp of what we know. It may be time to rewatch all the old episodes of *The Twilight Zone*...

2. Who's calling the shots?

Talk of *The Twilight Zone* puts me in the mood to keep the weirdness quotient notched up a level. And, in fact, when you start getting down and dirty in the borderlands, the weird stuff only gets weirder. And I do mean down. And I do mean dirty. For all that I see liminality pretty much everywhere, I'll confess that I'd missed what was underneath my feet — the soil.

It took an immersion in Merlin Sheldrake's *Entangled Life* to put that right and appreciate the obvious[5] — that the soil is poised between air and rock and is therefore a transitional zone all of its own, teeming with life, and critical for sustaining life on Earth. And within soil, it's fungi that live their lives in the cracks between other life forms, acting as communicators and facilitators, operating a massive infrastructure business underground, at a level that is all but invisible to us unless we know how to look.

Of especial interest in the context of noirish, *Twilight Zone*-y betweenity is the part of Sheldrake's book where he talks about hallucinogenic mushrooms, and the chemical psilocybin which is responsible for the effects they create. In terms of the discovery of shrooms' impact on humans, the assumption is that at some point in history, through natural curiosity and trial and error, people stumbled upon this quality of magic mushrooms, most likely in different locations at different times, and started to use them for their own ends. It feels such an obvious conclusion as to be barely worth making. But not so fast. Sheldrake uses a brilliant quote from the early twentieth-century philosopher A.N. Whitehead to overturn this orthodox viewpoint. (Remember that we've come across Whitehead before, as the author of *Process and Reality*. In this next quote, he was talking to the even more famous philosopher Bertrand Russell. I hope you appreciate the whiff of a dorveille vibe that we met earlier.) 'You think the world is what it looks like in fine weather at noon day. I think it is what it seems like in the early morning when one first wakes from deep sleep.' What Sheldrake is hinting at here is startling — the possibility that it's the fungi that are manipulating humans for their own ends, the kind of insight you'd only have if you see the world through the prism of that consciousness-slipping dream state when inversions of everyday reality take shape.

I know this sounds ridiculous, like some '50s B-movie nonsense (I'm thinking *When the Shiitake Hits the Fan*). But to a mycologist, in the context of the entangled lives of fungi, it's a reasonable speculation. After all, it's a matter of simple fact that certain fungi can — indeed, must — physically invade and take over the bodies of insects and get them to perform actions on plants that fungi can't do themselves. This is an evolved ability that is now critical to those fungi's survival. They are even known as zombie fungi (back to the B-movie theme). So, given that, it's by no means the most fantastical leap to imagine that fungi have taught humans how to get the hallucinogenic effect that many enjoy, and that they in turn derive a benefit from it. In this early-morning worldview, it's not humans using fungi; it's a transaction, a symbiotic relationship. It could even be that it's the fungi that are in control. As a theory, it's not without its challenges, but in the borderlands, the outlandish has a habit of asserting itself. It certainly appeals to me and took me right back to reading Kurt Vonnegut's *The Sirens of Titan* as a teenager,[6] an implausible science fiction romp, in which it turns out that the entirety of civilisation on Earth had been manipulated by a superior race in another galaxy in order to transfer a spare part to one of their spaceships.

3. In the forests of the night

> Woods have always been a place of inbetweenness, somewhere one might slip from one world to another, or one time to a former.
> — Robert MacFarlane, *The Wild Places*[7]

I want to talk about woods. I *have* to talk about woods. I *need* to talk about woods. No meditation on borderlands can ignore them. Robert MacFarlane's quote is once again acute — woods are classic liminal spaces, environments of suspension, where you just *feel* differently, where time has a conditional quality, where the air changes, where sounds carry in unusual ways, where your sense of location is disoriented, where the observational skills that support you around a cityscape desert you completely. Everyone has had the slightly frightening, slightly delicious sensation of being lost in a wood, all bearings misaligned, tracks that you assumed would take you back to your starting place mysteriously no longer there.

Although all natural features have potential symbolic power in storytelling, there is nothing to rival the mythic status of woods. If you need to add some dark magic to a fairy tale, reach for an enchanted forest. If you need a dog to discover an inadequately buried body in a contemporary thriller, a suburban wood will come in handy. Whatever the scenario, woodland always connotes something out of bounds — somewhere unpoliced, where the usual rules of civilisation don't apply — both familiar and strange at the same time, inhabited by owls, fairies, wolves, perhaps the odd lone sage or maverick who can handle the isolation and thrives in the ambivalent atmosphere. Growing up in Nottingham, you couldn't escape tales of Robin Hood, the heroic outlaw living in the greenwood in Sherwood Forest and coming on the occasional marauding trip into the city to defy the sheriff. Just look at a tiny sample of the roll call of fables, books, plays, TV, and films — *A Midsummer Night's Dream*; *As You Like It*; *Avatar*; *The Jungle Book*; *Twin Peaks*; *Little Red Riding Hood*; *Snow White*; *The Scarlet Letter*; *Beloved*; *The Lion, the Witch and the Wardrobe*; *The Lord of the Rings*; and on and on.

This symbolic role is so dominant that John Yorke, who we came across earlier in the Between Stories section, chose to call his landmark book about the structure of stories *Into the Woods*. He sets up the idea early in the introduction:

> In stories throughout the ages, there is one motif that continually recurs — the journey into the woods to find the dark but life-giving secret within. This book attempts to find what lurks at the heart of the forest.

As a setting or just a metaphor, there is nothing that says 'uncharted territory' more powerfully than a forest. Characters either literally or figuratively go 'into the woods'. We are so conditioned to this as viewers or readers that all it takes is a reference to woods, and our sense of alarm goes up a notch.

As Yorke says in passing, this role of woods and forests in stories is centuries old. Nicholas Jubber, in *The Fairy Tellers*,[8] a book that celebrates some of the great collectors of fairy tales through the centuries, takes a literal walk around the woods in hill towns near Naples to experience first-hand the landscape that inspired the first well-known anthologiser, Giambattista Basile. He sits among dappled branches to sit and read from *The Tale of Tales*, and has a similar explanation of the role of forests to the one that we've just read from John Yorke:

> The woods are where magic happens, and they dominate Giambattista's tales as much as the better-known German forest of the Brothers Grimm. In "The Flea", Porziella is dragged from her father's kingdom of "High Mountain" down into the forest, where "the rivers complained that when they flowed in the dark they tripped on stones, and the wild animals ... wandered safely through the thickets — in which no one ever entered unless he had lost his way."
>
> The poet's imagery for the forest switches between freedom and disorientation. You come to the forest to escape the hassles of court and town life — taxes, regulations, all the ways your life is knocked about by the powerful. But for heroes and heroines, a forest life is transient. It offers refuge

> until they can return to the court, to the castle, to prosperity and wedded bliss. Very few stories stage their happy-ever-after amongst the trees. Stay too long and you become a "man of the woods", an outcast ... a witch.

I'm especially drawn to this insight about the image switching. It's not enough that forests are a liminal space in their own right, but there is also a borderland within the borderland — you're in the woods, but is that a place of freedom from social constraint, or is it a place of uncomfortable loss of bearings? Or even, maybe it is both at the same time? Perhaps it's another case of 'be careful what you wish for'. That longed-for sense of liberation is great as a dream or aspiration, until you get it, and then you have no idea what to do with the freedom you've got.

Later, having examined other great fairy tellers, including the inevitable brothers Grimm and Hans Christian Andersen, Jubber returns to the theme of woods and forests. In fact, he realises he has very little choice, given that they are pretty much omnipresent in the tales he's been sifting through.

> When I started my first tentative steps on this trail, it felt as if the trees were too close together to show me the way. But slowly the light began to prise the trunks apart, and a path revealed itself, curling, occasionally forking, often narrowing, moving steadily towards the heart of the forest. And it was always a forest — whether the stories came from Italy or India, from the Ryazan region of Russia or the German Rhineland. For Somadeva, as for the Grimms, Giambattista Basile and Ivan Khudiakov, the forests are the places where characters are tested.

This same point again. Of course, a storyteller can test and transform their character in the context of their everyday life — and let's be clear, you can also come up with an equally stellar list of stories that do precisely that. But when the temptation to lob in an emotional intensifier to that testing is too great to resist, then it's amazing how often writers reach for a forest.

And the allure of forests continues. In recent years, Richard Powers's *The Overstory* has become a bestseller,[9] depicting forests in a somewhat different way to the usual trope. It features a set of characters who all appear to have stories that are disconnected from each other, until their narratives become entwined by trees. The opening story features the Hoel family, and an account of one of the ancestors of the family planting a chestnut sapling on their Iowa farmstead. The story of the different generations flies along at what feels like an absurd pace. As I started off doing that default thing that you automatically do as a seasoned reader — namely, identify with the first character you're introduced to — he was off the scene, dead, and replaced by his children. The same thing keeps happening. It's a disconcerting reading experience, until it dawns on you, very slowly in my case, that we are getting a chestnut tree's eye view of proceedings. In the time it takes the tree to get to something approaching maturity, three generations have come and gone. It's a skilful piece of show-not-tell scene setting and sets you up for the realisation that the real protagonists are the trees and forests, with a supporting role for those humans who understand their dignity and majesty within the wider ecosystem of life on Earth.

4. **To be shore, to be unsure**

If we need another iconic border in the natural world, we need look no further than towards beaches. Standing in the surf yields the liminal pleasure of transforming from land to water and back again. And then there is the transitory nature of beach materials — sand, pebbles, shells, seaweed, and flotsam and jetsam ejected by the tides.

The somewhat contradictory allure of the shoreline is captured with charm and poetry by Adam Nicolson in *Life Between the Tides*, a celebration of his lifelong fascination with rock pools.

> We still go to the seaside for consolation and simplicity. Demands and anxieties seem to drop away there; things still are as they were when we were ten. The rock pools still beckon, the gobies and blennies still shimmer beneath us. But there are ironies in choosing the shore as a theatre for reassurance. Even if its changes are dependable and rhythmic, it is thick with variability. A tidal coast is filled with that paradoxical quality: reliable unreliability, both closed and open-ended, both familiar and strange. Regularity toys with uncertainty there. Nothing is more predictable than the coming and going of the tide and yet nothing about it can be relied on: daily revelation and daily erasure, daily loss and daily reacquisition.

Exactly. I'm especially fond of the choice of an oxymoron there: 'reliable unreliability' is a quirky way to express that quality of beaches and shorelines that is part of the drama. The predictable rhythm and pure visual glamour of beach life is the draw, but they're not to be trusted. In one of his parables, Jesus talks about the foolish man who built his house upon the sand. There's no foundation of permanence here, and again we like that. It allows for something temporary, even transgressive — like the iconic adulterous kiss between Burt Lancaster and Deborah Kerr in the 1953 film *From Here to Eternity*. When the tide comes back in, all evidential trace that they were ever there will be washed away…

It's a theme that has been picked up again since, memorably in Alex Garland's 1996 cult classic *The Beach*.[10] Garland evokes the exotic allure of a hidden tropical beach paradise in Thailand, stumbled across by a British backpacker. The community that he finds there appears to be living an independent life of Edenic joy, fuelled by drugs. The beach creates the permissive backdrop in which this life is lived, and it's worth noting that, on occasion, Garland uses twilight as an intensifier of this liminal lifestyle: 'Red sky faded to deep blue, where a few bright stars already shone, and orange light threw elastic shadows down the beach.' But wait — perhaps there's something premonitory about the double use of classic liminal metaphors. Is all as it seems in paradise?

But in case we start to run away with the idea that beaches always symbolise some version of hedonism, they can also be used in entirely divergent ways. Ian McEwan's *On Chesil Beach* could hardly have a more different atmosphere hanging over it.[11] Set in a distinctly betweenish moment in recent history (1963, smartly in the middle of post-war austerity and the real start of the swinging '60s). The novella features a young married couple having their honeymoon in Dorset. Both are virgins on their (disastrous) wedding night, and both the book, and the subsequent film of the same name deal with the era's anguished attitudes to sexuality and the misery it unleashed on people trying to establish relationships in that atmosphere. Chesil Beach itself has a symbolic role. It's a 30 km-long, straight shingle beach that creates a lagoon on one side of it. One of the curious and famous aspects of the beach is the orderliness of its pebble size. If you know the beach intimately, it's said that you could know where you are on it if you had been blindfolded, simply by the pebble sizes underfoot. The couple in the book, Edward and Florence, had a plan to walk along the beach, 'to collect stones along the way and compare their sizes to see if storms really had brought order to the beach'. In the aftermath of their wedding night, this plan goes awry as they walk along the beach, which, with its lack of a sure footing, comes to represent disorder instead.

For my money, though, the jeopardy of the beach has never been bettered than by Kate Chopin in her 1899 masterpiece *The Awakening*,[12] the first feminist novel to make a true breakthrough in the United States. The main character, Edna Pontellier, is married to a successful businessman and has two sons. They take a vacation to a resort in the Gulf of Mexico. Once there, she meets and starts to fall in love with a younger man, Robert, who is the son of the woman who manages the resort. Edna is conflicted by her feelings for Robert and the duties she has as a wife and mother. It's not an accident that this all happens in a coastal resort, and throughout the book, both the sea and the beach reflect back at Edna the conflicting emotions that she is battling with. Read these short extracts. There is clear foreshadowing going on, and the intermingling of waves with snakes doesn't take a lot of interpretation.

> The sea was quiet now, and swelled lazily in broad billows that melted into one another and did not break except up on the beach in little foamy crests that coiled back like slow, white serpents.
>
> All along the white beach, up and down, there was no living thing in sight. A bird with a broken wing was beating the air above, reeling, fluttering, circling disabled down, down to the water.

...

> The foamy wavelets curled up to her white feet, and coiled like serpents about her ankles.

In 2021, I had the opportunity to explore this shoreline quality creatively in a collaborative project that was set up between a writers' group I belong to, called 26, and Bermondsey-based art dealership Eames Fine Art. Writers were paired at random with printmakers, and each pair was tasked with finding a common place (the name of the project) and creating a written piece and a print that brought out elements of the shared place of importance. The place could be specific, or a type of place, or somewhere mythic. I was paired with the Midlands-based printmaker Jason Hicklin, and, in conversation, the two of us quickly realised that it was beaches and shorelines that represented our common place. Jason had recently completed a set of walks and sketches of Porthmeor, near St Ives in Cornwall, and had this location in mind when we started discussing the collaboration. For my part, I already had my head in borderlands, and had been thinking about beaches as part of that. Jason tends to work in monochrome, and when he shared his first early draft of his Porthmeor prints, I was struck by how twilightish his skies looked. The possibility of doubling down on liminality, by trying to capture both the physical space, and the time of day, seemed too good to pass up.

Below is a reproduction of Jason's magnificent, brooding print, and below that, my written response to it. I make no claims to poetic skill, but what I was — and continue to be — drawn to in the conjunction of this time of day with this piece of landscape is the potential for an unmooring from the familiar, the everyday, and the expected, towards the contingent, slipping, ephemeral possibilities that arise briefly when these different fiefdoms jostle and negotiate with each other. You might remember samdhya, from much earlier in the book, as being the Sanskrit word for twilight.

Samdhya

This is rare thrill.

To watch this sky
cleave light and dark —
the eternal skirmish
that always goes to night.

Meanwhile feet are
sucked, pulled down,
mould and moulded
by sly sand.

Incoming fresh wave
a fizz of whites and greys
full of belief, but,
surprised by land,
retreats.

I am the twilight beach,
slipping between
implacable rock,
insistent sea.

Being that border.

5. **Full fathom five — the sea**

To state the obvious, people are creatures of the land. The sea is not our domain; we are not designed for it. We can spend some time *on* the sea or *at* sea, but without living there permanently. Unless we are in a submarine, we cannot spend any meaningful time *in* the sea, even with breathing apparatus. It means that whenever we are, at or on the sea, it's a provisional space. It nearly always represents a journey for us. Even if you're a trawlerman, it's a journey out and a journey back. In the context of this book, the significance is that any sea voyage, however long, is always spent between times on land.

Throughout our history as a species, the sea has held us in its spell. It has mythic power, symbolic power, and at a very literal level, it holds threat and peril. It's evident in the nautical metaphors that we use. The sea gives space to our unconscious, by releasing us from the solid ground that holds us in check. We talk of being 'unmoored', a direct lift from the nautical action of casting off from dry land, and being 'all at sea', or 'sailing close to the wind', 'giving a wide berth'. These are all phrases of disturbance or uncertainty, expressing the way that the sea impacts on feelings of loss of control, or unease. What we don't have are lots of nautical metaphors or phrases of certainty. When we want to imply that, we reach for *terra firma* — we talk of 'being grounded' or 'feeling rooted'.

The sea, then, is awesome for its volatility, its scale, its dynamism. Think of the incredible motion of waves, brilliantly caught in Japanese master Hokusai's work in the nineteenth century and more recently by British artist Maggi Hambling. Then there is that elusive, ethereal quality of light at sea, of which J.M.W. Turner was pre-eminent at representing. And then in literature, it's often the significance of journeying, questing, and the transformational power of the sea. For centuries, of course, sea journeys were the only alternative to walking or travelling by horse, and so it's no surprise that the roll call of many all-time classic works involve the sea as a central motif, but even recently it's true. Think of Yann Martel's 2001 Booker Prize-winning *Life of Pi*,[13] in which the central third of the book involves a 9-month voyage adrift on a lifeboat which Pi shares with a Bengal tiger. It's a scenario that takes some suspension of disbelief, but less than if the same pair were sharing a road trip in a Volvo, because with a sea voyage, it's implicit that we are talking about a setting for the unlikely.

But to return to those classics, we have Homer's *The Odyssey*, Shakespeare's *The Tempest*, and Herman Melville's *Moby-Dick*, but we could look at hundreds of others. None of those would exist without the sea. In *The Odyssey*, the key liminal theme is one of testing, rather like those initiation rites that we encountered earlier. The sea is the perfect proving ground for the testing ordained by the gods, with peril at every turn, including Odysseus losing nearly all his ships along the way.

And with *The Tempest*, it's worth remembering that Shakespeare was still writing at a time of maritime adventure but also tragedy — many lost their lives in the pursuit of gain, and the bottom of the sea is the depository of both, demonstrated with the beginning of Ariel's song:

> Full fathom five thy father lies;
> Of his bones are coral made;
> Those are pearls that were his eyes:
> Nothing of him that doth fade,
> But doth suffer a sea-change
> Into something rich and strange.

Note the way that the drowned man is transformed by coral and pearl in its 'sea-change' — quite the transition. The pursuit of riches and the means of failure are fused into one thing.

These writers understood that whereas we are at home on solid ground, the sea offers rolling fluidity. To humans, it's profoundly other, representing what we're not — it's where we confront our opposites. In the classic story architecture, the hero's need or desire is embodied in the antihero, and if that can be represented by an environment of otherness, so much the better. Step forward *Moby-Dick*,[14] and the demonic quest of Captain Ahab to extract revenge on the great white whale that took his leg on a previous voyage. *Moby-Dick* must be a contender for being *the* great novel of the sea. Like for Shakespeare and Homer, the sea for Melville can be a roiling, dangerous place. It's unknowable, unfathomable in every sense. This quality of being at the edge of our consciousness, of what we can control and be sure of, is the key point. Here is a long quote from it, but it makes the point about the sea as a space that defies human reason, certainty and command, and its extreme contrast to life on land, to what we know and what can be known.

> Consider the subtleness of the sea; how its most dreaded creatures glide under water, unapparent for the most part, and treacherously hidden beneath the loveliest tints of azure. Consider also the devilish brilliance and beauty of many of its most remorseless tribes, as the dainty embellished shape of many species of sharks. Consider, once more, the universal cannibalism of the sea; all whose creatures prey upon each other, carrying on eternal war since the world began.
>
> Consider all this; and then turn to the green, gentle, and most docile earth; consider them both, the sea and the land; and do you not find a strange analogy to something in yourself? For as this appalling ocean surrounds the verdant land, so in the soul of man there lies one insular Tahiti, full of peace and joy, but encompassed by all the horrors of the half-known life. God keep thee! Push not off from that isle, thou canst never return.

It is interesting to move sharply back into our own era and notice that the tone of the way that writers embrace the sea is different. Compared to the times of Melville, Shakespeare, Homer et al., there is on balance less jeopardy associated with sea travel, so the language that surrounds it is less apocalyptic. But what we have a lot more of is the governance of seas, as we saw vividly in the section on UNCLOS. Writers will still see seas as symbolic liminal spaces for personal reflection, but also as reflective of relationships with other cultures, other nations. I'm reminded of the way that the distance between the UK and the USA is often minimised by the Atlantic being nicknamed The Pond. If you think that's a one-off, then think again — Australia and New Zealand are separated by a four-hour plane flight but refer to the Tasman Sea as The Ditch.

I instinctively like both of these — it's around seeing seas and oceans as lines of connection, rather than separation.

Not long after Jan Carson's *Sea Borders* was broadcast on the BBC (from which this book's first quote derives), they put out another half-hour reflection on a slightly similar theme, this time considering the role of the Irish Sea as a membrane between Northern Ireland and Great Britain. Called *A Line in the Water*,[15] Neil McCarthy, an audio documentary maker, also uses a ferry, this time the one that sails daily between Birkenhead and Belfast, to explore the idea of a sea border. Brexit provided a political backdrop, given the fact that by this point the Northern Ireland Protocol had come into force, and thereby effectively enacted a highly charged political sea border somewhere down the middle of the Irish Sea. The whole piece is suffused with this uneasy invisible line: it's hard not to read something into the title being deliberately 'in' the water, not 'on' the water. There's a buried, elusive quality to this border, despite it being so recently conceived. During the course of his ferry crossings, he speaks to a variety of passengers that he happens to meet. Not once does he stumble across anyone who likes the border. Although in theory the Irish Sea can be seen as a division or barrier, overwhelmingly, for McCarthy's passengers at least, it's seen as a channel of communication, a connection. And therefore this new sea border runs contrary to the spirit that they feel exists between Britain and the island of Ireland, let alone adding economic and political complexity to a context that is fraught enough as it is. His final observation is this:

> The Irish Sea seems to be a body of water that brings people closer together and the very idea of having a border down it … I haven't met a single person who thinks that's a good idea. It's always been a connection between the two islands, Ireland and Britain. And it still is.

One of the most arresting insights to emerge from the piece, for me, is the notion that sea borders are just plain unintuitive, which we also saw earlier in Mike Parker's quote from *All the Wide Border*. There are many land borders that are contentious, emotional, disputed. But at least land is solid; we can choose to literally mark the land with fences, posts, signs, deploy all our physical apparatus of boundary making and nation building to shore them up. Or we can put the borders in places that make some natural sense — along rivers for instance. But a sea border has none of that. At an intuitive level, it feels like a border, if it's anything, is a land thing, not a sea thing. A bit like the Melville quote, seas belong to another emotional kingdom. For all that we know we need to do things like defend fish stocks through treaties that respect territorial waters, it still doesn't sit right. The clunkiness of UNCLOS is a demonstration of that. In the same way that Carson was teased by the intangibility of the line in the sea that divides Northern Ireland from Scotland, this new sea border's lack of physicality is as untrustworthy as the politicians that created it. As one of the people McCarthy meets ironically puts it, 'I think because of the waves, it moves a wee bit.'

But like all the other arbitrary borders that arise from nowhere to create separation, this sea border, created for expedient economic reasons, is up against the weight of history. The piece is cut through by a poem by Mark Ward, called 'Meridians', and it ends with a stirring question that brings the whole documentary to a conclusion.

> The sea that holds our shared past will define our future.
> History, friendship and family connections.
> The general toing and froing.
> And what cartographer can draw that line?

What cartographer indeed?

6. **Our revels now are ended**

Mark Ward's lines touch me in a soulful way. Earlier on, we looked at the dispiriting way that people are being increasingly pushed into tribal identities through polarising forces. It goes without saying that we're social animals, and we have a deep need to belong to our herd. It's one of the reasons we have borders at all. But if we are to have borders, then just as much we need to have our borderlands — spaces that are shared and communally owned, where we are enriched by difference and connection. It is for this reason that I wanted to end the book with seas. A central argument throughout has been that the ability to embrace borderland states, rather than feel threatened by them, is a skill that is right for our times. And if we're collectively not that good at it, then perhaps it's not too far-fetched to sense a correlation to the fact that few of us these days spend much of our time on ships. As people, we're having less of that experience of being held by water and allowing it to influence us by its intimate fluidity. We started the book with a quote from Jan Carson's *Sea Borders*, and I want to return to her at the end. She has an excellent take on this. In a second quote from her piece, she reflects on the way in which writers often need to find peace with existing in the middle of ambiguity, and that being on water captures that state of being exactly.

> As artists — the process of writing — we're very used to that kind of liminal space where you're uncertain and you're dealing with unknowns and you're trying to frame sense inside a big muddle. Usually… I find it really creative… The tide goes out, the tide returns. One land whispers to the other, and this is where my voice comes from.

As for writers, so for the rest of us. The borderlands — the spaces between — have an invitation to us if we want to accept it. They are many things: a playground; a place of respite and reflection; a wellspring of creativity; an empathy park, offering the opportunity to share and heal; an environment for exploring difference; a celebration of transition; a collaboration zone; a seedbed of abundance; a junction for making connections and discoveries; an incubator for insight and inspiration; a proving ground; a realm of magic and imagination; a space for exploring doubt, ambiguity, and uncertainty; a crossroads for decision-making; a meeting place for communion and exchange.

Above all, the spaces between exist in time, and that time is now. The borderlands are a present, in the sense of a gift, but also in the sense of a time to inhabit, and that time being this moment. To paraphrase Prospero from *The Tempest*, the revels of this book may be ended, but I hope that your betweenish revels are only just beginning.

AT THE BACK DOOR

When sharing this project with people, I've often been asked where my interest in the borderlands came from. It's not a question I've had to ask myself, because I've known the answer to it for a long time, and I'd like to close by sharing the story. For one thing, each person's borderland geography is unique to them, but offering a case study of my own may spark thoughts about your own spaces between.

In an echo of the way this book starts, I'm going to begin my own personal relationship to betweenism with a word. It happens to be my favourite word and has been ever since I stumbled across it in a book of underappreciated words about 25 years ago. The word is 'velleity', and very late in the day it occurred to me that there's a satisfying synthesis between velleity and my interest in all things liminal, which makes it feel like a decent place to start.

What it is? Velleity is a noun that is defined as the lowest form of volition. It's when you would sincerely *like* to do a thing, but not quite so much as to go out and *do* that thing, or even put in place the necessary steps. If you feel that way, then you can say that you have a velleity to do something. It's something you possess, a weak desire. It's a slight inclination, although not in the Leaning Tower of Pisa sense. I love the dictionary.com definition the best: 'A mere wish, unaccompanied by an effort to obtain it.' Utterly delightful. (I should call myself out really, shouldn't I? What I mean by saying that

I like the dictionary.com definition best is that I have the intention to go downstairs and check it in Chambers and OUP, but not quite so much as to go and do it.) Surprisingly, someone has gone to the effort of creating the adjectival form, which feels unnecessarily consequent. You can be a velletious person, if you are prone to episodes of velleity. I don't know if it's an extraordinarily knowing joke, but the normally exhaustive etymonline website suddenly gets very terse about velleity, as if it can't quite drum up the enthusiasm to give you the detail you crave. It just says, '1610s, from Medieval Latin stem of *velleitas* (from Latin *velle* "to wish, will.")' That's your lot, along with an apologetic Google Ngram that shows a strange, fluctuating pattern of 'popularity' for this scandalously unknown word. For the record, it seems to have been in a very gentle upswing since 1980, but the incidence is so low that it may only take a handful of fanatics like me to increase awareness of it. There is, though, a fabulous, somewhat obscure disclaimer at the bottom of the graph that reads, 'Ngrams are probably unreliable,' which makes me like them a lot more. It's a disclaimer that feels more bizarre the longer you think about it — 'The popularity of words can go down as well as up.'

Whenever I share velleity with people, they invariably say a version of 'I feel very seen,' or 'But that describes me completely. How come this word isn't better known?' To which I'm prone to saying something like, 'Velleity would, of course, like to be more famous, but just can't put in the necessary hard yards to get higher up search engine optimisation…' I confess that I did briefly own the domain name for velleity.com. I was initially surprised that it was available, before realising that, well of course it hadn't been taken, and then I felt guilty that I had transgressed by doing something so active. I discreetly allowed my ownership to lapse. I must get round to seeing if it's still available…

But I digress, because it's now dawned on me that the positivity people tend to feel for velleity (including me) has a lot to do with its betweenish quality. It sits in a connecting space that has fierce kick-starter intention on one side, and bone idleness on the other.

Both are strong, powerful phenomena in their own way, but they lack a bridging thought. Velleity is that bridge, the modest enabler of a respectable, gentle motivation that can be quietly put off without ever being discarded. It means that your intention can sit in a liminal space all of its own, rather like the idea of writing this book did for about 6 years, before velleity eventually had to be put to one side.

* * *

I have to say, for a book that's all about flux and flow, the finality of an ending is a complex thing. At a certain stage in the writing, my eldest son, James, asked me whether I had an ending for it, and I confessed to him that, at that point, I had quite a few ideas to finish it with. As an excellent storyteller himself, and very much in the spirit of John Yorke's 'journey there, journey back', he asked, 'Do any of them end where you started? The honest answer then was no, but he helped to crystallise something I was dimly aware of — that I had unfinished business with the first border that I'd grown up with.

I do accept that this isn't great news for you. Having stayed the course throughout this, you are entitled to a fantastic payoff — such as me going over Niagara Falls in a barrel, to experience the full drama of one of the world's great border sights; or sailing along the Danube, to take in the river that creates a natural border between four different sets of nations. I can only apologise, but one aspect of borders that I've come to realise with greater force through this odyssey is that you ultimately have to make your peace with the ones that most define you, and as anti-climactic as that may be for you, for me that means the Nottinghamshire–Derbyshire border just outside Long Eaton, which is on the Derbyshire side.

As a boy, I grew up 1.3 miles from that border, on the Nottinghamshire side. But what this adjacency did *not* do was to give me joint sympathies to both counties. I was fiercely

Nottinghamshire and have remained that way. It's not something that can easily be rationalised. But it can be explored. When I was young and still at home, I would cross over this border only occasionally, but when I did, it made some kind of emotional impact. In that era, local football rivalries were starting to intensify, and Derby County and Nottingham Forest had both had meaningful success for the first time in either of their histories, in both cases thanks to the mercurial management of Brian Clough. It created a powerful sense of tribalism, which older people told me had not existed before. Derbyshire, and Derby in particular, suddenly had an enemy status, and this border symbolised it. They were resolutely not-Nottingham, in the classic otherness sense of negatively defining your tribe that we've already seen. (In a rather excellent nod to healing the uncomfortable borderlands opened up by football rivalry, the two cities have renamed the A52 that connects them The Brian Clough Way. Classy.) Several years later, my mother moved to Long Eaton (what? How could she?), and I then often had to make this curiously unpatrolled border crossing while she was still alive.

In addition to the highly specific border that forged my sense of identity, there was also the wider regional aspect. Although memory's a tricky beast, I'm certain that I did have a distinct sense of living in the Midlands, and that at its most literal, it meant that you were neither north nor south but in a middle zone. My confidence is based on memories of car journeys we sometimes made a little bit further north. You didn't have to go very far before you were seeing colliery winding gear and lots of industrial architecture that was quite different industrial architecture from anything we ever saw in Nottingham, but in spirit very much like the reproduction Lowry picture of the grim industrial northern cityscape that our mum had up on our dining room wall.

Every now and again, some indication of what it might mean to be a Midlander would occur. For instance, at the age of 10, in my last year of junior school, our then form teacher, the redoubtable Mr Brown — a man with such vast eyebrows that it looked like an entirely independent lifeform had taken root on the upper reaches of his craggy yet benign face — told our class that because we lived right by the river Trent, we existed at the point that divided the country in its pronunciation of the word 'scone'. According to him, north of the Trent it rhymed with gone, and below the Trent it rhymed with stone. I loved this. He asked for a show of hands regarding how we all pronounced it. I can't remember the specific split now, but I do recall that it was a genuine division, which, to my 10-year-old mind, was proof of Mr Brown's assertion, because you'd expect people that lived in the middle to be divided in their pronunciation. How exciting! (You took your excitement where you could in those days.)

The point is, I've carried this scone belief around with me my whole adult life: it's been one of those crumbs of knowledge that (normally) sits in my subconscious and contributes in a minute way to my sense of identity. To me, being a Midlander is bound up with notions of seeing both points of view, existing without sharp definitions and absolute clarity of opinion. I mean, hey! We don't even take sides on contentious matters like the pronunciation of baked goods.

Therefore, imagine my consternation when, through the gift of the internet, I discovered that Mr Brown's factoid about scone (or scone, if you prefer) pronunciation was in large part incorrect. When, in my role as your intrepid scone researcher, the time came to fact check this, I came across an actual scone pronunciation map, as you can see below (sometimes the internet is simply miraculous. It leaves no scone unturned). And it turns out that in fact we were living towards the southern tip of the only substantially sized part of the UK where a dominant number of people rhyme scone with cone. I'm a 'gone' man, for the record. There is a slight balance of 'cone' rhymers in the London area, and in Cornwall, who we must concede know a thing or two about these controversial confections.

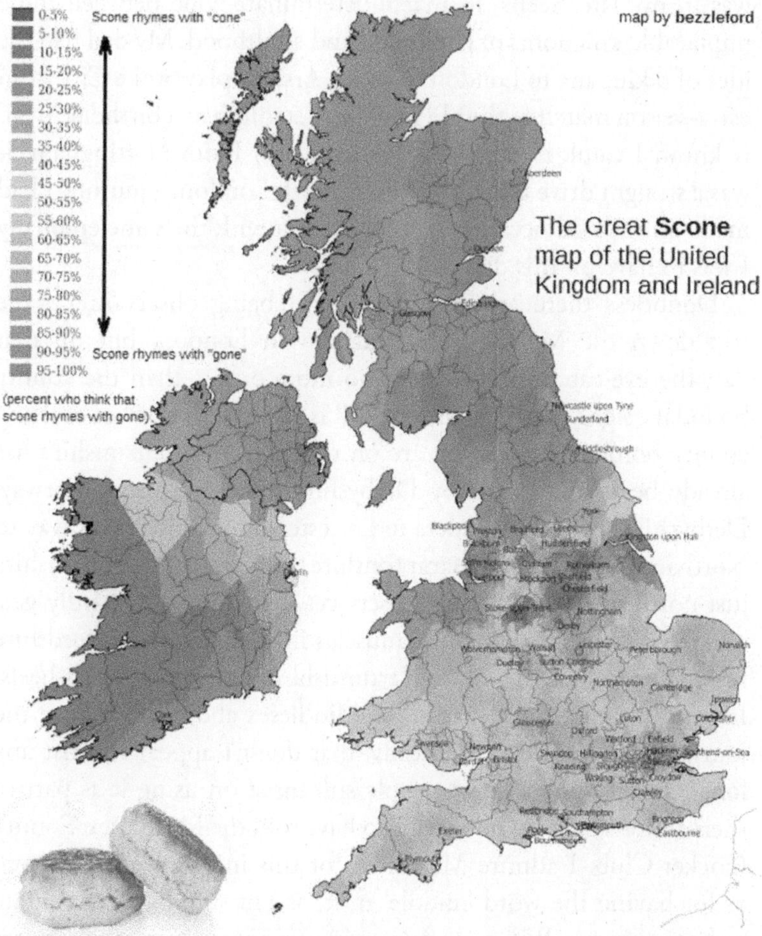

In the light of this new evidence, I've had to let go of my prior position as some kind of unofficial border guard of national scone pronunciation, but the information came too late to change the affirmation that Mr Brown's revelation gave me about my position as a Midlander.

Dial forward a few years, and I can still recall the first time that borders properly took hold of my imagination. The details are hazy, but this much is clear: it was around the time of my birthday. I was in my later teens, in that indeterminate zone between those implacable kingdoms of childhood and adulthood. My dad had the idea of taking me to London to watch Arsenal play Stoke City in an early season match at the old Highbury stadium as a birthday 'treat' (I know. I think it was 0-0. Thanks, Dad.) From Nottingham, it was a straight drive down the M1 to north London, a journey I had made on the odd occasion before, but not with the same epiphany I was to have on this day.

Doubtless there are infinite ways of being observant on the trip down the M1 from Nottingham to London, but on that day, the eye-catching thing was no more or less than the county boundary signs. It was then, and still is today, a journey of crossing county borders. Before you are on the M1, Nottinghamshire has already been supplanted by Derbyshire. Once on the motorway, Derbyshire swiftly surrenders to Leicestershire, which gives way to Northamptonshire. Northamptonshire turns into Buckinghamshire just north of Newport Pagnell services, which in turn hardly gets a look in before Bedfordshire muscles in. But before Bedfordshire has its feet under the table, Hertfordshire is snapping at its heels. In former times, there used to be Middlesex about this part of the journey, but as discussed already, that doesn't appear to exist any longer, even though some people still insist on using it as part of their address, and no one seems to have told the Middlesex County Cricket Club. I admire Middlesex for this indeterminacy, as well as for having the word 'middle' in it, as I'm sure by now you are only too aware. But nowadays, without any notice at all, you're into Greater London, which may or may not be a county or even a correct name for anything.

In any case, the teenage me, for reasons of aforementioned local football enmity, being keen to leave Derbyshire, looked out for the approaching Leicestershire sign. As it came, I could see the back of the equivalent Derbyshire sign on the other carriageway, and I noticed with a mild shock that there was something of a gap. They weren't literally at the same point. It took a second or two of driving, at Dad's mildly daring 75 mph, to traverse the gap between the two signs. What was going on here? Where were we in that moment? If we thought we'd crossed into Leicestershire, but cars in the opposite direction 100 m away thought they'd crossed into Derbyshire, we couldn't both be right. Or could we?

My interest was piqued. Sure enough, the same phenomenon happened at the Northamptonshire 'border', and again at the other borders down the motorway. I was thrilled by these moments (I realise these 'thrills' aren't the best look, but hey). For about a dozen or so seconds of the entire journey, I appeared to be in no county, but between two of them, a conditional, fleeting space. It's a space I've enjoyed occupying ever since, at any opportunity.

But I was to learn that not everyone does. A few years after that experience, I was working in my first job after graduating. I'd had 3 years living in Norwich, studying at the University of East Anglia, and landed a job as a bookseller in the same campus bookshop I'd been a customer at while being a student. The team that worked there were a mixture of people from elsewhere who had moved to Norwich along with local people, born and bred in Norfolk. Amongst this second group was one woman, named Sandra, whose father worked in some agricultural capacity. He lived right in the middle of Norfolk, which is a pretty big place as English counties go, being the fourth largest. Once a year, as Sandra told the story, her father had to go to an agricultural show in King's Lynn, which, whilst still firmly in Norfolk, was a mere 10 km along the A17 from the Lincolnshire border. However, this was far too close for her dad's comfort. He'd never left Norfolk in his life, had no plans to, and this was as close to leaving as he ever got. In the run up to the annual visit, he had to take tranquillisers to get him through the ordeal.

I heard a similar story from a local Norwich friend a little while after this. In this case, it was my friend's mum, with a similar lifelong residence in Norfolk, who had suddenly had the urge to visit London. David duly set off to drive her down, but they never made it. She had to ask him to turn the car round and come back home. They'd managed to get all the way through Suffolk and into Essex, but that was as far as they got.

Both of these stories stayed with me — long before I started thinking of this book, but after I'd already become interested in the notion of identity and how borders contribute to it, especially when, in truth, most county borders in the UK are not objectively that significant. And yet, for individuals, they can be. It's too easy to have a comedic side-swipe at people from Norfolk — I've done it myself — but what it does have is a powerful sense of place. It exerts a pull on its people, and that counts for something. As someone who feels the same gravitational pull about Nottinghamshire, I've got nothing but fondness for the stories of Sandra's dad and David's mum.

I'm thinking back to those parts of my border backstory now, as I stand between the Nottinghamshire–Derbyshire border signs on the outskirts of Long Eaton. As with those county borders I noticed on the drive to London with Dad, there is a gap between the two county border signs on opposite sides of the A6005. This time, because I'm not driving past, I've got the time and opportunity to examine the signs. Along with the county logo, the Nottinghamshire sign says, 'Welcome to Nottinghamshire' and then underneath, 'Robin Hood's County'. As if to underscore this reference to the legend of Sherwood Forest, a tree has started to grow at the bottom of the sign and curls its way up the post, partially obscuring the sign. The Derbyshire sign, on the other side of the road, has the county name in green capital letters, with the historic heraldic symbol of the county on top of it. Underneath, a separate sign asks you to 'Please watch your speed.' Not to be outdone by the Nottinghamshire sign's tree, the Derbyshire sign is starting to get overwhelmed by nettles and brambles and has ironically been hit by something off to the left-hand side that wasn't watching its speed, because the metal is damaged and scuffed, and that post is skewwhiff, leaning back into the vegetation. It takes about a dozen paces to walk between the two signs. The gap is filled by a flat bridge that motorists wouldn't notice, and in fact I'd never realised it was there before either, but it takes you over the top of the modest river Erewash. In mid-September, in a burst of hot weather, the view south-east from the bridge's brick wall is charming and unexpected. The river is busy, flowing away from me in swirling eddies downstream, hemmed in by trees, trembling in full leaf and almost touching each other across the stream of water. Overhead, a pair of common terns make their way to their colony on Clifton Pond, one of many stretches of water in the former gravel pits of the nearby Attenborough Nature Reserve, where the Erewash ends its journey, just short of the River Trent. Behind me, the traffic noise on the road is incessant, with cars, buses, and vans going in both directions the whole time. But that's fine. Nature and machinery are connected through motion. As Heraclitus said: 'Everything flows, and nothing remains still.'

Apart from me. Here I stand, motionless, in my own very first liminal space, my own primal, boyhood borderland. The me that likes all this flux, ambiguity, shifting sands, insert indeterminate metaphor of choice. A rare pedestrian gives me a curious look — it's not a place you'd expect to find someone standing still. My hunch is that he and all the other cyclists and motorists are too familiar with the border signs to register anything at all when and if they see them, and the occasional visitor that's passing through will give them no more than a casual glance.

While stood here, I'm also thinking about an article I read a couple of days previously in the online version of the Nottingham Post, which was about the affiliation that people feel who live in Long Eaton. It started in an interesting way: 'For those who live close to county borders, picking a shire can sometimes be a bit of a problem. While many border towns fall neatly into one or the other, some are a little more blurred.' *Hello*, I thought. *This is interesting — my kind of article*. The point it went on to make is that Long Eaton is technically in Derbyshire but has a Nottingham postcode, and falls far more into the gravitational field of Nottingham than Derby. Therefore, a few locals were interviewed to get their perspective, and inevitably there were views expressing both sides of the debate (I realise the word 'debate' may be over-egging the pudding here…), along with those who thought it was half and half. But I was most caught by one interviewee that started by saying 'That's a hard one, because sometimes I think I'm just here.'

Well said, because that really is the entire point. I'll have to leave here before long, rejoin the flow of life. But for now, I'm just here too. Between the two border signs but allowing the feeling of the border to melt away, dissolve. Enjoying the satisfaction of the border being a literal bridge, another fine liminal metaphor, if another one was needed. Reflecting on having, just before this, visited our mother's grave a couple of miles away. She was a great fan of T.S. Eliot, and we had a line from 'East Coker' in *Four Quartets* engraved onto her headstone — 'In the darkness shall be the light, and in the dancing the stillness.' I'm thinking about the way in which everything contains its opposite, including so many of these themes that have captured my imagination: heroes and antiheroes, truth and lies, rival countries and cities, the past and the future, and so on. I'm also delivering a gentle note to self that should have occurred to me before, but which bubbles up as I look down on this beguiling, flowing river border. Rather than standing on one side of a partisan divide, with the apparent security of having your tribe behind and alongside you, the better, ultimately richer, and more fulfilling place to be is between.

NOTES

On the Threshold

1. Jan Carson, *Sea Borders*, Jan Carson. https://www.bbc.co.uk/programmes/m0003cm6

Words

1. Percival Everett, *The Trees*, Influx Press, 2022
2. Roland Schimmelpfennig, *Liminal*, Maclehose Press, 2023. Many thanks to Alix Berber, co-founder of *The Liminal Review*, for pointing out to me that the translator of this book has made an interesting decision in the English version of the title. The accurate translation from the German title would be 'The Line Between Day and Night'. In fairness, it's just possible I may not have picked the book up with that title, so it does show you something about the significance of titles…
3. Open Spaces Society, https://www.oss.org.uk/
4. Frederick Jackson Turner, *The Significance of the Frontier in American History*, 1893
5. Jaroslav Dokoupil & Tomas Havlicek, 'Border and border region, theoretical aspects, identification and determination' in *Acta Universitatis Carolinae: Geographica*, 2002
6. Adam Nicolson, *Life Between the Tides*, William Collins, 2021

Being Between — Liminality

1. Arnold Van Gennep, *Les Rites de Passage*, 1909
2. James Crawford, *The Edge of the Plain*, Canongate, 2022
3. https://ich.unesco.org/en/USL/enkipaata-eunoto-and-olng-esherr-three-male-rites-of-passage-of-the-maasai-community-01390
4. https://maasai-association.org/ceremonies.html
5. Dimitris Xygalatas, *Ritual: How Seemingly Senseless Acts Make Life Worth Living*, Profile Books, 2022
6. Tim Robinson, *Stones of Aran: Pilgrimage*, New York Review of Books, 1986

Between Ideas

1. Heraclitus, *Fragments*, translated by Brooks Haxton, Penguin Books, 2001
2. William James, *Pragmatism and other writings*, Penguin Books, 2000
3. William James, *Essays in Radical Empiricism*, University of Nebraska Press, 1996
4. Michael Foley, *Life Lessons from Bergson*, Pan Macmillan, 2013
5. A.N. Whitehead, *Process and Reality*, Simon & Schuster, 1979
6. Ferdinand de Saussure, *Course in General Linguistics*, translated by Roy Harris, Bloomsbury, 2013
7. Iain McGilchrist, *The Matter with Things*, Perpetua, 2021
8. Carlo Rovelli, *Helgoland*, Allen Lane, 2021
9. David Spiegelhalter, *The Art of Uncertainty*, Pelican, 2024

The Betweens of You

1. David Bodanis, *Einstein's Greatest Mistake*, Little Brown, 2016
2. Anil Seth, *Being You*, Faber & Faber, 2021

3. Douglas R. Hofstadter, *Gödel, Escher, Bach: An Eternal Golden Braid*, Harvester Press, 1979
4. Henry David Thoreau, *Walden*, 1854
5. John Kaag and Clancy Martin, 'At Walden, Thoreau wasn't really alone with nature', *New York Times*, 10 July 2017
6. John Banville, *Eclipse*, Picador, 2000

Between Times

1. Daniel Kahnemann, *Thinking, Fast and Slow*, Farrar, Straus and Giroux, 2011
2. L.P. Hartley, *The Go-Between*, Hamish Hamilton, 1953
3. Ted Gioia, *Music: A Subversive History*, Basic Books, 2019
4. Gabriel Garcia Marquez, *One Hundred Years of Solitude*, Jonathan Cape, 1970
5. Colson Whitehead, *Harlem Shuffle*, Doubleday, 2021
6. A. Roger Ekirch, *At Day's Close: Night in Times Past*, W.W. Norton, 2005
7. Robert Moss, *The Secret History of Dreaming*, New World Library, 2014
8. George Szirtes, *Reel*, Bloodaxe, 2004

Between People

1. Rob Poynton, *Do/Improvise*, Do Books, 2013
2. Ian MacDonald, *Revolution in the Head*, Fourth Estate, 1994
3. Keith Johnstone, *Impro*, Faber & Faber, 1979
4. Robert Feldman, *The Liar in Your Life*, Twelve, 2009
5. Schweizer and Levine, 'Are liars ethical? On the tension between benevolence and honesty'. Research paper, Wharton, University of Pennsylvania, 2014
6. https://www.bbc.co.uk/news/uk-politics-56624437
7. Gordon Kerr, *A Short History of Coffee,* Oldcastle Books, 2021
8. Maria Konnikova, *The Confidence Game*, Canongate, 2016

9. Ezra Klein, *Why We're Polarized*, Profile Books, 2020
10. https://jamesclear.com/why-facts-dont-change-minds

Between Stories

1. John Yorke, *Into the Woods*, Penguin Books, 2012
2. Irene Vallejo, *Papyrus*, Hodder, 2022
3. Bruce Chatwin, *In Patagonia*, Jonathan Cape, 1977
4. Tim Prentki, *Applied Theatre Reader*, Routledge, 2009
5. Ali Smith, *Spring*, Hamish Hamilton, 2019
6. Mike Parker, *All the Wide Border*, Harper North, 2023
7. Italo Calvino, *If on a Winter's Night a Traveller*, Secker & Warburg, 1981
8. Laurence Sterne, *Tristram Shandy*, 1759–1767
9. Peter Brooks, *Seduced by Story*, New York Review of Books, 2022

Between Places

1. Derek Mahon, *The Hunt by Night*, Oxford University Press, 1982
2. Benedict Anderson, *Imagined Communities*, Verso, 1983
3. Paul Kennedy, *The Rise and Fall of Great Powers*, Unwin Hyman, 1988
4. Lewis Baston, *Borderlines: A History of Europe Told from the Edges*, Hodder Press, 2024
5. Jussi Laine, 'Threats, Challenges, and Finnish–Russian Cross Border Security Co-operation: A Finnish Perspective', ResearchGate, 2015
6. Ben McIntyre, *The Spy and the Traitor*, Viking, 2018
7. Tom Chivers, *London Clay*, Penguin Books, 2021
8. Paul Farley and Michael Symmons Roberts, *Edgelands*, Jonathan Cape, 2011

The Betweens of Nature

1. Robert MacFarlane, *The Old Ways*, Hamish Hamilton, 2012
2. Beatrice Forshall, *The Book of Vanishing Species*, Bloomsbury, 2022
3. Joan Didion, *Blue Nights*, Fourth Estate, 2011
4. Lars Mytting, *The Reindeer Hunters*, MacLehose Press, 2022
5. Merlin Sheldrake, *Entangled Life*, Vintage, 2021
6. Kurt Vonnegut, *The Sirens of Titan*, Delacourt, 1959
7. Robert MacFarlane, *The Wild Places*, Granta, 2007
8. Nicholas Jubber, *The Fairy Tellers*, John Murray, 2022
9. Richard Powers, *The Overstory*, Heinemann, 2018
10. Alex Garland, *The Beach*, Viking, 1996
11. Ian McEwan, *On Chesil Beach*, Jonathan Cape, 2007
12. Kate Chopin, *The Awakening*, Stone and Co., 1899
13. Yann Martel, *The Life of Pi*, Knopf, 2001
14. Herman Melville, *Moby-Dick*, Bentley, 1851
15. Neil McCarthy, *A Line in the Water*, BBC, 2021

THANKYOUS AND WITHOUT-WHOMS

I've never liked the phrase 'last and by no means least', and in any case, the thankyous must start with a 'first and foremost', and that is to my wife, Elen Lewis, who first told me that this was my book way back in 2012, and has exhorted, encouraged, and been my first editor ever since. I don't believe it would have seen the light of day without her insightful sure touch on so many occasions. My sons, James and Tom, have also lived through the book at great length too, both contributing ideas and perspectives that have been of immense value, along with their partners, Jess and Suze, respectively.

I'm indebted to friends who have either offered excellent feedback on reading sections of it, or their belief in the project. In particular, big shout-outs to Neil Baker, David Bodanis, Andy Hayes, Jamie Jauncey, Gordon Kerr, Noel Murphy, Bren Pointer, Chris Rushby, John Simmons, and, especially, Elise Valmorbida, whose Guardian Masterclass on borders and remote advice through her genius *Happy Writing Book* stiffened my resolve many times. I'm also not forgetting the whole Dark Angels crew at Aracena in the autumn of 2023: Neil, Gillian, Tara, Craig, Michelle, Ettie, and Lloyd. A more enthusiastic crowd of readers and listeners couldn't be gathered together. It was during that autumn that my business partners Ro Pocock and Caroline Whitehill generously released me from work to get dedicated time to finish the first manuscript, and I'd be at least a year away from finishing if it hadn't been for the luxury of those weeks. Thank you both.

As for the content itself, there are a good number of other people who have contributed specifically to the book, either through fresh thinking, book recommendations, introducing me to other people to speak to, or being willing interviewees. It's a joy to acknowledge them all, so here goes: Alix Berber, Iain Carruthers, John Curran, Vincent and Rebecca Eames, Alys Franzmann, Annie Hillinger, Louise Horner, Sarah Jay, Tony Laverty, Kymberly Loeb, Tim Marshall, Mary-Ann Ochota, Cherry Potter, Rob Poynton, Katie Slater, Michael Walling, Natasha Ward, Tom Woodnutt, and John Yorke.

As for the finished book, huge thanks to master printmaker Jason Hicklin, who understands liminality as well as anyone and happily donated the cover art. And of course, to Zer0 Books' Editor-in-Chief, Tristam Adams, who had immediate and instinctive belief in the idea, and whose editing has been astute, wise, and generous in equal measure.

Thanks to you all.

CULTURE, SOCIETY, & POLITICS

Contemporary culture has eliminated the concept and public figure of the intellectual. A cretinous anti-intellectualism presides, cheer-led by hacks in the pay of multinational corporations who reassure their bored readers that there is no need to rouse themselves from their stupor. Zer0 Books knows that another kind of discourse — intellectual without being academic, popular without being populist — is not only possible but already flourishing. Zer0 is convinced that in the unthinking, blandly consensual culture in which we live, critical and engaged theoretical reflection is more important than ever before.

If you have enjoyed this book, why not tell other readers by posting a review on your preferred book site.

You may also wish to subscribe to our Zer0 Books YouTube Channel.

Bestsellers from Zer0 Books Include:

Poor but Sexy

Culture Clashes in Europe East and West
Agata Pyzik
How the East stayed East and the West stayed West.
Paperback:978-1-78099-394-2 ebook: 978-1-78099-395-9

An Anthropology of Nothing in Particular

Martin Demant Frederiksen
A journey into the social lives of meaninglessness.
Paperback: 978-1-78535-699-5 ebook: 978-1-78535-700-8

In the Dust of This Planet

Horror of Philosophy vol. 1
Eugene Thacker
In the first of a series of three books on the Horror of Philosophy, *In the Dust of This Planet* offers the genre of horror as a way of thinking about the unthinkable.
Paperback: 978-1-84694-676-9 ebook: 978-1-78099-010-1

The End of Oulipo?

An Attempt to Exhaust a Movement
Lauren Elkin, Veronica Esposito
Paperback: 978-1-78099-655-4 ebook: 978-1-78099-656-1

Capitalist Realism

Is There No Alternative?
Mark Fisher
An analysis of the ways in which capitalism has presented itself as the only realistic political-economic system.
Paperback: 978-1-84694-317-1 ebook: 978-1-78099-734-6

Rebel Rebel

Chris O'Leary
David Bowie: every single song. Everything you want to know, everything you didn't know.
Paperback: 978-1-78099-244-0 ebook: 978-1-78099-713-1

Cartographies of the Absolute

Alberto Toscano, Jeff Kinkle
An aesthetics of the economy for the twenty-first century.
Paperback: 978-1-78099-275-4 ebook: 978-1-78279-973-3

Malign Velocities

Accelerationism and Capitalism
Benjamin Noys
Long-listed for the Bread and Roses Prize 2015, *Malign Velocities* argues against the need for speed, tracking acceleration as the symptom of the ongoing crises of capitalism.
Paperback: 978-1-78279-300-7 ebook: 978-1-78279-299-4

Babbling Corpse

Vaporwave and the Commodification of Ghosts
Grafton Tanner
Paperback: 978-1-78279-759-3 ebook: 978-1-78279-760-9

New Work New Culture

Work we want and a culture that strengthens us
Frithjof Bergmann
A serious alternative for humankind and the planet.
Paperback: 978-1-78904-064-7 ebook: 978-1-78904-065-4

Romeo and Juliet in Palestine

Teaching Under Occupation
Tom Sperlinger
Life in the West Bank, the nature of pedagogy, and the role of a university under occupation.
Paperback: 978-1-78279-637-4 ebook: 978-1-78279-636-7

Color, Facture, Art and Design

Iona Singh
This materialist definition of fine art develops guidelines for architecture, design, cultural studies, and ultimately, social change.
Paperback: 978-1-78099-629-5 ebook: 978-1-78099-630-1

Sweetening the Pill

or How We Got Hooked on Hormonal Birth Control
Holly Grigg-Spall
Has contraception liberated or oppressed women?
Sweetening the Pill breaks the silence on the dark side of hormonal contraception.
Paperback: 978-1-78099-607-3 ebook: 978-1-78099-608-0

Why Are We the Good Guys?

Reclaiming Your Mind from the Delusions of Propaganda
David Cromwell
A provocative challenge to the standard ideology that Western power is a benevolent force in the world.
Paperback: 978-1-78099-365-2 ebook: 978-1-78099-366-9

The Writing on the Wall

On the Decomposition of Capitalism and its Critics
Anselm Jappe, Alastair Hemmens
A new approach to the meaning of social emancipation.
Paperback: 978-1-78535-581-3 ebook: 978-1-78535-582-0

Neglected or Misunderstood

The Radical Feminism of Shulamith Firestone
Victoria Margree
An interrogation of issues surrounding gender, biology, sexuality, work, and technology, and the ways in which our imaginations continue to be in thrall to ideologies of maternity and the nuclear family.
Paperback: 978-1-78535-539-4 ebook: 978-1-78535-540-0

How to Dismantle the NHS in 10 Easy Steps (Second Edition)

Youssef El-Gingihy

The story of how your NHS was sold off and why you will have to buy private health insurance soon. A new expanded second edition with chapters on junior doctors' strikes and government blueprints for US-style healthcare.

Paperback: 978-1-78904-178-1 ebook: 978-1-78904-179-8

Digesting Recipes

The Art of Culinary Notation

Susannah Worth

A recipe is an instruction, the imperative tone of the expert, but this constraint can offer its own kind of potential. A recipe need not be a domestic trap but might instead offer escape — something to fantasise about or aspire to.

Paperback: 978-1-78279-860-6 ebook: 978-1-78279-859-0